The Ragged Edge

For Mary Johnson, for creating and then for so long sustaining a voice whose resonance has been and will be felt far beyond our imagining.

THE RAGGED EDGE

THE DISABILITY EXPERIENCE FROM THE PAGES OF THE FIRST FIFTEEN YEARS OF THE DISABILITY RAG

EDITED BY BARRETT SHAW

The Advocado Press

"Excavation" by Kenny Fries first appeared in *The American Voice*.

"A Test of Wills: Jerry Lewis, Jerry's Orphans and the Telethon," "On the Barricades with ADAPT," "The Power of One Person," "Why the Nation Doesn't Have Attendant Services," and "Unanswered Questions," Copyright by Mary Johnson.

The Ragged Edge:
The Disability Experience from the Pages of the First Fifteen Years of The Disability Rag.

Copyright 1994 by The Advocado Press.
All rights reserved.
Printed in the United States of America.
For information, write to:
The Advocado Press, P.O. Box 145, Louisville, KY 40201.

ISBN 0-9627064-5-0

Library of Congress Catalog Card Number: 94-79440

CONTENTS

INTRODUCTION

When I assumed the editorship of *The Disability Rag* last October, I did so with both excitement and trepidation. I was honored to be inheriting a magazine that had just received the *Utne Reader's* Alternative Press Award for Best Special Interest Publication, a magazine whose influence has grown to be almost ridiculously incongruent with the number of its sales. But I was fearful of perhaps not being able to keep it going at its customary full-tilt charge. Having been closer to *The Rag* than to the disability rights movement as a whole, I tended to see the magazine as very much the product of the vision and effort of its long-time editor and co-founder, Mary Johnson.

Soon after I arrived, the staff decided that a suitable way to celebrate the completion of *The Rag's* first fifteen years and to honor Mary's stewardship of all but one of them would be a collection of excerpts from the magazine over the years. A short "best of" collection from the first five years is still a popular item, and so much has happened since then!

I started rereading old issues with, I think, some preconceptions. I think I thought a *Rag* survey might serve as a concise history of the disability rights movement. I figured the book as another "best of." I supposed that a large number, if not the majority, of the articles I'd want to use would be by Mary Johnson. I was wrong on all counts.

That concise history came out last year. It's by Joseph P. Shapiro and it's called *No Pity: People with Disabilities Forging a New Civil Rights Movement* (Times Books). Which is not to say that the complete history has been told. For one thing, it's still in its early stages. Even at that, there are many other angles to explore from the starting points he gave. But *this* book didn't turn out to be a history.

Neither is it the best of *The Rag*. I found way too much high-quality writing to call this small a selection "the best." And a lot of it was *not* by Mary Johnson, although it must be said that over the years the bulk of the straight reportage as well as the editorial opinion was hers. But ideas and images and stories and visions came from many writers. They began to coalesce, as I looked at them in relation to each other, into a mosaic or, better, a collage that altogether made a coherent and compelling picture.

Any reader who has been familiar with *The Rag* for many years might be likely to think that the dominant theme to emerge would be one the magazine has long been associated with, such as access, or images of disability in the media. And maybe there will be collections on those topics later. But what insisted on being expressed first was simply — or rather, not so simply — the experience of being a disabled person in American society today.

To give some background, *The Disability Rag* first appeared as a four-page newsletter in January 1980. It was produced and distributed locally by two Louisville, KY, women, Mary Johnson and Cass Irvin, who were involved with grassroots disability rights organizations and who wanted to provide a way to give people with disabilities and others a place to read about and debate often undiscussed disability issues. By the mid-'80s, *The Rag* was a small but powerful national magazine.

In the first few years, much of the writing was done by Johnson and Irvin, but as a national audience grew, *The Rag* began to be seen as a place where writers with disabilities could find an audience that would understand the experience they were writing from — an audience that they didn't have to be heroic for or submissive to, but to whom they could speak their anger and frustration or declare their emerging pride. It was a meeting place for what came to be called the disability community to debate ideas, to be unafraid to argue differing opinions or rally together behind common causes. It was an outlet for the products of a blossoming disability culture.

This book, as I said, is a collage of those ideas and opinions and blooms. Or perhaps the name taken by another magazine of disability culture — the kaleidoscope — is a more appropriate image, for I found that as I tried to break down the picture into cohesive sub-topics, just to draw up a coherent table of contents, the parts kept wanting to move and rearrange themselves. In other words, those sub-themes were so overlapping and interlocking that the grouping of articles became somewhat arbitrary. "Public Stripping" and "Auschwitz on

Sesame Street" could as easily been in the section on oppression as where they are. The articles on telethons could have been in the section on images, but they seemed to deserve their own. And so on.

It is hard to unravel the tangled, knotted ball of the disability experience — isolation and differentness versus a common identity; images of weakness, vulnerability, enforced childishness, learned helplessness versus defiance, willingness to make waves and change the status quo; pity, destroying dignity, and its other side, fear, fear of our differentness, our "imperfection," as if perfection were humanly achievable; and then our own fear, raw fear of attitudes that would destroy our kind, whether by genocide, selective abortion, euthanasia, assisted suicide or rationing of care. This book attempts to weave a rough but strong cloth from these gnarled strands, to give the *feel* of the disability experience.

Such a cloth would not have a neat, finished selvedge, but a ragged edge. This is a good image for the way people with disabilities live, at a rough and often ravelling interface with the rest of society. Daniel Callahan of the Hastings Center used the same image in his book *What Kind of Life: The Limits of Medical Progress* (Simon & Schuster, 1990), but not in quite the same way. He used "the ragged edge" to describe the limits of the achievements of medicine. No matter what breakthroughs and "cures" are accomplished, the organism thus preserved longer will only be open to other kinds of decline and depredations. A powerful insight, but he uses it to justify limits to certain kinds of care.

People are scared of living on the ragged edge. True, all the medical tinkering in the world has not shown that the human organism does anything other than break down eventually. Some people have become so afraid of this normal course of things that they would rather die than face it. Having had this view projected onto them, they tend to project it on the rest of us and think we'd all rather die than not be perfect machines. This is not the case. Ironically, it is people with disabilities who could best make them see the value of life on the ragged edge, life with some physical limitations, even if it were saddled with external barriers and barriers of attitude. And how much more so if it were not?

Because many kinds of difference are feared and shunned,

the disability experience has been a different experience. We are told there are now 49 million people with disabilities in America — about one in five. There are many kinds of disability and many degrees of each. Some are more stigmatized than others. But the fact that one in five Americans has one ought to make it evident that having a disability is no more abnormal than having straight hair or an epicanthic fold. Variety is normal. If perfection were possible, it would be dull.

As preface, Cass Irvin describes *The Rag's* mission from the perspective of more than a dozen years ago. Then listen to *The Rag's* writers. If you have a disability, you will hear your sisters and brothers speaking to you. If you don't, you will hear something you need to hear.

Barrett Shaw, Louisville, KY, July 1994

PREFACE

Why We Do What We Do

Cass Irvin

Quite often we, the editors of *The Rag,* have said to our readership, "This is *your* paper. Write to us, make comments about what we publish and submit materials." And you are beginning to respond — sometimes more than we have room for.

The choices we make about what we can and cannot print are not arbitrary. The *Disability Rag* is considered to be a product of a "disability press" and the role and function of that disability press has changed a great deal in this country in the last 20 years.

Twenty years ago, printed materials, newsletters or magazines focusing on the area of disability were mainly professional publications about medical or rehabilitation concerns, or they were "how-to" or "how I succeeded" or "how I accepted — and you can, too" publications for disabled people. Few if any publications looked at disabled people and saw civil rights issues at the core of our lack of access, education and employment.

The disability press (that is, all publications for and by disabled people in this country) is beginning to change its image. It is beginning to take its role more seriously. It is beginning to do what the feminist press has done for women in the past decade. The disability press is beginning to help us see ourselves as we really are — not as society tells us we are. We today, like women ten years ago, must realize that society imposes the obstacles we are encouraged to overcome, not our disability. We must realize that we are not any more "less than normal" than women are "the weaker sex." The disability press must provide to disabled people the vision and the models that testify to the rightful place of disabled people in our society.

The disability press should serve its audience by providing a view of how it ought to be, what can be and what it is for some of us now, but not all of us — not yet.

A disability press's role is to view the world, our society, through a disability lens. It should explore issues relevant to all people and illustrate the disability impact these issues have. Nuclear power, the next war, the abortion issue impact upon disabled people as much as do health care benefits or full employment.

A disability press needs to provide its readers with a frame of reference to hang those visions on and thus begin to make them real. We need to know that as disabled people the feelings we are experiencing because of our situation are real and valid and not abnormal. . . .

Until *The Feminine Mystique* was published, women had no reinforcement for their feelings. That book told them it was okay to feel unfulfilled by marriage and motherhood. Until that publication, many women hated themselves for their assumed inadequacies.

The Feminine Mystique exemplifies the function of the feminist press.

The role of the disability press is to record and preserve our present and our past. It exists to speculate about our future. And its role is to point out the relevancy each has to the other. *The Rag* has not published articles on F.D.R. just because he is one of our folk heroes. We publish them because he is a part of our history and his role as a disabled person in his society helps us understand our role in today's society. Unlike most minority groups, we do not have our own culture and traditions. But we do have a past and we should learn about it and feel pride in the accomplishments of our forebears and we should feel anguish about how badly our people have been treated. There are parallels to both in our future.

"The pen is mightier than the sword." Printed words are strong tools for change. And the language that we use defines and shapes our perceptions of ourselves. What is more important still is that our language shapes society's perception of disabled people. When you hear disabled people debate "disabled" vs. "handicapped," you are hearing a people in the process of defining themselves.

If we have not quite settled on the most appropriate, universal term, it is only because we have not defined ourselves totally yet. Many of us are just beginning to feel a sense of identity with the community of disabled people; our feelings of pride for our name have not fully evolved yet. But we are beginning to correct others when they call us by the wrong name.

Looking out for, observing and refining all of these elements are essential tasks of a good disability press. *The Disability Rag* adheres to this philosophy and strives for quality writing in the area of disability. And we encourage our readers to submit articles that will shed light on or analyze issues affecting the status of disability. We accept articles that help create a climate of opinion about disability. We must — due to space limitations — discourage personal narratives unless they contribute to the vision of disability in America.

With this issue, *The Disability Rag* celebrates its second anniversary. We hope we have grown in these two years, and we hope to be around for 20 more — at least.

January 1982

COMING TOGETHER

Aphasia

Edward L. Hooper

"**B**abe, would you geth the egllaatrr buttten? Boy, I must really be beat."

We took the elevator up to physical therapy. By the time we arrived, an incredible imploding feeling had overwhelmed me. I'd lost my source of language. My world was shrinking as if I were falling into a deep well, with my wife's face at the top, getting smaller and smaller. Through the smallness and dimness I could see the panic wrenched on her face.

I'd been saying things like, "raghhitttifrmmdgg, son-of-a-bitch, sssxazzuttt." I could curse with tutored clarity but the rest was nonsense to everyone else. Only I could understand.

I could hear my love's frightened voice: "Please don't try to ask anything. Don't talk. Rest. Stay quiet, please."

"Ghrrappl drrrddippll cccoppykk?" I wanted to know what was going on. My head was a can of alphabet soup overstocked with consonants. Gibberish spilled out of my mouth with every r, d, and t, shaking my wife Cindy to the bone.

Cindy and a couple of therapists had stepped outside the partition for a moment, and I could hear their frantic whispers: "Get a blood pressure cuff! I think he's had a stroke!"

"Nooooooooooooooo!" My fall was now at light speed.

"Please, oh, please, no; no, not a stroke!" I pleaded within myself.

A neurologist was waiting for me on the medical floor. "Can you count to ten?" he asked me.

"Four, two, nnnii . . ." I responded.

"Who is the President of the United States?"

My brain was a pinball machine. Amid the clanging and clatter, I kept waiting for TILT or Game Over. There was a disconnection of thought and language, and I squirmed and struggled for what could have been a month with the answer I wanted. Then, "Jellybeans. Jellybeans. Jellybeans. NO! Son-of-a-bitch! Goddamnit! No, jellybeans, no, no . . ."

Then the neurologist pulled the plug on me. "What's your wife's name?"

"Mary!" I blurted. "No, no . . ."

God! I'd called Cindy Mary! The mental implosion was complete: I was trapped in a black hole of the mind.

Cindy was at my bedside. Her face faded and cleared, faded and cleared, faded . . . She was trying to comfort me. But my calling her Mary wasn't reassuring either of us. I had a headache and tried asking Cindy (calling her Mary) for some Tylenol, but I had the letters jumbled like an anagram, so when it finally came out, it sounded like Nellyt. Naturally, she couldn't understand, which only served to infuriate me.

"Nellyt! Nellyt! goddamnit, son-of-a-bitchin' bastard!"

My swearing soon turned to crying, and Cindy's eyes were red with tears, too. Was this how it would end, here in the rehab hospital, in the darkness of my mind, my wife looking on helplessly?

Around 3 a.m., the nurse came in and asked me, "Who is the President?"

"Ronald Reagan. Ronald Reagan! Ronald Reagan!"

Oh, God, I thought, "One, two, three, four, five, six, seven, eight, nine, ten! Two times two is four! Four times four is sixteen! A hundred, a thousand, ten thousand! Oh, baby! George Bush! Walter Mondale and Geraldine Ferraro! Eight times seven is 56! Go tell Cindy! GO TELL CINDY!"

My 18-hour struggle with aphasia had been caused by a reaction to an antibiotic.

Irene, a "stroke patient," took physical therapy the same hours I did. Therapists at rehab had to do a lot of doubling and tripling with patients — time's money, you know.

Irene worked very hard in therapy. I was amazed at what she'd accomplished. She was doing it all — bed, bath, in and out of her wheelchair, starting to walk a little, on and off the toilet — and I'd presumed her occupational therapy was going well, too.

Irene was quiet. Aphasia did that. It made her understand that others didn't understand; so silence, in Irene's case, was a method of dealing with her frustration. But she followed instructions like a trooper. I now realize I'm prouder of her in retrospect — in rehab, I was always secretly envious of those who could do more than I could.

Irene's husband and son came to visit her often, and I was happy the day I heard she'd soon be going home. But a few days later, I encountered Irene in therapy crying, and refusing to do any therapy. She was headed for a nursing home. She had not had a voice in her fate, though she'd spoken clearly through her actions and accomplishments that she was ready to resume life at home — her own home.

I overheard her husband talking to the doctor and therapist. "She doesn't understand a word I say. How can I care for her?"

"She understands *me,*" the therapist insisted, as if she'd said it before. "Try to be patient with her. Help her."

"Home is the best place for Irene," the doctor told her husband. "It will give her an environment conducive to recovery."

"It's easy for you people," Irene's husband was protesting. "You don't have to take care of her day and night. I work. I can't. I'm sorry."

That's all I heard. All — except the sobbing of Irene. It was a lonely sobbing, so much like the loneliness I'd felt, ever so briefly, two months earlier. I knew she was trapped inside herself, with tears the only residual of her hope.

I never heard what happened to Irene. No one seemed to want to know.

Seeking the Disabled Community

Edward L. Hooper

A phasia is a devastating disability. It envelops the
mind, giving it no access to the outside world. In this way,
it renders the person devoid of any way to call out for her rights.
Eventually, without support and understanding, a person with
aphasia simply loses hope.

Society treats our disability movement as though it has
aphasia. Our words — no matter how clearly we communicate
them, no matter how many facts we marshall, regardless of our
intentions to participate in mainstream society, for the good of
all — are as if spoken clearly only in our own minds. It's as though
we're making sense only within ourselves. Society hears it as so
much gibberish.

How many times can we say, request, insist, proclaim,
scream that we do not want pity; that we do not like the
paternalistic attitudes of others; that we are disabled people
whose physical disabilities do not make us lesser people —
disabled *people;* that we are neither heroes nor villains; that we
are alive because we want to be, not because we are simply using
life as a waiting room for an appointment with death? How many
times before even a fragment of what we know to be true will be
understood by society as something more than nonsense?

We become frustrated. Time and again we speak the words,
demonstrate our worth in society (when given equal chance),

only to be denied basic understanding — the understanding that must precede our being accorded basic human dignity and equality.

How many times have you tried to explain your feelings about disability, only to be greeted by the blank face of solace or bewilderment?

Those of us with the capability to communicate are finding that we can channel our frustrations outward to our brothers and sisters, who really *do* understand disability.

I think it's that understanding that defines, for me, The Disabled Community. *E pluribus unum* is not some cutesy motto they decided to put on our currency; it defines common purpose. How many of us with disabilities have it?

I am often bemused by the statistics that say there are 30 to 40 million people with disabilities in this country.

Someone better tell 25 or 35 million of those folks that they're part of this big group — because they haven't a clue. If you use a wheelchair, try going up to someone with a hearing aid and explain to them that you're both in the same community. Good luck!

Perhaps the Census questions should look at our understanding of ourselves as disabled.

Alone, each of us will end up like Irene, trapped within ourselves. We'll end up accepting a lesser existence — or not wanting to bother with life at all. That's why it's critical that we reach more and more disabled people. Within our community, the disabled community, we can console, complain to, empathize with and care for one another.

Then maybe we can look back into society's eyes and say, "See, it's *you* who need help, not us. We will be patient but stern, repetitious in our discontent, angered at your indifference, relentless in our purpose. And in time, with our guidance, you may learn."

It's easy to succumb to futility when your ideas are consistently dismissed as gibberish. But despite the dubious statistics about our numbers, there are many who *do* understand, who are of common purpose: they are The Disabled Community.

They're out there to help us find peace in our thoughts, and give us a sense of excitement that will, by comparison, make my remembering President Reagan's name seem like a tranquil snooze.

Society has shuffled us around, not trying to understand us, not knowing exactly whom, or what, they're shuffling. If we don't vigorously acknowledge disability to ourselves and forge The Disabled Community, we will never be acknowledged.

August 1985

Like Squabbling Cubs

Mary Jane Owen

Of course we hate to explore the nasty question: "Why don't we seem to 'get it together' the way other civil rights movements have?" But explore it we must.

Like other minorities, we struggle with the pain and humiliation of overt prejudice and subtle discrimination. Why has our struggle not brought us the same sense of group identity? Sometimes we say it's hard to organize around having something in common — disability — that none of us really wants.

But the children of slavery came together around physical characteristics that the majority society taught were ugly. "Black is beautiful" seemed an audacious assertion when it was first made.

We undercut each other's efforts. We act as if we don't really like each other. We don't share networks. We fail to give each other credit for success if it's in *our* area of expertise. We act as though we can gain credibility only as individuals — not as a class. Those of us with the financial resources to make substantial contributions to the Movement rarely put our cash where our rhetoric is.

We act like starving wolf cubs squabbling over too few tits. We don't even seem to notice when the source of our sustenance gets bored and walks off, leaving us snapping at each other.

This is not a pretty picture of our Movement. But it seems apt.

Recently I noticed that I fit the image of one of those greedy wolf cubs rather more closely than I liked. I realized I wanted and needed credit for my ideas. And I felt angry over the lack of financial reward for my contributions. I am not proud about these insights. But perhaps they explain some common attitudes within our Movement.

It was at this point that several friends and I began to discuss how important our jobs are to us who have disabilities. As we talked, I realized the concepts of "vulnerability" and "security," examined together, seemed to illuminate some things about how we behave in our own Movement.

Those of us with disabilities are precisely the people who prove to society how frail and vulnerable the human creature is. We prove in every way that "it" can happen to anyone, anywhere, anytime. That reality often frightens nondisabled people into avoiding us.

It also frightens many of us. We know, from the gut out, what it feels like to have some system of the body fall apart. The sword has fallen and broken our thin thread of potential perfection. We are already flawed. *And if it happened once, it can happen again and again.*

Maybe we have learned to compensate at our present level of functioning. But what about the next assault? How much can we be expected to overcome? We are vulnerable, in the worst way, to the future.

I once read and hated a book on stress by Hans Selye. Selye asserted that we are each born with a certain fund of resilience which we draw upon but never replenish. I deplored the idea.

But time and experience have caught up with my rash optimism. In maturity, we learn that each of us has a limited ability to cope with stress. As disabled people we also learn that controlling stress requires controlling our environments.

Once we have given up the role of being cared for by our family — or the state — how can we possibly accumulate enough resources to guarantee we retain the critical element of personal control over our lives which we have struggled so hard to acquire?

Those questions, which are unavoidable, make us concerned with our own security.

I thought of friends I knew who'd achieved some measure of success. One has great wealth, but seems afraid to share or spend it. Another has a secure and generous income, but cannot be convinced it will continue, so she squirrels away resources against a fearsome future and deprives herself of current pleasures.

And me — I realized I faced the inevitable decline which age brings, and wondered how long I would continue to be able to support myself. While in the past I shared my ideas and expertise freely, I had come to want the security offered by recognition and financial reward.

As disabled people, we must deal with the issue of vulnerability. Each of us might justifiably conclude, "If I don't create a personal support system — which requires financial security — I'll lose control over my life's options. To assure my independence, I must assure my own security." When each of us sees the world this way, our sense of community is endangered. We become like wolf cubs.

Will an awareness of these fears and needs of ours weaken the Movement? I think not. If we can name the demons which assault our drive to work together, we gain a measure of control over them. Such insight can give us compassion when we observe our peers acting out the terror of vulnerability.

Independence and self-direction are scary. But they are the basis for mature and productive living. The challenge is to help each other through and out of individual terror as we work toward the development of communities of support for people throughout life — communities that allow us all dignity and options. Compassion for each other's fear, a vision for each other's freedom: somehow this seems to me to make our political goals clearer.

We need some phrase we can use to remind each other that striving to be a full participant in society today is not simply a little game we can play when the mood strikes us, but a serious, every-day-of-the-year struggle to alter some pretty prevalent myths and images about freaks and other "flawed" entities.

We need to remind ourselves that as single individuals we cannot change these limiting perceptions. Society continually generalizes about our "class" — even while we may not acknowledge the similarities.

Exceptional disabled people may inspire the media to promote "supercrip" tales about what it is like to be disabled in America today. But such recognition of individual merit has done little to alter the basic mindset of fear and loathing about those qualities which society still believes handicap human potential.

During the 1960s, when a black activist disrupted group effort, that individual was brought into line with a reminder: "Don't try to Mau Mau us." That meant: Save your angry rhetoric for a more appropriate target than your brothers and sisters in the struggle for civil rights.

When that same group said to someone who identified strongly with the white aggressor, "Don't be an Oreo," everyone was reminded that, no matter how hard one tries to find a place in the larger society, black people carry their blackness with them.

We need an intimate and familiar way to speak as clearly and tersely to our peers; a way to convey lifetimes of common understanding. Enough of squabbling over too limited resources and opportunities! Enough of sops offered to turn the rage of frustration into bland despair! We are not the enemy of our personal goals; the danger lies in our common and too-often-buried fear and distrust.

March/April 1985

Malcolm Teaches Us, Too

Marta Russell

Spike Lee's film shows us a Malcolm X who is a true cultural revolutionary thinker, one who saw the importance of speaking about what it meant to be black living in a white-supremacist society. And there are parallels to be drawn between the disability rights movement and the movement Malcolm X called for. There are questions to be asked about being disabled in a physicalist society similar to those Malcolm asked about being black in white society.

Malcolm's most important message was to love blackness, to love black culture. Malcolm insisted that loving blackness was itself an act of resistance in a white-dominated society. By exposing the internalized racial self-hatred that deeply penetrated the psyches of U.S.-colonized black peoples, Malcolm taught that blacks could decolonize their minds by coming to blackness to be spiritually renewed, transformed. He believed that only then could blacks unite to gain the equality they rightfully deserved.

It is equally important for disabled persons to recognize what it means to live as a disabled person in a physicalist society — that is, one which places its value on physical agility. When our bodies do not work like able-bodied persons' bodies, we're disvalued. Our oppression by able-bodied persons is rife with the message: there is something wrong, something "defective," with us — because we have a disability.

We must identify with ourselves and others like us. Like Malcolm sought for his race, disabled persons must build a culture which will unify us and enable us to gain our human rights.

As we see in Lee's film, the white man's dictionary itself became a revealer of truth for Malcolm. With help, Malcolm discovers that the word "black" is coupled with evil, degeneracy, death and the order of darkness, while "white" is linked to goodness and purity of an angelic order.

When disabled people go through the same exercise, what do we learn? That "able-bodied" is defined as fit and strong. That "able" is defined as "having great ability," "competent." "Disability" is defined as something that disables or disqualifies a person, is a physical incapacity caused by injury or disease. To "disable" is to "deprive of some ability," to "make unfit or useless." And "handicapped" is defined as "suffering from a mental or physical disability."

You bet able-bodied people wrote this dictionary! Our "disability" label has not been taken yet as politically or personally empowering for disabled persons newly embarking on the trail to self discovery.

Many of us insist labels are unimportant. Wrong! Exploitation and oppression are given power through language. In our hierarchical society, it is the social implications of words that do us the greatest damage. Malcolm X knew this. By evolving his self-image, and by changing the words used to describe himself and his race, Malcolm knew he could make the old words disappear, too. Who calls an African American a negro anymore? We inherit language. Our children will inherit language we use today.

In my dictionary, the word "disability" is preceded by the word "dirty" and followed by the word "disabuse." Let's disabuse ourselves of the able-bodied definition of disability and suffer no more.

If we identify as disabled people, then others should be called "nondisabled." It gives them less power over us. Nondisabled people should not participate in our identification process. The recent coinages of "people with differing abilities" and "physically challenged" are far worse than "disabled." Our socioeconomic and political history teaches us that what we really are is *disvalued* persons.

When a sympathetic white girl asked Malcolm X what she could do for black people, he answered, "nothing." Part of our oppression as disabled people is in believing we need nondisabled people to do things for us. We may need them to be our attendants; we do not need to give our personal or socioeconomic power over to them. We need services, we don't need to be "taken care of."

Before his spiritual transformation, Malcolm inflicted pain on himself to straighten his "nappy" hair to the more desirable look of white people's. What do we do to ourselves to look nondisabled? We go through painful, expensive surgeries to correct our "defects." We submit to the wiles of the medical profession who promise to "cure" our disabilities. Some of us will endure great pain to be able to stand up and walk rather than use a wheelchair, so as to have straight bodies that look more desirable than a cripple's body. Like Malcolm, disabled people must learn to celebrate our own bodies and respect who we are.

Like Malcolm who, before his conversion, preferred the company of white women, many of us feel it's a status symbol to have a nondisabled partner. We see it as a mark of success. Like Malcolm the Black Muslim who came to terms with his race and married an African-American woman, we need to question our motives for forming relationships with nondisabled persons.

Malcolm's characterization of his people into "house Negroes" and "field Negroes" has parallels for us, too. The "house Negro" lived in the master's house, cooked, cleaned and did the master's every wish, often to his own degradation. When the "field Negroes," living among themselves, planned an escape, the "house Negroes" rarely went along. They became known as Uncle Toms. In the disability community we have our Uncle Toms, too — we call them Uncle Tiny Tims. They're thankful for whatever crumbs they're given by nondisabled people; they fear the stigma of associating with the rest of us. Uncle Tiny Tims are addicted to the charity — the enslavement — mode of thinking. They're ashamed of being disabled and will not identify with our movement. You won't hear Uncle Tiny Tims refer to themselves as "disabled."

When we wonder where the mass of disabled people are, we must recognize that many still hold to the Uncle Tiny Tim slave mentality.

Though Malcolm X largely considered Martin Luther King, Jr., an Uncle Tom, I think he'd agree with King's contention that freedom is never voluntarily given by the oppressor but must be demanded by the oppressed. And that leads to the real question: Where are the real leaders in our community? By leaders, I mean those capable of empowering others to celebrate who they are — disabled persons —rather than running from it; to embrace who they are, not disown it; to associate en masse with one another, indeed, to prefer it to nondisabled people's company — in short, to love disability.

When we can love disability, then we will have a real movement, not a token one. Thank you, Malcolm X.

March/April 1993

Disability Culture Rap

Cheryl Marie Wade

Disability culture. ***Say what?*** Aren't disabled people just isolated victims of nature or circumstance?

Yes and no. True, we are far too often isolated. Locked away in the pits, closets and institutions of enlightened societies everywhere. But there is a growing consciousness among us: "that is not acceptable." Because there is always an underground. Notes get passed among survivors. And the notes we're passing these days say, "there's power in difference. Power. Pass the word."

Culture. It's about passing the word. And disability culture is passing the word that there's a new definition of disability and it includes *power*.

Culture. New definitions, new inflections. No longer just "poor cripple." Now also "CRIPPLE" and, yes, just "cripple." A body happening. But on a real good day, why not C*R*I*P*P*L*E; *a body, hap-pen-ing.* **(Dig it or not.)**

Culture. It's finding a history, naming and claiming ancestors, heroes. As "invisibles," our history is hidden from us, our heroes buried in the pages, unnamed, unrecognized. Disability culture is about naming, about recognizing.

Naming and claiming our heroes. Like Helen Keller. Oh, not the miracle-worker version we're all so familiar with, but the social reformer, the activist who tried so desperately to use her celebrity to tell the truth of disability: that it has far more to do with poverty, oppression and the restriction of choices than it has to do with wilted muscles or milky eyes. And for her efforts to tell this truth, she was ridiculed, demeaned as revolutionaries often are. And because Helen Keller was a survivor, and that is the first thing any culture needs — survivors who live long enough so that some part of the truth makes it to the next generation.

Helen Keller was a survivor, so she pulled back from telling the fuller truth; that's often what survivors have to do: they have to swallow the rage, wear the mask, and, yes, pull back from telling it exactly like it is so that there might be a next generation. And so, Helen Keller, a survivor, we honor you as our ancestor, our hero.

Naming and claiming our hidden history, our ancestors. Like the thousands of mental and physical "defectives," singled out for "special treatment" by the Nazis. Yes, disability culture is recognizing that we were the first victims of the Holocaust, that we are the people the Nazis refined their methods of torture on. So we must honor these unnamed victims as our ancestors, we must raise their unmarked graves into our consciousness, into the consciousness of America so it never happens again. And just as Native Americans insist the true name of discovery is genocide, more and more of us insist that the true name of "right to die with dignity" (without opportunities to live with dignity) is murder, the first syllable of genocide.

Naming and claiming our ancestors, our heroes. Like all those circus and carnival freaks, the first disability performance artists. Those rowdy outcasts who learned to emphasize their Otherness, turn it into work, a career, a life. Oh, it may have been a harsh life, sometimes even brutal, but a life: they kept themselves from being locked away in those institutions designed for the excessively different that have always been such a prominent part of the American economy. And so we claim these survivors as our ancestors and we honor them.

Naming and claiming our ancestors, our heroes. Now most of you probably know the story of James Meredith, freedom fighter, African American, who helped break the color barrier, the racial barrier to higher learning by insisting he had a right to an education; *insisting.*

And without that insistence, the doors of Ole Miss would have remained closed. But do you know the story of Ed Roberts, cripple freedom fighter, disabled man, who, armed with self-esteem and a portable respirator, broke the disability barrier to higher learning by insisting he had a right to an education, by insisting that the doors to the University of California at Berkeley be opened, and by doing so, laid a significant brick onto the foundation of the Independent Living Movement? Independent! Living! Movement! The language of it! — that revolution of identity and possibilities for disabled people. The independent living movement. Oh, you may never have heard of it. It never made it onto prime time. Norman Mailer did not rush out to capture its essence in 30,000 words.

Yet it took root; it grew; it spread all across this country, all around the world — because there is always an underground. Notes get passed among survivors. And the notes we're passing these days say: there's power in difference. Power. Pass the word.

So what's this disability culture stuff all about? It's simple; it's just "This is disability. From the inside out."

Culture. Pass the word. Now maybe the word is the moan and wail of a blues. Maybe it's the fierce rhythms and clicking heels and castanets of flamenco. Maybe it's outsider art. Passing the word. Maybe the word is authentic movement, that dance that flows from the real body notes of cripples. Maybe it's the way pieces of cloth are stitched together to commemorate a life, to remember a name. Maybe it's American Sign Language, a language that formed the foundation of a cultural identity for a people, Deaf people, and bloomed into ASL performance art and ASL mime.

Culture. Sometimes it happens over coffee or on a picket line. A poem gets said and passed along. And passed back. Amended. Embellished. And passed along again. Language gets claimed. Ms. Gay. Crip. Guerrilla theater becomes theater with a soul. Teatro Campesino. The Dance Theater of Harlem. And, of course, WRY CRIPS Disabled Women's Theater. Radical. True. Passing the word.

Culture. Maybe so far you've been deprived. Maybe right now the primary image you have of disability is that of victim. Perhaps all of you know of us is Jerry's Kids, those doom-drenched poster children hauled out once each year to wring your charitable pockets dry.

But I promise you: you will also come to know us as Jerry's

Orphans. No longer the grateful recipients of tear-filled hand-outs, we are more and more proud freedom fighters, taking to the streets, picket signs strapped to our chairs.

No longer the polite tin-cuppers, waiting for your generous inclusion, we are more and more proud freedom fighters, taking to the stages, raising our speech-impaired voices in celebration of who we are. No longer the invisible people with no definition beyond "Other," we are more and more proud, we are freedom fighters, taking to the streets and to the stages, raising our gnarly fists in defiance of the narrow, bloodless images of our complex humanity shoved down the American consciousness daily.

And these changes, they will happen, just as the Independent Living Movement happened, just as the Rehabilitation Act's 504 regulations for access happened; just as the Americans with Disabilities Act — the most comprehensive civil rights law ever written — happened.

Because there is always an underground. Notes will be passed among survivors. And the notes we're passing these days say, "There's power in difference. Power. Pass the word."

Disability culture. What is it really all about?

It's this.

And *this.*

And **this.**

Yeah, this—

COMING AT YOU FROM
THE INSIDE OUT.

September/October 1992

IMAGE AND IMAGES

Survivor

S. L. Rosen

"Is he dead?" they whispered, lifting me onto the stretcher and shoving me quickly into the ambulance.

"No. He's one of the survivors."

I call myself a "survivor." I have survived death. Survived in a world that doesn't know what to make of people like me, true; but survived nevertheless. That should be worth something.

A lot of people use the word "survivor" today. There are survivors of bad economic times. Survivors of divorce. People survive layoffs, psychological traumas, deaths of spouses. [People are now calling themselves brain injury survivors and cancer survivors too; incest survivors, spouse abuse survivors.]

The word "survivor" is uniquely suited to one group of people: People who survive accidents, diseases, who survive what would have been almost certain death just a few short decades ago. And people deformed, born with cerebral palsy, with stutters, cleft palates, open spines. People whom society has trouble imagining at all — the sideshow people: freaks, geeks, crips, gimps, people who look funny, talk funny, walk funny. The halt, the lame and the blind, as the Bible says.

In much earlier times many of us were killed. The ones of us who weren't existed as survivors.

Sometimes, we were saved for a purpose: to provide en-

tertainment, perhaps, or to serve as an omen, or token, of The
Other. We have been ridiculed, tortured, locked in chains,
locked out of sight of day. We survived — perhaps because we had
no other choice. But nonetheless, we survived.

No other word could unite us quite as clearly as the word
"survivor."

It finds common bonds among so many different people, in
so many diferent physical conditions. For it does not deal with
the state of our bodies at all but with a political reality:
survivorship.

"Survivor" unites us politically and socially. We are not
alike in our physical conditions — as we know too well when when
looking for coalition. But we are alike in experiencing oppression — an oppression focused on the status our bodies signal to
our oppressors. We are different because of our bodies; but for
that reason we are also alike. And we are all oppressed the same
way, for the same reason: our bodies are different; therefore, we
are not normal. This one fact unites us. Our status throughout
our oppression is survivors.

Attempts have been made before to unite us with a word
that recognizes the social reality of our status. That's how
"handicapped" was born. It attempted to unite us by stating that
we were all "handicapped" (or put at a disadvantage) by society.
But it soon acquired a negative ring: it has made us sound like so
many social service cases. And the fact that it was an adjective
— "handicapped" — didn't help things, either: "Handicapped"
what? That has always been a problem. The solution was always
to call us "THE handicapped" — something that grates on our ears
and means, really, nothing at all.

"Disabled" was our own way of fighting this label. But
"disabled" is in many ways even worse: it is, itself, a negative
word. True, we can look to the success of "black," which was also
originally a pejorative term. But black, as a word, is neither
negative nor positive. It's only a color. True, in white culture,
"black " has been used to convey evil, but that meaning was
thrust upon the word; it was not inherent in the word itself. But
you cannot get away from the fact that "disabled" means "not
able." There is no other meaning.

"Survivor" is a real word. It is not negative; it always
conveys a sense of wholeness, of skill in just those ways we have
had to be skillful. And it defines us both socially and politically

within the framework in which we have had to live all these years. We have survived medically, morally, politically and economically. Those of us who are involved in the struggle to end our oppression are, simply, survivors.

There is no better word to define the reality that belongs uniquely to us. We persist in enduring continuous medical humiliation, lack of privacy, lack of respect, constant tooling around on our bodies; blithe promises of cure, prohibitively expensive devices for moving about, confinement in nursing homes, confinement in back rooms, dependence on the mercy and good will of people who take care of us (because we are not allowed the technology to take care of ourselves), deplorable economic conditions, life on SSI, blockage from buildings. And yet we continue to work for change. What are we if not survivors?

There has been a move recently to coin "cute" words: "handicappers," "exceptional" and "physically challenged" come to mind. What are we trying to do? The intention is good: we're looking for a way to make it all sound so positive. But it ends up sounding like pablum.

"Survivor" does not sound like pablum.

It is no good to invent an identity. If we do not choose an identity freely, it has no meaning for us. We will still be defined by the oppressors. And how can we build a pride if we are defined by our oppressor, if our existence is plotted by our oppressors?

Until we define our existence, in a word we ourselves have chosen, we will never be free.

I have chosen my word: survivor.

May 1983, reprinted May/June 1991

Thoughts on Thinking Differently

Tanis Doe

During all the work I have done with the disability rights movement, working against inaccessibility, for support services, equal education for deaf people, independent living for severely disabled people and political lobbying at the national level, there has been a steady message invading my thoughts: fear. Yes, fear. Call me phobic, but I believe that fear is our greatest handicap in society.

No matter how many articles are written and read, no matter how many media campaigns are held or accommodations are made, the very last disability to be understood, accommodated and then accepted will be disorders of thought. We can't seem to accept the idea of thinking differently. By "We" I mean everyone, people who identify as having disabilities and people who don't because we have a hierarchy of disability that puts mental illness and mental disabilities among the least desirable.

It is difficult enough to accept differences in physical appearance, speech, behavior, ways of coping, etc. But people are afraid of thinking differently.

Perhaps I should personalize this, or "own" it, and say that I am afraid of thinking differently, too. I can assure you that I already think differently than most. I am both qualitatively and quantitatively "different" in my thinking. I am certainly more radical than the norm; still, I am open-minded. My thoughts are interconnected so that one small idea will trigger several related concepts and set my mind in a search mode looking for similarities and differences, applications and storage.

It is not like a computer; I have a very human brain. I believe thinking and feeling are intertwined. I have often felt and thought that I feel more than do normal folks; and I certainly think more than is normal. I cry easily at movies and books. I anger easily at injustice. I can quickly rationalize either side of an argument — and I can be quite convincing. Aha! sounds like a lawyer, an actress, or a psychoneurotic, eh? Precisely my point.

The way I think is so deeply entrenched in how I feel and who I am that I am really terrified at the thought of thinking in any other way. I have memory disturbances, vertigo, partial seizures and experience brain "fog" on a regular basis, and these affect me far more drastically than my being deaf or using a wheelchair. Recent health problems have made me fear brain damage, and recent hospitalizations, combined with psychiatric consultation, have forced me to confront my own sanity or lack thereof. I will openly admit to going through one or two "clinical depressions," suicidal tendencies, workaholism, emotional instability (and liability), uncontrolled anger and even self-destructiveness.

Anyone who reads this who knows what "clinical depression" is will understand that even by itself without all my other "thought" differences, the effects of depression alone are devastating. I can remember knowing, believing with all my mind, that there was no way out. No one would help me because I was helpless, hopeless and humorless. I did think of death as an option that would bring relief. I also had the responsibility of caring for a child, though, so I had to discount suicide as the method of coping. Many others have not been so lucky. Depression affects you holistically — your appetite, your energy, your sense of self, your concentration, your sleeping habits, your every mood and thought. Depression may (or may not) be a social construction (or deconstruction) but it is a very real and frightening condition to those of us who experience it.

It is scary to think and feel so differently that you desire death as an escape. Any sane, so-called "normal" individual should be afraid of those types of uncontrolled differences. All people are afraid of loss and will grieve the loss of a friend, loss of vision, loss of a leg, and loss of independence. But it is beyond imagination to cope with the loss of sanity or loss of self.

Having worked with people labeled with a mental handicap for many years, I believe that this fear also applies to retardation. People cannot bear the thought of not thinking in the way they are used to — "normally." Each person has his or her own way of thinking, but we are — yes, I am, too — afraid of losing that natural ability or being left with "lesser" powers. This could be why Alzheimer's disease receives so much attention. We are all afraid of losing our minds.

People with disabilities often argue that it is not the disability that needs removal but the barriers. Let us be disabled, as that is who we are, they say; but allow us some dignity and equality. Yet millions and millions of dollars are still spent on the prevention and rehabilitation of various disorders and disabilities. But for mental health and mental disabilities, there is less hope and less help. For people who have mental health disabilities in addition to other, sensory, physical or mental disabilities, the system is even less accommodating.

Sheltered workshops still exploit people labeled "mentally handicapped" under the guise of "training." People labeled "mentally ill" are being systematically abused medically, pharmaceutically, physically and socially, both inside institutions and out.

Street people are left with no homes, no support; they wander in medication-induced trances unless they have sold their prescription drugs for food, cigarettes or alcohol money.

I believe that society will learn to accept physical, sensory and learning disabilities, including the now trendy concepts of codependence, alcoholism and addiction. This will happen long before mentally related disabilities are dealt with. Homophobia, anti-semitism and bigotry may all be relics of the past long before people with mental health disabilities are accepted into the community.

People are sooo afraid of the unknown! Imagining how to live in a wheelchair, or be blind, may be a frightening challenge, but it is far more tolerable and concrete than trying on a mental disability. My belief is that we people labeled "mentally ill" or "mentally handicapped" will be the last to enjoy any true experience of equality. That's because we think differently.

March/ April 1992

Boutonnieres

John R. Woodward

*T*he only image of persons with disabilities to come out of
the 1992 Republican convention coverage was one of the
most regressive features to appear on the national airwaves all
year.

The feature, which aired on CNN Headline News several
times the night after the Republican convention had adjourned,
explored the "human interest" in the sheltered workshop at
Homewood Flossmoore High School outside Chicago where the
students made boutonnieres worn by Republican convention
delegates.

"Far away from the spotlight in Houston, at this suburban
Chicago high school, 16-year-old Inan Shalati is one of the faces
behind the boutonnieres," Margaret Lowrey of CNN intoned. On
screen, Shalati — described as "blind, with cerebral palsy" —
struggled with labored speech as she explained that she could
put boutonnieres together: "People are amazed and that, because
we don't see the flowers, and they think, how can you put them
together?" Rather than allow Shalati to finish explaining how
she manipulates the components of the boutonnieres, Lowrey
broke in to declare her "a triumph of the spirit over bodily
bonds," along with four of her friends in the workshop, each of
whom also participated in making these "amazing" boutonnieres. "They are special," said Lowrey, "overcoming physical

and learning disabilities to make the patriotic ornament, and show that they, too, have something to contribute." Does any of this sound familiar?

"I feel good knowing that somebody out there is going to be touched by what I'm doing," Shalati said. Without in any way taking away from her personal pride in her accomplishments, I feel awful that she has been exploited so thoroughly: first made to work in sweatshop conditions that no nondisabled person would legally be required to endure unless he or she were a convicted felon, and, second, held up to the world as an inspirational example — as if her impairment were her oppression and not the archaic attitudes that condemn her to toil over these "patriotic ornaments" instead of receiving an education.

The sheltered workshop at the Homewood Flossmoore High School is supported by a federal grant from the Job Training Partnership Act. The original purpose of the JPTA (a program devised in the early 1980s by then-Senator Dan Quayle to replace the Great Society-era Comprehensive Employment Training Act, or CETA) was to prepare people who had received inadequate educations for jobs in the private sector. Evidently it didn't occur to Lowrey to question why JPTA is supporting sheltered workshops, or why boutonniere-making has replaced education at Homewood Flossmoore.

This is nothing new, of course. As a former reporter, I am constantly startled by the behavior of my former colleagues when they go out to report a feelgood story about "handicapped people." Journalistic objectivity, research, the questioning attitude — all of them go out the window when the goal of the story is "human interest" about persons with disabilities "overcoming" something.

"It has uplifted their spirits," said instructor Larry Barron. "Oh, they talk about it all the time, they met incredible people!" Lowrey coyly suggested that perhaps none of the people his students has met is as "incredible" as Barron himself.

"It was his idea to make boutonnieres for the 1989 Inaugural, Desert Storm soldiers, Pearl Harbor's fiftieth anniversary and to circumnavigate the globe aboard the space shuttle Discovery." Barron's most incredible skill may be his talent for jumping on trendy bandwagons that would do credit to the best Madison Ave. public relations firm. His talent misfired at least once, though: the 30,000 boutonnieres made for the Democratic convention were not used.

"I was kind of hurt that the Democrats didn't use them," said one student at the workshop. A scowling Barron took a harder line: "We put our heart and soul into making a difference and it obviously didn't with the Democrats."

There isn't anything original I can say about the tone of the CNN feature. Lowrey's patronizing attitude and the whole cheery philosophy of "overcoming" are well known to readers of *The Rag*. It is not "extraordinary" when large numbers of people with disabilities are taught to perform simple assembly tasks by rote. It is not "inspirational" when nondisabled people find a way to exploit the labor of people in sheltered workshops and at the same time surround themselves with an aura of sainthood. It is disturbing, however, to see these myths manipulated for political gain. If the Republican Party sees the Homewood Flossmoore boutonnieres as a positive image of the contribution people with disabilities can make in a Presidential election, what does this say for the future of the ADA, or the future of our movement's leaders? If CNN couldn't find any more profound disability-issue story in the Republican convention than this, what does that say about our image in the media?

I'd like to report that the tone of the CNN feature made Barron uncomfortable. I'd also like to explain why the Republican Party managers accepted the boutonnieres and tell you what they thought of CNN's piece on the Homewood Flossmoore High School sheltered workshop. I'd also like to tell you that their Democratic Party counterparts turned down the unsolicited boutonnieres because they were deemed to be exploitative and in bad taste. Unfortunately, I can't tell you any of these things. The Homewood Flossmoore High School declined to return my calls, as did the Republican National Committee media office, the Clinton campaign headquarters and CNN.

In the end, it's just another "amazing crip" story. All that sets the Homewood Flossmoore boutonniere story apart from a thousand others is the juxtaposition of this story with one of real importance: the Presidential election. How sad that of all the things that could have been said about our issues in this election, boutonnieres are the "issue" that will be remembered?

November/December 1992

Toward a Theory of Radical Disability Photography

Anne Finger

The Creatures Time Forgot: Photography and Disability Imagery.
By David Hevey; additional text and photographs by Jo Spence
and Jessica Evans. London and New York: Routledge, 1992. 226
pages. $19.95 softbound.

*I*n one black-and-white photograph, a white person in a
manual wheelchair is shown in an elevator reaching for the top
button, just out of reach. "Everyone assumes I won't want to get
to the top," the text reads, adding underneath, "Our biggest
handicap is other people's attitudes." The name of the British
charity that ran the ad, The Spastics Society, appears underneath, in print larger and darker than any of the rest of the text.

In another photograph, this one in color, an Asian girl in
an elaborate "dress-up" costume of silver, magenta, purple and
white rests her chin in her hands and looks frankly and warmly
at the camera. There is no outer sign of the girl's disability; only
the photo's inclusion in an exhibition commissioned by the all-
disabled Graeae Theatre Company marks her as disabled.

Both of these photographs appear in disabled British
photographer David Hevey's *The Creatures Time Forgot: Photography and Disability Imagery*, certainly the most valuable book
yet published about disability and artistic practice and one of
the most important books to come out of the disability movement

on either side of the Atlantic. The theoretical models that Hevey outlines have relevance far beyond the field of photography. Providing the first sophisticated analysis of disability and aesthetic practice, going far beyond the notions of "positive" imagery and the unearthing of disabled heroines and heroes, Hevey's work is vital to all disabled artists and those seeking to create a disability culture. Hevey's approach to the photographic representation of disabled people is to look first at what has been the dominant imagery, in both charity advertising and in contemporary photography, and then to suggest means by which disabled people can put ourselves in the picture.

The first photograph described above appears in many ways to be "progressive," and certainly it's a change from the tragic faces and find-a-cure mentality that activists both in the U. S. and Britain have protested so vigorously. But after reading *Creatures* we bring a more critical eye to even such "reformed" charity advertising. Before we can really read this advertisement, Hevey insists that we have to understand what charity is: that in order to read the image, we need to know what the task of that image is.

Hevey points out that charities function to "bind up the wounds of society"; that their *raison d'etre* is to work for amelioration of such wounds, rather than for fundamental social change that would prevent such wounds in the first place; most importantly, that in locating the oppression in the impairment itself (that is, in the body or mind of the disabled person) rather than in the social organizations that actively exclude and oppress disabled people (from the state on down to the family), charities, by their very nature, turn away from social and political change and toward individual "help the handicapped" solutions. Not only does the charity industry as a whole function this way under capitalism (and what a relief it is to read a book about disability that isn't scared of naming capitalism as a source of our oppression!) but each individual charity must compete with other charities for "the charitable dollar." Thus, charity advertising aims at simultaneously creating an image of "its" disease or impairment and of that particular charity as the custodian/savior/earthly representative of all those with that dreaded impairment.

Creatures next looks at how charity advertising goes about doing this. Almost invariably in black and white, the visual image used in charity advertisements is frequently one of dependency, strangeness, isolation. The written text, however, often offers "objective, scientific" facts about the disability and suggests the possibility of its being cured. Thus while the text is offering a rational way of understanding and lessening fear of the disability, the image above it is busy inculcating both fear and loathing.

Recently some charity advertising has begun to focus on "attitudes." Hevey writes, " 'Attitude change' is the charities' dream of social change without political action. . . . [It] asks disabled and non-disabled people to disengage from the physical world of inaccessible construction and enter a mapless world of hope."

Let's return to that initial advertisement: significantly, the person's back is to the viewer. Is the person male or female? The unstyled hair and unisex jacket could belong to either gender; one has to look very closely to see what is (probably) the hem of a skirt. What we have here isn't androgyny; it's the state of being neuter. It is the wheelchair that the person sits in that becomes their salient feature. The person is white. (I might remind readers that Britain is a much more multi-racial society than we in the States generally assume it to be.) If the person were Black or Asian, the message would be confusing: The "Everyone assumes I won't want to get to the top" could be read both in terms of disability and in terms of race — and clearly any kind of an analogy between racism and ableism is one that works against the aims of charities. Significantly, passivity is still enshrined in the disabled person's action. While s/he stretches forth a finger for the top elevator button, s/he will clearly never reach it. What does s/he feel? Anger? Bitterness? Frustration? No one knows. S/he remains a blank. What is s/he going to do about it? Not organize a demonstration, but rather hear a meek plea for "attitude change" made on her/his behalf.

Creatures makes it clear that no amount of reforms, of making disabled people "part of the process," of having "positive images" in charity advertising or on telethons will solve these problems: they are intrinsic to the charitable enterprise itself. "What constructs itself as the heart of a heartless nation is itself one of the great bastions of oppression of disabled people," Hevey writes. "The real 'tragic flaw' of this form of disability representation is the existence of the . . . charity itself."

Having examined charity advertising, Hevey turns his attention to the work of contemporary photographers. Disabled people are often excluded from such work; but our inclusion, when it occurs, is often not a step forward. Examining the work of Diane Arbus, Gary Winograd and Jean Mohr, he finds that we are often used as freaks and grotesques, as visual expressions of social anomie, or else rendered (as in the work of Jean Mohr) as symbols of innocence and nobility.

Hevey's writing is at its strongest when he roots his discussion in his personal history: his entry into the world of photography through being a seafront "smudger," taking pictures of vacationers posed in front of a local landmark, while at the same time regarding his "real self" as a painter, an art student, a creator of high art. Or when he talks about the work he did as an assistant to a photographer for a business magazine, watching the process whereby the images of men who were physically falling apart were transformed into bold and powerful "captains of industry." He used the techniques he acquired in these environments in his work photographing disabled people: shooting in color, encouraging the subjects to be active participants in the process (and making clear to them that the process did not aim to represent "victims"). Thus the photograph of the disabled girl in her dress-up costume, in which she presents herself as she wishes to be seen. Hevey's work, many examples of which are included in this volume, is broad-ranging: from the collaborative portraits from his "A Sense of Self" exhibit to the parodic re-enactments for "In the Charity Camp." One of the photographs from the latter exhibit, "Thank you for putting us in colour," shows two women seated at table with picnic remains (white bread, pink ice cream, a cake that says "Tragic But Brave"). One looks glum (the way kids in MDA Telethon posters looked before MDA realized it had to clean up its act) and the other (tagged with her first name, in case she should get separated from the other handicapables on the outing) looks plucky and grateful. Hevey's work is at its strongest when he's mocking ableist attitudes or when he returns the stare of ABs.

In his final chapter, "Revolt of the Species!: A Theory of the Subject," Hevey examines the work of theorists Victor Burgin, Susan Sontag, Alan Sekula and Jo Spence, who question the modernist belief that a photograph has a single, inherent meaning. Instead, they see meaning as produced by the viewer, who makes it part of a complex web of pre-existing and ongoing beliefs and assumptions. However, though Hevey agrees that we can never assign any plastic image a fixed, indeterminate meaning, he asserts that we do need to look at the task to which an image is put. He also insists that we must do more than critique what has been done — we must become active participants in the process of creation. We need to look *out* from the photograph as well as looking *in* to it: we need to look at how "people enter, control or direct imagery as subjects." Hevey turns to radical theater, which he sees as offering a blueprint for radical disability photography. Citing the work of Augusto Boal, he says that radical photography, like radical theater, must reject "tragedy in favour of mobilization." In other words, disability must cease to become a sign —whether of innocence, of the overall injustice of the human condition or of inherent stain. Representation of disability must rather be part of an overall liberatory project. Hevey talks specifically about his own photographic work — how he undermines the passivity many disabled people experience in the face of the camera through a workshop process that explores the roots of that passivity and that enables the person photographed to also participate as a photographer.

The final two chapters offer differing perspectives on disability. One is an interview Hevey conducted with the late Jo Spence, who discusses her personal experience with cancer and medical treatment. Spence is down to earth and makes explicit how her working-class background intersected with her experiences on (and off) the medical assembly line. Jessica Evans traces the historic construction of the category "mentally handicapped" and discusses the projection of able-bodied fears onto disabled people. She points out that in charity advertising, "the mental state of the subject appears to be manifested in the visual appearance of the body. . . . charities' obsession with the bodily mark betrays an irrational and even sadistic impulse which clearly contradicts their humanist claims."

The Creatures Time Forgot is a brilliant book. But I found it uneven. Hevey discusses charities at great length in the first two chapters, making points that, while important, could have been condensed; the final section, where he develops his "theory of the subject," goes by too quickly. At times his work seems more accessible to someone familiar with photographic processes and theories — and unfamiliar with disability — than *vice versa*. The book would have been stronger had he integrated a feminist analysis more deeply into his work: for instance, when he talks about Diane Arbus, he throws out some fascinating suggestions about how she used disabled people to express her own alienation from the family. I wish he had followed up on those hints more; I'm fascinated with how women artists make use of disabled people as subjects for their work, especially at points where women artists are moving into new territory — how disabled people become the "other's other."

But these shortcomings only stand out because Hevey's work is so impressive in its range and complexity. Both in his theoretical work and in his photography, David Hevey breaks striking new ground for our movement. This book belongs on the shelf of every disability rights activist and every disabled artist.

November/December 1993

Giving It Back

Cris Matthews

*T*wo years ago Gail Linn — my best friend through most of grade school — died. Yet I found out only a week ago — accidentally.

Taking a nostalgia drive through the old neighborhood, I noticed the wheelchair ramp that had taken up most of her parents' yard was gone. I was unprepared for the news that my old friend was gone too.

We were diametric opposites, she and I. She was blonde; I have dark hair. She was shy at school, not popular; I was outgoing and had lots of friends. My parents were divorced; her family even included a live-in grandmother! She excelled at everything academic, including perfect penmanship. I was smart but struggled with math; my writing was a more "distinct" scrawl. She was five months older than me. Throughout grade school we were best friends.

Freshman year of high school meant different homerooms, different classes and even different bus routes (yes, in those days we were bused to "special" schools.) Most of the friends we'd made in grade school still hung out with me; Gail Linn could be with my crowd at recess after lunch. By then I was a hippie. Gail Linn was still Gail Linn.

When I transferred to yet another gimp school, my ties to my former friend ended in the blur of adolescence and the unrelenting roll into adulthood. Through grapevines and assumptions I knew our lives had taken quite different paths. I had been on an adventure with thousands of experiences in my catalog and twice as many lessons learned. I struck out on my own and sometimes paid dearly for it, but ended up richly rewarded. I'd traveled a bit, been involved in disability civil rights confrontations in the streets of our city and was now managing to live on my own.

Gail Linn's academic brilliance brought her an offer of a full scholarship, including room, board and attendant service at a Big Ten University, at a time when gimps like us just didn't go to college. She turned it down, though, because she couldn't bear to leave home. There she stayed until she died.

When I returned to my hometown after having been away for several years, I'd once made an effort to call her, curious to see if the woman who had always had the best of everything was still on top.

We chatted, and I learned her grandmother had died, her brother moved away and sister had married — and that Donna's husband really liked Gail Linn. Poor Donna, I thought: even marriage hadn't given her an escape from her demanding older sister. Gail Linn told me that she and Donna would go to an occasional Barry Manilow concert or this or that. I saw Gail Linn was still insulated from my harsh realities.

I didn't tell her how hard it was for me to find someone to get me up in the morning. I glossed over the last broken heart I'd had; I didn't mention how I was afraid of getting old. I told her, instead, about my job. I told her I was learning to drive, and that I was now volunteering at the same summer camp that 18 years ago she'd gone home from after two days.

I realized I still knew her. I remembered the look of uncomfortable disagreement she'd wear when you knew she just didn't get it. She'd kind of shrink into herself when something seemed too much for her, in all her academic brilliance, to think about. She'd smile weakly, divert her eyes. "Oh, uh-huh," she'd say.

There wasn't much to say after that conversation. We'd hit a wall, reached an impasse even nostalgia couldn't penetrate, leaving me searching for what it had been that had held us together so long ago.

She called only once after that; I don't remember what it was we talked about. When I moved to my own place, I entertained the idea of inviting her and her parents over for dinner, to show them what people with disabilities could accomplish in these modern times. But I knew my purpose was only to gloat, so the invitation was never extended.

When I met my beloved Dave, the thought of calling Gail Linn occurred to me. But then I recalled a tearful conversation we'd once had because a neighbor boy hadn't liked her. She'd been crazy about him and he knew it. He'd told me privately once that he didn't like Gail Linn much, but that he'd come over because her mother had always been nice to his widowed mom. He'd proceeded to point out to me the things I'd thought only I noticed. He'd mocked, while I'd sat numbly, divided inside between loyalty to my defenseless friend and relief that I wasn't alone in my view of her. Through all the nights Gail Linn had weepingly prayed for Joey's conversion, I writhed in guilt, knowing the truth.

I couldn't tell her about Dave. I was afraid I'd be gloating — over finally having the one thing Gail Linn didn't.

When Gail Linn's mother told me about her daughter's death, she revealed a few things that underscored for the final time the differences that had helped us drift apart.

Gail Linn was involved in her church's young adult club. On overnight trips, her brother would go along and handle her care, because he could still lift her. The family knew nothing of attendant services — or even lifting devices that would help other women to lift her.

Her mother told me that Gail Linn, when she went down the block, would take along a cordless phone to call home in case she got in trouble. At the end of her block is an accessible bus route; Gail Linn probably never knew it existed. She would not go on her own any farther than the cordless phone would work. A beautiful city, a calm neighborhood and an accessible bus route at her door — she turned them all down. A free ticket to higher education, summer camp and access to all kinds of interesting other adventures. She couldn't cope.

I took comparatively wrong roads; traded common sense for intrigue so often it became habit. I opted for the gravel road instead of the yellow brick one. I spent so much time on self-loathing that I nearly became a burnout who could only identify friends by which barstool they sat on. My physical health and mental attitude were so poor that I almost lost my life. Much of my experience has been a voluntary boxing match. But the victory has come in a life richer than I could have predicted. Still, Gail Linn's death has made me examine my life as I've never done before.

I feel rage when I think of her life, and its lurking, stereotypic "happy cripple" motif, used as a standard for the rest of us. In school Gail Linn was demure and quiet. She followed instructions, did what she was told and never deviated from the path others presented to her. So pleased were they with her gentility! They always asked me why I couldn't "be like Gail Linn."

They didn't see the after-school side of Gail Linn. They didn't see that the instant she was lugged up the stairs to the main floor of her family home, Gail Linn became the queen of all she surveyed, using her disability to lord it over her siblings. Donna came third even though she was the middle child (Jack, her brother, was the youngest, but his gender granted him household priorities). Once home, Gail Linn became loud, bossy and spoiled. The transformation was practically unbelievable.

Is the rage I feel resentment? It would have been so much easier for me had I never gone away to school, never gotten a job; if I'd never done anything more than was offered me within the two-block radius of my mother's home. The stresses of recruiting and managing attendants, paying bills or even figuring out what to eat each day could have been traded for a comfortable, predictable life with my mother. Maybe I resent Gail Linn for taking the cushy route.

Could my rage be frustration? Frustration at knowing that Gail Linn had been in a unique position for someone with a disability at that time in society — that her brain could have opened countless doors for her? Frustration knowing that she might have written her own ticket, and still ended up with a cushy life — that she had earned herself? Frustration thinking that, had she done that, she could have given something back?

She had a chance to bust a stereotype. Instead, she accepted it. That she had a life of relative ease is not what so enrages me; it's the way she accomplished it.

A major roadblock to our community ever gaining power is that we're handed things. Gail Linn's family handed her a life;

Social Security handed her a check. Gail Linn handed back the cute, acquiescent gimp routine that telethons are so fond of promoting. Thus she got her needs met.

Are we better for living this kind of life? Did she make a difference in anything in the time she spent on earth?

I can't begin to judge the worth of a person's life, particularly when I so often question my own. And who can actually fault someone for the harmless, innocent choices they make as they move across the continuum? But why have we made it so easy for gimps to do nothing? And why do we as a community allow so many of us to do so damn little?

My mother says there can be only one Albert Schweitzer. But each of us has the chance to make some little impact on our world. It doesn't mean that every person with a disability has to have a job or be involved in politics. It simply means that individually we should find something to get interested in that reaches beyond our dwellings, more than two blocks away. Instead of allowing others to keep us content by feeding us, providing us shelter and care, let us find a way to return something.

This seems particularly important for those of us who don't work, whose hours aren't taken up in work and work-related activities. There's endless opportunity to find ways to give back. Volunteers are needed everywhere. In a volunteer situation it's often easy to see the results of your efforts. If transportation is a problem, find out what you can do where you are. Go to the library and help another person learn to read. Get out the phone book and pick out a few organizations that look interesting and call to see if you can do something from your home. Take a class. Get a pen pal. Do something. Turn off the television and do something.

There is nothing wrong with accepting benefits the government has designed for us. Such benefits help many of us stay out of institutions. But to spend our days and nights doing nothing with our lives is pure selfishness. Those of us who do are simply taking advantage of the still-popular opinion that people with disabilities needn't worry about anything; that someone will take care of it all and we don't have to lift a finger to do anything about it — that we can simply take our checks, meet our immediate needs and vegetate.

Employed gimps are not above reproach. There's plenty of

time to do nothing after hours. Even if we accept that the stress of preparing for, traveling to and from work and being on the job are compounded by the presence of a disability, most of us can find an occasional hour or two to do something for someone else.

Organizers complain that there are never enough people to do all that needs to be done. They then pile so much work on themselves that they end up getting nothing done. Maybe we should turn our attention to those who benefit from the sweat of activism and find out why there is so much inactivity among us. Perhaps we should be thinking of ways that make surrender to the happy cripple role less attractive. It might take coming out of our high-and-mighty leadership modes and really listening to those in our community like Gail Linn whom we write off because they don't fit our expectations.

Involvement of any kind makes a statement that's unmistakably clear. It says that our lives are not defined by entitlements, public assistance programs or others' definitions of who we should be. When we immobilize ourselves we're affirming what Jerry Lewis has claimed is gospel — that we have nothing in our lives worth mentioning. That our lives as people with disabilities are devoid of productivity or goals; that nothing should be expected of us.

When we get outside ourselves, though, even for an instant, we not only enrich ourselves as individuals and as a community, but we strengthen a world which is in desperate need of help.

Look at ADAPT. Whether one agrees with their tactics or not, the fact is that they are able to mobilize more of us than any other organization has ever been able to. This is largely due to the fact that they reach out to those of us who have been considered by others with and without disabilities as valueless and shown us our worth.

Not everyone can be a leader. But ADAPT leadership understood a long time ago that leadership is meaningless without folks who are willing to fight the battles. And by having the sense to include all kinds of us with disabilities, they have built a power base that made even Bill Clinton take notice. Every person at an ADAPT action is made to feel his or her own worth. They know that their efforts as individuals count; that their being at an action makes a difference. And they all share in the victory.

All ADAPT members reach outside themselves whenever

they confront the issues ADAPT takes on. No nondisabled person who ever encounters an ADAPT action will ever look at people with disabilities in the same way again. Even if they disagree with ADAPT's tactics, they'll be changed — ADAPT has underscored for them in a big way what many of us preach: that individuals with disabilities are not all willing to be "Jerry's Kids." ADAPT makes people who have disabilities think about themselves again, and think about where they fit in the world. Even if they don't agree with what ADAPT does, or how it does it, they at least have been forced to think about why they disagree. For once they're not numbly accepting someone else's dictates.

ADAPT folks have done more with their lives than suck up resources. Along with others, they laid the groundwork for what would become the Americans with Disabilities Act. So did many people with disabilities who grew up before the days of access. Instead of staying home, they got out and rolled down driveways and into streets, because there were no curb cuts. They went to college; they did things that none of us could begin to know about, things that began to change the face of disability and make it possible for activism to start. Most didn't sit in front of government offices or block buses, but they did something.

So can each of us. Gail Linn may not have ever joined ADAPT, but had I taken the time to understand her, maybe we could have hit a common chord that might have encouraged her to use that marvelous brain of hers for some good cause. Maybe not; but it would have been more difficult for her to ignore the world around her had some of us activists planted the seeds.

It boils down to who controls our lives. We might think we do; but every time Jerry Lewis snivels his way across America, he takes away our control. Every time one of us decides it's easier to just take what we can take, Jerry Lewis wins. If we let people like him win, then we have no business complaining when we can't get jobs, or the services we need, or even access to the local grocery store.

It isn't up to me to decide what Gail Linn's life amounted to. But as long as I can, I will continue fighting anyone who sees our lives as pitiable — including those of us with disabilities who hold that view. I will do my best to help battle the forces that keep people like Gail Linn from doing just one little thing for someone or something outside themselves. And I will never ever again entertain the thought that I could possibly have been happy on the same road that Gail Linn chose.

A popular country song speaks to the choices we make. He could have made different, less complicated, easier choices in life, the singer croons; but he would have missed a lot in the process: "I could have lived without the pain, but I'd have had to miss the dance."

Some of us are dancers. We fly across the floor in our wheelchairs, turning them, moving them, spinning them around to the music around us. Sometimes there are patterns, sometimes it's freeform. Onlookers may not consider this dancing, but it is to us. It is celebration. This is why we dance.

Some make it to the dance, then wait for someone to lead them through the steps. Few realize it's OK to invent the steps. They leave without enjoying all the dance has to offer. If someone had encouraged them from the floor, they might have danced a little, once in a while.

Others simply don't come to the dance at all, because they can't imagine how such a thing is possible. Since they can't conceive of the dance, it doesn't exist for them. They live and die without making any difference — to anyone or anything. They sat back and took all the favors, all the handouts, all good deeds done for them, without ever trying it for themselves. Whether they lived or not seemed to make no difference.

Had that song been popular when I was a kid, I might have told those so anxious for my conformity why I couldn't be like Gail Linn. " 'Cause I gotta dance," I would have said. "And Gail Linn won't learn how." They couldn't have understood. But 25 years later, I am so glad I didn't change. What a stunningly beautiful dance I would have missed!

Gail Linn's mother summed up her daughter's life: "Well, at least all her sufferings are over." I didn't ask, but I kind of figured that she wasn't talking about the short illness at the end. My life has to be more than a testament to suffering. Existence on this earth must, in some small way, be better for my time here. Gail Linn convinced me of this. Maybe that is the meaning I've been searching her life for.

July/August 1993

Questioning Continuum

Carol J. Gill

Continua are in fashion these days. The farther we drift away from each other in society — the more that classism divides us and violence tears us apart — the more some people seem determined to project unity, or at least continuity, onto humankind. I don't believe this "reframing" of reality helps anyone. It trivializes the experience of us who must face the cold facts of marginalization while it ignores the value of our different experience.

There's a concept in statistics called "regression toward the mean." It says that measurements tend to cluster toward the average or middle. Anything extreme is unlikely to be repeated. For example, if my average time of swimming a lap is 40 seconds but one day I have an incredibly short time of 25 seconds, all factors being equal, my next time is likely to be longer — closer to average.

Sometimes I think human preference is ruled by this law of probability. Many people are distressed by the unusual. They want it normalized, brought to the middle where they are. In fact, it's the rare person who feels perfectly comfortable with anything discrepant from her/his realm of familiarity.

I think this tells us a lot about the continuum-seekers. They need someone to tell them it's all a bad dream, that there really are no discrete differences between people or their experiences of life. They like hearing that what's important is that we're all part of the same human family. This takes away the confusion, loss of control and untidiness of genuine diversity. It eliminates both the tension of admitting you may be unable to completely understand someone different and the "stretch" of accepting their culture as valid anyway.

True confessions: I am an ex-homogeneity-junkie, myself. In college I rhapsodized over constructs like brotherhood and fellowship (not yet seeing any gender considerations there!). It served me twice to idealize unity. First, it seemed like the path out of my own marginalization, i.e., disability would be insignificant in the universal family. Second, it made it so much easier for me to accept poor people and gays and cultural/racial minorities if I could simply imagine they were all like me under the skin. I wanted to believe differences were illusory. Along with many other pubescent idealists, I longed to dump the melting pot into the Cuisinart and make a pablum smooth enough for me to swallow.

But my black and gay and Jewish friends refused to go gently into that good blender. They insisted on being exactly what they were (and letting me know exactly what I was!). I got over the rejection and disillusionment to learn that it wouldn't kill me to be tense over differences. I even learned that I could be enriched by cultures I didn't understand, cultures that didn't exist for my enrichment. I learned that both the world and my own mind were big enough to encompass messy, noisy heterogeneity — that people didn't cease to exist as human beings because they didn't resemble me, that I could interact with them without pulling them toward the middle. I could appreciate separate colors without needing them to be my rainbow.

When I was growing up, my father frequently talked about a man that he worked with who came from Japan. He really liked this man. He would visit the guy's house and then come back and tell us all the ways he was different: the foods he ate, his furnishings, his clothes, the way he counted on an abacus, the way he reasoned about life. My father's world view was enriched by his association with that friend. His accounts conveyed tremendous respect without ever needing to find ways the man was similar to us.

Respect is a key concept in accepting differentness. Many years ago, I was sitting on a stage with Judy Heumann and an interviewer asked us what we found most disturbing about others' attitudes toward us. Judy said she most resented their need for us to be nondisabled. I'm ashamed to say I didn't totally get it then, but I do now. There is a great lack of respect for who I am as a disabled person conveyed by people who either wish I could be normal or who need to see my disability as an unimportant part of me.

So when is a person disabled and not something else? I tend to think you're disabled when society says you're disabled. I agree with activists who believe that "disability" is mostly a social distinction — one that is triggered by some physical/sensory/mental/functional/cosmetic difference. How much of a difference is significant enough to count as a disability? That's usually decided by the majority culture tribunal. What is barely noted in some cultures can be a great stigma in another (e.g., being born with a missing digit). In sum, I believe disability is a marginalized status that society assigns to people who are different enough from majority cultural standards to be judged abnormal or defective in mind or body.

There seems to be an underlying social requirement that in order to qualify as a disability, the defect must lie beyond the individual's immediate control. Maybe by working hard, the disabled person can improve, but not too easily. If persons can control their impairment at will (occasional recreational drug use; charley horses) they are not seen as disabled but as "bringing it on themselves." However, if they are unable to stop hurting themselves, they may be seen as disabled (someone with an addiction). Similarly, if they "brought it on themselves" but now can't reverse it, they are disabled (someone injured via driving drunk).

Although I am emphasizing society's role in determining disability status, I am not suggesting that, in the socially ideal world, all physical, mental and sensory conditions would be irrelevant or unnoticed. I am not a complete environmentist or cultural relativist on this score. Many people who are considered disabled now would still have an experience of "differentness" in a more accessible and socially accommodating world. I believe I would be one of them. I would still experience struggle, pain, slowness, and things I couldn't do the way most people could (e.g., run spontaneously) even if I had all the human and technical help currently imaginable. (I admit my imagination is limited — I don't know if something like virtual reality, for example, would be the ultimate leveler of experience.) Further, I would still have a disability history or heritage behind me affecting my worldview. No, you can't take that away from me.

But in the ideal world, my differences, though noted, would not be devalued. Nor would I. Society would accept my experience as "disability culture," which would in turn be accepted as part of "human diversity." There would be respectful curiosity about what I have learned from my differences that I could teach society. In such a world, no one would mind being called Disabled. Being unable to do something the way most people do it would not be seen as something bad that needed curing. It would be seen as just a difference. Differences might make you proficient in some contexts, deficient in others, or not matter at all. For example, if I can't run, I might be an inferior messenger if time is critical. However, my inability to run might just as likely have stimulated me to address time more creatively or to develop ways to send messages swiftly that are as efficient as running, or vastly superior. In other words, ideally, even if I had a difference that might hinder me in some contexts, I wouldn't be judged *generally* deficient because a recognized feature of Disability culture would be the fact that such limitations can be fodder for innovation and for a rich and valuable human experience. Once again, respect.

Returning to the present world, given my understanding of disability as a social status, what about people who say they are disabled but society does *not* so label them? What about things like alcoholism, chronic fatigue, compulsive behaviors? Conditions like these seem to be judged by society as either too insignificant or too voluntary to be real disabilities. Consider also the borderline conditions, like eyeglasses, limps, the fingertip lost in a factory accident, the gradual hearing loss with age, the so called slow learner at math. These are the differences most people downplay out of embarassment or fear of social devaluation. They are also the differences some pull out of their back pockets when they want to prove that there is a continuum of disability or if they have something to gain from being disabled — a parking space, priority treatment, a place of power in a disability organization. Are any of the above disabilities? (The terrain is looking a little gray, but since I started the discussion with my own thoughts, I'll humbly continue — hopeful that readers will understand that I'm just taking a stab at an analysis that I think is important to continue through others' responses.)

I would say that it's possible to have a disability without society's agreement. Society may simply be too ignorant about some disabilities to include them in the classification. If the public knew how "debilitating," involuntary, and physiologically-based such conditions as alcoholism and chronic fatigue were, it's conceivable these would be viewed more generally as disabilities. The critical issue seems to be whether they affect life functioning or are weird enough by society's standards that they would be labeled disabilities once they were fully revealed. Anything potentially labeled as a disability by society is a disability, in my book.

But I *have* met people whose claim to disability truly annoyed me. I find it hard to embrace as brothers and sisters those folks who spend their whole lives comfortably in the nondisabled world without any mention of personal disability until a disabled person challenges their authority to speak for us. Then they justify their position of profit or leadership in a disability organization by trotting out their spectacles or trick knee or rheumatiz'. "Actually, we're all disabled in some way, aren't we?" they ask. "No!" I say. If the only time you "walk the walk" of disability is when it's convenient for you and you even admit your disability has little impact on your life and no one regards you as disabled, give me a break — you ain't one of us! You aren't in danger of the marginalization we experience or expect on a daily basis.

Here's a possible rule of thumb: If a person who has *not* been labeled disabled has some physical, sensory or mental difference or limitation that does *not* significantly affect daily life and the person does *not* present himself/herself to the world at large as a disabled person, chances are the person is not disabled.

Is it a disability if it's invisible? If it's disabling enough to affect your life, it's also potentially visible. Your learning difference, your fatigue, your pain or depression could all be revealed under certain circumstances. You know you have a "real" disability when you know society will label and marginalize you once your difference shows.

I am increasingly tired of disabled people who don't believe the hidden disabilities of others are significant or "real" disabilities. But I also have a hard time with people whose disabilities are completely unapparent who complain of being "shut out" by the disability community. If you are not willing to openly identify as disabled, I'm sure you have your reasons, but don't be surprised if you are taken for an AB. If you are truly disabled you must realize why we need sometimes to shut the nondisabled world out — why we need to grab precious privacy, community and identity for ourselves when we can. I could not belong to the Black Student Union (BSU) at my school, and after I learned how oppression robs a people of their power and identity, I understood I had no place there. I also knew some African Americans who could and did pass for white. They knew without complaint that the price of entry into BSU was identifying as black. I have heard retorts from some persons with hidden disabilities along the lines of: "What do you want me to do — wear a sign?" Well, if that's the only way you can think of to "come out" as disabled, I recommend you get suggestions from a gay friend or ask yourself if you really want to be a part of the disability community.

What about nondisabled people who say they belong in our community because they experience disability through a loved one? Nondisabled people, no matter how much they love us, do not know the inside experience of being disabled. Moreover, they are in a position to escape the stigma. They can leave our sides and go out among strangers as "normal people," if only for a few minutes of peaceful anonymity. They may know the day-to-day pressures of being associated with a disabled person, they may deal with their own stigma for loving us, and they may grieve for our oppression (and their own if they share our lives), but they don't know the relentless feeling of dealing directly and inescapably with both the difference and the public invalidation it inspires. That stiff smile, that condescending pat, that flight of stairs, that slick elevator devoid of braille signs, that loneliness on prom night, that aching just to live our lives without having to argue for equality — unfortunately, they are ours.

Are people with illnesses disabled? Only when they have the temerity to neither get well nor die. Society has a niche for ill people. They should be on the move, traveling the arc from health to sickness and back to health. There's another niche for people with terminal illnesses. They should move from health to death. If they know their manners, they get on with it, too — no "lingering." If you remain in the limbo of ill-health for too long and you can't do everything you used to do the way you used to do it when you were healthy, you get stigmatized. And that stigma sure looks and quacks like disability stigma. People who linger in abnormal states, who don't work normally, or who need help acquire a status of invalidation.

Looking at the connection between illness and disability another way, people who learn to live with chronic illnesses often demonstrate the same resilience, modified values and creative pragmatism that mark the disability culture. Chronic illness and disability seem to teach people similar lessons about life. Furthermore, some illnesses definitely make people disabled (e.g., ALS) while some disabilities lead to problems that are painful, progressive or weakening to the point of being experienced as not just a difference but as a sense of real malaise.

To my mind, people with lingering illness are definitely in the club. This used to bother me because I didn't like reinforcing the misconception that all disabled people are sick or dying. Who needed more stigma? True, some of that discomfort may have been my own prejudice and denial about illness. Still, robust disabled people with stable conditions — for example persons simply born without a body part — would not seem to qualify in any way as ill. I think it makes sense at times to keep a distinction between disability and illness because prejudice against "healthy" disabled people offers a pure case for studying what ableism is all about. People with disability can experience horrendous discrimination and abuse simply because they look different. Until we learn more about how this compares to discrimination based on illness, I favor keeping a line, however flexible, between illness and disability, or seeing them as two entities with a large area of overlap, neither one subsumable into the other.

I am left with many questions that I believe would be helpful to answer: Are disabled, ill and elderly people similarly stigmatized because of society's dread of disability in each group? In other words, is it all just disability prejudice, or is there an illness stigma separate from a disability stigma (Is contagion a factor?) and an aging stigma separate from both? What part does appearance play? How much is due to public fear of our dependency on others? What about others' belief that we can't do enough of the things that AB's think are essential to life to be considered attractive or fully human? How much is due to our perceived lack of power and our reminder to others of *their* vulnerability to loss/change? I appreciate the ideas of disabled scholars, including Irv Zola and Harlan Hahn, who have tackled issues involving disability v. illness and the components of disability prejudice. But I think we need to continue exploring the remaining unknowns, especially when so many of our children are being "integrated" and "included" in the mainstream in the belief that this will result in, among other benefits, a reduction of disability prejudice in AB's proximate to them.

I'm already bracing myself for the criticism of the "human race" brigade. I expect to be accused of encouraging divisiveness when we should all be promoting our common experience and goals. Let me respectfully submit that people with disabilities, including myself, have not created our own marginalization. We got that from society. Now we must find the best way to survive that fact physically and emotionally.

If we've learned anything from other oppressed minorities it's that you gain nothing from efforts to assimilate into the culture that devalues you. We will never be equal if we accept token acceptance as slightly damaged AB's. Politically and psychologically our power will come from celebrating who we are as a distinct people. I'm not content being a pale version of the majority culture. I want to be a strong version of something else — different but equally valid. (I'm being humble here; in fact, I believe a fully articulated disability culture that honors differentness and interdependence would be a vast improvement over the corrupt intolerant culture I was born into!)

As the British Disability Arts activists said so often during their 1993 tour of the U.S., the struggle shouldn't be for integration but for power. Once we have power, we can integrate whenever we want. Once we command respect for who we are, we can afford to join forces with the rest of the human family, free from the danger of losing our power, losing ourselves. The "respect for who we are" has to start with us. We need to work on our own heads about who we are, our value and the value of our culture. When we develop a stronger identity as a community, we can really serve notice on society, or integrate into it, from a position of strength — on no one's terms but ours.

March/April 1994

THIS IS OPPRESSION

The First Taste

Cass Irvin

The very first friend I had after I had polio was the daughter of the woman my family paid to come take care of me. She was my age, and even though she was paid to be my friend, we got to know each other and she taught me a lot. She lived in the real world, and I didn't.

Every other Saturday, she would come take me out. Sometimes we'd go downtown.

Yellow cabs were roomy in those days. Angela, my wheelchair and I would all fit in the back seat. (There wasn't any "special transportation for the handicapped" in those days.) It must have been about 1959.

One day we decided we go take in a movie at the Mary Anderson. Angela pushed me up next to the ticket window, and went up to the window herself. She asked the man at the window what time the movie started. He told her, and she told me. Then she asked him how much it cost, and he told her and she told me.

We figured out that we had enough money, so Angela put the money up in the window and said, "We'd like two tickets, please."

"Sorry, I can't let you in there."

I asked the man, "Can't I sit in the aisle in my wheelchair?" I knew that when I had gone to the movies with my family, my father had lifted me out of the wheelchair and put me in a seat.

I had known that it was a fire hazard.

But now the man said, "Not you. Her," and pointed to Angela.

Angela just stood there, and I just sat there. Finally, we went away.

I became totally embarrassed for her. It was the first time, I think, I had ever felt embarrassed for someone else. It was so humiliating! All that time! She had asked, "What time is the movie?" and "How much is it?" and he hadn't said anything until she gave him the money!

I was indignant. Angela wasn't. She was used to it, expected it. I could not understand why she could not be let in. She could walk! I couldn't walk; I could understand why — I totally accepted why — I might not be allowed to go in — but I could not accept for anything that she could not go in.

"I'm gonna tell my daddy about this!" I told her.

I was sure he'd call the management and straighten things out. We'd write to the papers, we'd create a big stir; we'd embarrass them!

It was my first experience with racial segregation. I had not known before what that kind of segregation meant. I didn't know then that it was the norm of the day, and that it would take a great deal more than my daddy writing a letter to get things to change for Angela.

I had assumed it was perfectly all right for me not to be able to go in. I know now that this, too, is segregation when it happens to us today. It's segregation, just like it was for Angela. But people don't call it that. For us, it's "special." But what they mean is segregation.

For blacks, it was "separate-but-equal" that kept Angela out of the Mary Anderson Theatre. For us, today, it's "special."

It's going to take a long time for us to recognize that it's segregation in our case, because they call it "special." Such a nice word! How can you criticize somebody when they're doing something "special" for you?

"Oh, please, ask us if you have a problem," people tell us, over and over. "We're more than willing to help you. We want to; that's what we're here for — to do whatever 'special' thing we need to do for you." How can you criticize people for that?

Two years ago at a performance of *The Elephant Man* at the Macauley, I felt exactly what Angela must have felt that afternoon at the Mary Anderson. When those ushers and the box office manager came over to me, I felt sick inside. I felt humiliated. I felt embarrassed. Put down because I wanted to sit where my friends were going to sit. I was causing a problem; I wasn't being a good girl and going to the back row.

I felt so mad and so hurt that night at the Macauley that I hardly know what happened during the rest of the play.

It's easier to denounce an injustice toward someone else than to let yourself feel it when it happens to you. Being humiliated is a bad enough experience; but to rise up and draw attention to it!

We're made to feel that we're supposed to know better. That we brought this humiliation on ourselves. We should know better than to try to sit somewhere we don't belong. How awful of us for creating a problem for the ushers!

And so, we accept our "special" services, just as Angela accepted segregation. It's hard to throw away what society's taught us. It's hard.

February 1983

The Room of Pain and Loneliness

Edward L. Hooper

"I have a picture of that room. It's in my head even now. There's a toilet. There's an elevated bathtub — the kind that lets them slide you in from a hospital bed. There's two other bathtubs in there, too — regular ones.

"Two frosted windows there, there in drab, green walls. A big, heavy door. A lot of chrome in there. And a cold floor. A cold, cold brown tile floor."

At the D.T. Watson Home for Crippled Children in Leetsville, PA, and particularly in the keen memory of Tom Zabelsky, it served a very different purpose. It was a closest. A sterile closet.

"The room — the whole institution — had no warmth. It was sterile. Sterile and cold." It was in this room that Tom remembers being confined. For hours. For days. Alone.

The very night Tom arrived at D.T. Watson, as he remembers it today, he fell out of bed and broke his hip. He doesn't know how he fell, he says; he didn't have the strength or ability at the time to move his body, he remembers that.

And though X-rays were taken which confirmed a break, neither he nor his parents were told about the injury for months — and then, according to Tom's mother, they found out quite by accident, when a nurse let it "slip out" one day.

He was little, he was hurt. And he cried.

"If you don't stop crying we're going to put you in The Room! *By yourself!*" Tom recalls the words today — years later. They punctuated, he says, the abusive actions and attitude he felt all his days at the D.T. Watson Home for Crippled Children.

Tom was sent to The Room too many times to count. Perhaps that's why he remembers The Room so clearly — because 5-year-old children do fuss and cry — especially "crippled" children with newly broken bones, rehabilitating from polio. Tom spent what seemed to him like years isolated in that sterile closet.

If Tom didn't obey, if he wasn't quiet, the casters would be unlocked on his hospital bed and he'd be wheeled into The Room. Wheeled into The Room to contemplate his incorrect behavior. He remembers he was always made to feel he'd done something bad.

But he didn't know how to meet the Home's expectations of what "being good" was.

"God — then I was in that room, how I prayed I could go to sleep so the time would pass faster! But I couldn't sleep," he now says. "No one seemed to care that I was lonely or in pain. I'd call — cry — for my mother. But nobody came.

"I couldn't express myself to anyone. Of all this, the whole experience at D.T. Watson, what I remember most is the loneliness."

Tom did learn, during the two years he was to spend at D.T. Watson, how to limit the time spent in The Room. He simply learned to obey the "don't fuss, don't cry" rules. Regardless of the pain, wants or needs.

D. T. Watson, he says, was an expensive convalescent home — "for rich kids." He was able to stay there only through money from The March of Dimes.

His body was tended to, after a fashion — and he was fed. But one could scarcely say he was "cared for." To this day he cannot remember a smile, or even a friendly face, except on weekends during visiting hours, when stern, forbidding faces turned warm and caring — at least until parents went home.

Why didn't Tom Zabelsky tell his parents about The Room they put him in when he wasn't "being good?" He doesn't really know, he says; it took him 34 years to finally tell his mother about the abuse he felt at the D.T. Watson Home.

Finally he comes up with another reason: "I guess," he tells me, "I thought it was just something I had to endure.

How many disabled people in this country are enduring abuse? If society even knew the numbers, large as they would be, would they care enough to do anything?

I was shocked to learn that the Nazis had exterminated a million disabled people during the '30s and '40s. Yet the very thing that shocked me into disbelief and anger has been met by the media and society at large with a shrug — an insignificant, obscure historical footnote to the Holocaust.

Society cares more about *all* people in the '80s, doesn't it?

And abuse is now "out of the closet," right? We read all the time about abuse: child abuse, spouse abuse, abuse of the elderly. It's all being aired now. As a society, we're beginning to say we'll not turn our heads anymore, that those responsible will be held accountable. Aren't we?

Disability's abuse closet seems locked as tightly as ever, teeming with what by all sketchy accounts is a Pandora's box of unspeakable nightmares nobody seems to want to touch.

I know a 21-year-old man who, for over a week, had not been bathed, moved, or even allowed a toilet. His bowels became so badly impacted that the contents of his small intestine had started backing up into his stomach. He was finally hospitalized, with pressure sores, a urinary tract infection and the impaction. He'd been abused. By his mother.

The man won't blow the whistle on his mother, though. Nor will countless other disabled people come forward to accuse their families or attendants of crimes against their humanity. They simply endure.

They endure slaps, punches, burns, isolation, neglect. Insults, intimidation, theft. Lack of personal care, physical restraint, sexual molestation. And more. They endure it.

Why?

Abused people are afraid things will only get worse if they do try changing things themselves. Most complaints about abuse of elderly people and children, even most complaints of spouse abuse, come from third parties or professionals who suspect the abuse, rather than from the victims themselves.

Certainly backlash from an already uncaring or violent person is a legitimate, logical fear for someone disabled who's being abused. And even if they were to escape their subjugation, where would they go? To the dreaded nursing home? They must surely think of all this. And so they remain silent.

Or perhaps they internalize the abuse, thinking that somehow they've done something bad, something to deserve whatever physical or psychological bruising they get. Or perhaps the victims are ashamed — for themselves and their abusers. They feel these are "family" matters, best kept private.

Perhaps simply being disabled is enough; that both victim and abuser genuinely believe that "that's just the way it is when you're disabled. Shut up and be happy you're getting anything at all!"

Day after day after day, like Tom Zablesky, disabled people endure.

We acknowledge spouse abuse, child abuse, elder abuse. But we don't acknowledge disability abuse. Not yet.

This needs to change. We all know the problem exists. The short-term effects of disability abuse are terrifying; the long-term effects are psychologically devastating.

But we keep the abuse "in the closet." That's the metaphor we use — our metaphor to describe things in society we deny or are most ashamed of. Yet Tom Zablesky lived that in-the-closet metaphor. To him, it was no metaphor. It was real: The room of pain and loneliness.

Is the disability community ready to open the closet, to confront the reality of disability abuse, to face the dilemmas, to tell the horror stories?

March/April 1988

Disconfirmation

Billy Golfus

Doctor Professor George Shapiro in the Speech-Communication Department of the University of Minnesota is always talking about baseball.

He gives examples to explain basic ideas about communication, like a pitcher pretending to ignore a batter just before he strikes him out. He says that being ignored can affect a lot more than your batting average. Now, the thing is, he thinks communication is real important. He's a professor who has given his whole life to studying it so he sort of sounds like Mick Jagger in that line from *Everybody Needs Somebody to Love:*

"If everyone here'd listen to my song tonight, it would save the whole world."

There's this thing called Disconfirmation. Fancy word, huh? It sort of means being ignored. Not exactly, but close enough. Disabled people are just one group that gets disconfirmed a lot. Everybody's experienced some watered-down version of it.

Dr. Professor Shapiro is a rooting fan of this book by Watzlawick, Beavin and Jackson, *Pragmatics of Human Communication.*

They quote William James, who everybody calls the father of psychology. James wrote about Disconfirmation.

"No more fiendish punishment could be devised, even were such a thing physically possible, than that one should be turned loose in society and remain absolutely unnoticed by all the members thereof."

It happens to everybody that I know that's disabled. Happens with friends and family, happens with these do-gooder social systems. For a long time I figured I was the only one; then I was talking with Sandy Ford, a nurse who does research with the Hyperbaric Chamber at Hennepin County Medical Center.

We were talking about how all my friends split after the accident.

"It happens EVERY time. EVERY time." says Sandy Ford. "Like we've got a guy injured, I don't know, this week. And he's 32 and he has this cute little fiancée that's there holding his hand. That's there crying. Weeping, weeping. All this stuff. And. Unless he has an extremely good recovery she is NOT going to hang in there.

"And when I see high school kids come in. The first three weeks there are kids everywhere. I mean, they're flockin' in here and everyone is suddenly John's best buddy. I mean, everyone has known him since a baby. Everyone is a good friend.

"And all you gotta do is sit back and watch. If, outside of his family, he winds up with two people that will stick with him for six months — and some people will stay six months — but at a year, if you have one person who stayed with you, you're pretty lucky.

"Strokes. I think a lot of times they don't split. If you've been married for fifty years and your wife or husband has a stroke, you're probably not gonna split.

"But now you take head injury, and the biggest population is males between the ages of 16 and 25. Now they don't have that same long bonding with friends. Even if they're married, they don't have the same history of bonding. Friends invariably leave. I daresay even with strokes, their friends leave."

Sandy offered this paradox; for some people, if their friends didn't leave, they probably wouldn't have done as well. Weird, huh?

The explanation for people getting in the wind, leaving, is always the same: "They probably don't know how to handle it." That's a cliché everybody uses. People want to be nice and not point the finger too hard. I've heard that line literally dozens of times. One of my best buddies, Kay, 73 years old and legally blind, has heard it about some of her own kids.

"It's different people that you come to know after the injury," Sandy Ford went on. "And I do think some catastrophic things can happen and some good things come out of it. And I DO think it's catastrophic when all your friends walk out on ya."

My friend Stevie, the writer, said having your friends leave happens to everybody. I want to say pure and simple: not all at once or the same way as it happens to people who have been hurt or handicapped, it don't.

But ever since the accident everybody's all the time telling me what's happening with me. Stevie the writer's got this thing that it's very hip to turn the obvious on its ear. "They didn't leave," he said. "You left."

He really said that.

Having all these people go away and ignore you IS fiendish punishment. Some people have walked by me on the street and pretended they didn't recognize me. Like, you NEED interaction with other people. On the other hand, baby, if they're gonna go, let 'em go.

Watzlawick and the gang go on to say that Disconfirmation says, in effect, "You do not exist."

Having all these people split was painful. Probably the worst of them were the "old friends" who acted like everything was OK and we'd "work it out." And still split.

It caused me to look at love and trust real different.

Because Disconfirmation, just by saying what a friend isn't, also says what a friend is. Dr. Professor Shapiro, because he is a college professor, talks about several "defining" — that's the way they talk — things: He says a friend is honest and present and "I can be imperfect with them." That means that the people who split or the people whose actions say "You do not exist" ain't really friends anyway. No loss. In fact, a gain. "Present" means someone who's there and gonna be there. So having people leave is lonely, but just a painful clearing of dead wood.

Your do-gooders are, a lot of them, in this artificial-friend role. But they ain't friends of mine. I'll tell you that. They are going to treat you like a client and not a real person. You as a real person are Disconfirmed. And you better fit their image of how a helpee should act. And be grateful.

Disconfirmation is like being ignored," I explained to my friend Jerry.

"Like DVR (Department of Vocational Rehabilitation) is doing to me?" Jerry asks.

"That's it. You can get a hint that the do-gooder programs can't see you and therefore can't communicate just by their use of acronyms. Make up three or five letters in a row and you've got a social service program."

"If you don't fit their program or their system, then you're out of place," says Jerry, starting to get the idea. "They wanted me to go through five days of testing. And I said I've got a file about a mile long that's got all the testing you could possibly want. It's like fucking communicating to, to . . . to nothing!"

Do you see what this has got to do with Disconfirmation? Jerry's being ignored. They can't see him because they've got a "program."

Whenever I try to leave a message with my DVR counselor's secretary she always says that she'll take a "VERY BRIEF" one. In other words, she hasn't got time for my messages. She has real work to do. That's Disconfirmation. You don't count; you don't exist, remember? In fact, I think you've got to have taken a class in Disconfirmation or you can't be a secretary in the first place.

I got inaugurated into that do-gooder meat grinder when I went for help from Jerry Waldman at at the Jewish Family and Children's Service.

He was one of those who didn't see much wrong with me. Mom told me about watching a TV program on closed head injury and all the brain-damaged specimens were complaining that nobody could see much wrong. I remember saying to Jerry Waldman, "I'm crippled."

"YOU'RE NOT THAT CRIPPLED," was his loud insistent answer. When he thought that you didn't catch his meaning he spoke LOUDER AND CLEARER.

He saw me walking with difficulty, unable to use one arm, some difficulty talking. Not even in a wheelchair. I mean, HE wasn't having no trouble walking. And HE wasn't having no trouble with his memory.

If you ain't been through this junk, how much empathy you gonna have, anyway?

"My problems," according to Jerry, were because I was out of work. "People get a lot of their good feelings about themselves from their jobs," he told me. So jobs didn't have jackshit to do with paying the rent and buying food — they were about "good feelings!"

Later, when Jerry Waldman became the director of the agency, he sent me to The Jewish Vocational Service, an arm of his own agency. Talk about the Three Stooges! They give you all these tests to figure out what you should be. Or at least what you want to be.

Why the hell didn't they just ask me? It would have saved a lot of time. Their testing is what my friend, Father Robert Lesch, calls self-validating. They subtly asked, "True or false: I would like the work of a prissy doily-embroiderer." And it's like we're waiting for the results of the tests to see what I should be. Honest to God, they seem to see those tests as closer to the Stone Tablets that Moses found than to the tea leaves they are. But if they run the tests, then they're covered. "See? It says right here . . ."

They gotta have something to DEMONSTRATE that they're doing something. In the meantime, you don't exist except as you fit into their program or "help their statistics" (their funding, their jobs). "Did you ever actually find anyone a job?" I asked Mary Hiemenz, my DVR counselor.

"Sure," she said. "If I didn't think this really helped people, I wouldn't do it."

But I get the Disconfirmation from Mary, too. I almost want to say she can't help it, it's not her fault. She's got two or four hundred clients — I never can get it straight — so you would expect a certain amount of Disconfirmation. How the hell is anybody going to get any attention among that many clients? In contrast, I depend on her for simple things just to operate. Like a ribbon for my printer, or computer disks. And if there's a SNAFU, it might take me days to reach her. Real help is almost impossible.

So, even though I believe that she's on my side, the system is set up to disconfirm people. Trying to reach her drives me right up the wall. You put somebody at the other end of the line that really doesn't care if they're reached or not — which is most of them — and the message that you get is that you're invisible. You don't count. Because that's what Disconfirmation is: the message that you don't exist.

If you're disabled, you've gotten that message.

Unfortunately, I've seen disabled people buy into that crap.

Disconfirmation from friends and family is ususally painful but obvious. The do-gooder helping professions have so many, many ways of doing it that it's a lot subtler. They say things like, "There's nothing wrong with their program, you understand. YOU DON'T FIT."

Or they teach "learned helplessness" because it gives them a *raison d'être*. Mary Hiemenz talks about seeing a bunch of counselors "holding on . . . petting this person and hugging them. And of course she's afraid to leave that environment." My friend Jerry asks, "Is this program set up to keep me there or is it just the way I'm looking at it? Some of this stuff just keeps you in these things. Myself, I get amazed at it."

Now I suppose you want to know what that's got to do with Disconfirmation? Well, they can't see you — you don't exist. You just become this icon to give their empty lives meaning. Or work out their own problems. Or to help their statistics.

Somebody asked me if Disconfirmation was intentional. You betcha it is, sometimes. Sometimes cruelly intentional. But if they can't see you, how can you even think of holding them responsible for anything? The essence of Disconfirmation is it allows the disconfirmer to escape from drama. You can't call it. They say — with a pitch and tone of voice that says you're crazy — "I didn't DO anything."

Well, that's a judgment call. I think that we are all interdependent on each other. If you see someone drowning and don't at least try to pull them out, that's murder. But that kind of Disconfirmation goes on every day with "friends" and family and the do-gooders. And you CAN'T call it. It's subtle but it can damage you. And you won't even know you were hit.

Chris Ringer, who does workshops for the "helping professions," says "in talking to these people an interesting theme seems to emerge, which is that a lot of them grew up in families where there was something wrong."

Mary Hiemenz talks about hearing people say, "I got into this field because I had my own family problems and I thought it would help me." I've heard them say that. Haven't you?

Chris Ringer thinks it has to do with control needs that they learned as children. "A lot of people in administration, or managing helpers . . . were saying, 'These people get overly involved in other people's business. They won't listen to what the clients want. They don't know when to stop. They can't put it away when they go home. And it's like their job's not a job. It's their identity."

My friend Jerry describes how that control shows up in getting you into the program that THEY like. They like to dictate what THEY want you to do. Jerry has trouble reading, and they didn't want to have to pay for a program for him to learn reading. Jerry asked, "How you going to deny me that program when that's the basis of what I want to do?

"Then the next month they paid for it. I don't know if they get off on some kind of power/control. I was supposed to react by saying, 'God, you're wonderful!' But I've noticed they always let you know what they are doing for you. What are you supposed to say? 'Thank you very much?' I guess I appreciate it, but I don't care to have someone let me know about it all the time.

"Do they ever do that for you? Let you know how wonderful they are and what they're doing for you? Doesn't that shit get to you?" my friend Jerry asks.

Do you see how denying him a reading program is a combination of control and Disconfirmation? You with your individual problems don't exist. You're just there to show them how much control they have over people, or to "work out" their own problems, or to let them have confirmation of how truly wonderful they are. Get it? The ones who walked away or ignore you are so much easier to deal with. That crummy behavior is almost a gift if you look at it in the right way.

First thing to do about Disconfirmation is to be aware when you're being disconfirmed. It's not so easy, and there's no 800 number to call. "Important" people can disconfirm you because they're so busy and you're so unimportant. When somebody won't take your phone calls ("He's in a meeting") or doesn't get back to you or promises whatever and then doesn't, those are pretty clear signs. But you can also be Disconfirmed with a smile.

My friend Sunnyland always talks about the showbusiness types who say, "You're beautiful, baby. Don't ever change. Let's do sushi sometime," over the shoulder.

That's Disconfirmation. All I can tell you is that my survival in the world is a little easier knowing that it exists and knowing what to call it.

November/December 1989

Cowboy Justice in Tiburon

Arthur Jacobs

Watch your step in Tiburon, partner . . .

I walk with a cane, have a paralyzed left arm, a speech impediment, long hair and a good education. I meet old friends from college in Tiburon, CA, on October 20, 1991. We climb aboard a fast boat and cruise over to see the fire in Berkeley. We race back to shore because my friends have to catch a plane to Dallas. The wind blowing in my hair from the speed of the boat makes me look wild. We arrive back on shore, and my friends drop me off at a bus stop and drive off to the airport.

The bus does not leave for twenty minutes so I go to get some coffee at Sam's Café. "Café" is a misnomer; it's actually a bar. I order a beer instead of coffee. Joking around with the bartender and the few people at the bar feels pleasant. Even with all the noise at the bar, people take time to understand my funny-sounding voice. I wander out onto the back pier, where people are sitting under the late afternoon sun, which is occasionally blocked by the black smoke and soot from the fire, eating, drinking and talking.

Walking around the pier, I talk to people now and again. It is quieter outside, so it is easier for people to understand me. Walking by one of the owners, I can tell he's curious about who this wild-looking, long-haired person is. I certainly seem out of place, walking around enjoying myself, my shirt unbuttoned, my hair waving and curling every which way, limping with a cane made out of a mahogany tree limb and carrying a beer bottle in my pocket.

I have the bottle in my pocket because my left arm is paralyzed and can't hold anything. I use my right arm to hold the cane, so if anything is going to be carried, into my pocket it goes.

The owner is immediately cautious. He approaches me and says people have been complaining about me; that I'd better leave or he will call the police.

"Who complained?" I ask, surprised, but he will not tell me. So I refuse to leave. He says he will call the police. "You are free to," I respond.

He might as well have said, with a Western drawl, "Stranger, I'll give ya till sundown to get out of town," because the next thing I know Officer Naugh comes in with a backup officer. It could just as easily have been Sheriff Naugh and his deputy marching into the saloon with pistols on their hips. They had pistols.

Naugh, figuring that I do not need my cane and that it might be a dangerous weapon, takes it from me. When I tell him that I use the cane to walk, he does not believe me. (Personally, I think he is acting like a John Wayne prototype.) They order me to leave with them.

When we start to leave, Naugh sees that I have a hard time walking and really do need the cane. He tries to give it back, but I do not take it. I am mad now! I am forced by police (John Wayne chasing the bad guy out of town) to limp out of a café, in Tiburon. Proudly but slowly I limp out of the bar. As we go out, a number of people tell the officers that I am innocent; even one of the bartenders tells the police there must be a mistake.

The enforcers of the law do not listen, however. How could they? The police are only actors in this real-life movie, and they only take orders from their director. I wonder who their director is?

Being thrown out of the bar would have made a good story had it ended there — or if I'd then jumped on my horse and ridden proudly into the sunset. But there's more.

I was given a choice between a de-tox center and a jail. I ask them to *take my alcohol level.* I am not drunk; they are persecuting the wrong man. They refuse. If they're not going to cooperate with me and take my alcohol level, I'm certainly not

going to cooperate with them. I let them decide where they want
to take me (I keep forgetting I'm the bad guy in this real-life
motion picture.) They decide to take me to the de-tox center,
where they start ordering me around, to which I say, "as long as
I have to take orders, you had better lock me up." Naugh agrees,
but he's angry. Now he'll have to do paperwork. They bring me to
the San Rafael Jail, where I sit four hours in a holding cell
because supposedly I am drunk. It is humiliating.

I am released with no charges filed. My blood was never
checked for alcohol. Moral? Watch your step in Tiburon,
pardner — especially if you move differently and still have the
audacity to enjoy yourself. There's a good chance you'll be run
out of town.

July/August 1992

Hate

Barbara Faye Waxman

*W*ith the passage of the Americans with Disabilities Act, the federal government affirmed "that disabled persons have been subjected to a history of purposful unequal treatment" in our society. This monumental piece of civil rights legislation was the result of Congress's recognition of a history of discrimination toward disabled workers, tenants, consumers, students, passengers, patients and citizens in this country.

Yet ironically the government has not acknowledged the presence of a deeper layer of harmful conduct which also violates the civil rights of disabled persons: violence springing from hate.

While the Bush Administration and the 101st Congress were deliberating over the ADA, they were concurrently in the process of passing the national Hate Crimes Statistics Act, P.L. 101-275.

The federal government and some state legislatures, including California, Connecticut, Idaho, Illinois, Maryland, Minnesota, New Jersey, Oklahoma, Pennsylvania and Virginia, have begun to respond to reports of an increase in incidents of "antiminority hate crimes" by passing laws to collect and analyze information regarding crimes which are motivated by bigotry and bias. As required by the Hate Crimes Act, the U.S. Attorney General is to "acquire data for the calendar year 1990 and each of the succeeding 4 calendar years, about crimes that *manifest evidence of prejudice* based on race, religion, sexual orientation or ethnicity . . . " [italics added]. Hate violence, as defined in the act, includes crimes of murder, non-negligent manslaughter, forcible rape, assault, intimidation, arson and destruction, damage or vandalism of property.

Disabled people were not included by Congress in the list of protected classes in this major piece of hate violence legislation. Congress apparently did not think disabled people comprised a "high risk" group facing personal violence. However, states which have passed hate crime data collection legislation — California, Connecticut and Oklahoma — did include disability as a characteristic which places individuals at risk for hate crimes.

While crimes motivated by hatred toward groups specified in the federal law are treated by Congress as social injustices, when based on disability they are seen in a wholly different light. In various criminal statutes, such as dependent adult legislation, disability-biased crimes are seen as random acts of passion rather than violence — the presumption being that disabled people provoke and invite abuse due to their behavior or attributes. (This double standard is the same as that evident in criminal laws dealing with presumption of rape: that women tempt men and then cry, "rape.")

But the truth is that anti-disability violence is produced by a whole series of ideological structures that legitimatize oppressive behavior. Disabled people face a pattern of oppressive societal treatment and hatred, much as women face misogyny, gay men and lesbians face homophobia, Jews face anti-Semitism and people of color face racism.

The crimes which the Act focuses on seem to be overt and organized violent acts such as gay bashing, the Howard Beach incident, cross burnings and vandalism of Jewish synagogues and cemeteries. Sandra Lambert, a disabled feminist writer, thinks of disability-related violence as a less explicitly violent form of oppresssion. "Disabled people aren't shot down in the streets of South Africa or the urban United States. They aren't killed as they go camping with their lesbian lover. There are never TV images of disabled people being beaten, shot or set on by dogs."

Yet data about rape, child sexual abuse, incest, sexual

harassment, battery, neglect, defamation and other forms of violence directed at disabled people indicate that they are much more likely to be targeted for violence than their nondisabled cohorts. Though FBI statistics and state-collected disability-related child abuse data do not reveal the scope of violence against disabled people, other studies show appalling rates of victimization. Ongoing research estimates that sexual violence directed at disabled people is one and a half times that directed at nondisabled people of the same sex and age. Moreover, the literature on the incidence of intentional harm inflicted on disabled children shows that any factor which advances the parent's perception of the child as "different" or "difficult" greatly increases the likelihood of abuse. Studies on abused children found that as many as 70 percent of that group showed evidence of physical or mental disabilities prior to the actual abuse. There are reports that mental retardation increased by eightfold the probability of an abusive attack.

Many violent acts against disabled people are overt: the vandalism and fire bombing of a community-based home inhabited by disabled adults who were threatened and beaten; the murder a few years ago of Cary Dickenson, a multiply disabled man found stuffed into the trash can of a Southern California library (an incident deemed by authorities a cruel prank turned tragic); the abuse of a 9-year-old Northern California student with multiple developmental disabilities who was repeatedly thrown into a cold pool by the teaching staff until she went through the required swimming motion — an instruction technique which included forcibly pouring hot pepper sauce into the student's mouth numerous times to force her to "keep quiet"; the arson two years ago of a 40-foot wooden wheelchair ramp belonging to James Lundvall, a paraplegic who is in a coma as a result of smoke inhalation (the Denver police, who called this a "random" act, were surprised when the arson occurred again 48 hours later); and the shooting death of two-and-a-half-year-old Eric Bernstein by his mother, who contended that she did so because the boy was not responding to treatment for his multiple disabilities, and as a result had her sentence reduced from first- to third-degree murder. It has not yet occurred to the authorities that these overt acts were hate crimes.

When violent crimes against disabled persons are exposed, federal resources such as the "Protection and Advocacy" system, set up to focus on institutional abuse and neglect, are supposed to help. In 1986, the Subcommittee on the Handicapped of the Senate Labor and Human Resources Committee, together with the Senate Appropriations Subcommitteee on Labor, Health and Human Services, Education and Related Agencies held three-day hearings on the treatment of institutionalized persons who are "developmentally disabled and mentally ill." The hearings were the culmination of a nine-month Senate staff investigation of conditions in state-operated facilities.

"During the three days of testimony," Senator Lowell Weicker, former Chair of the Subcommittee, wrote, "Subcommittee members heard example after example of mistreatment of the nation's mentally disabled citizens. We heard from parents, advocates, administrators, journalists, employees and residents themselves. We heard of physical violence, rape, unexplained deaths and filthy living conditions. We heard of young people tied naked to the floor in four-point restraints for days, as well as other instances of inappropriate uses of restraint and seclusion. And we heard that these conditions existed in public facilities that were receiving substantial amounts of federal funding and were certified to be providing active treatment to residents."

Violence toward disabled people has thus been part of the federal record for many years, and P and A's have continued to uncover abuse throughout the institutional system. Why was this evidence not utilized to ensure that disabled people were among the protected classes in the Hate Crimes Statistics Act? Why has Congress, after hearing numerous descriptions of abusive treatment tantamount to a pattern of violence, continued to treat this violence as situation-based, rather than bias based?

A major reason for the consistent denial of hatred as a motivation for violence against disabled people is that we are not perceived as constituting a viable, separate group in society. A recent Louis Harris survey of disabled Americans reported that 74 percent of us feel some common identity with each other and that 45 percent see ourselves as a minority, in the same sense as people who are black or Hispanic. When hate crime policymakers exclude the disability community from the Hate Crimes Statistics Act, they ignore the evidence that disabled people in the aggregate constitute a political entity. They ignore the fact that when a disabled person is targeted for violence, she is attacked not simply as an individual but as a member of a minority group.

Nondisabled people are strongly inclined to deny the success of a disabled person. They perceive it as the disabled person "making the best of a bad job." This reaction is apparently required to safeguard the nondisabled person's belief that his own appearance and capacities are important and infallible. Disabled people who present positive personality and behavior traits such as being successful, outgoing and warm may not only be helped less, but may experience more covert anger from nondisabled people. These traits, considered desirable in nondisabled people, may not be held desirable in disabled people. Successful and assured disabled people violate their "stigma role requirements of suffering and acknowledged inadequacy" — in other words, they refuse to "stay in their place" — and nondisabled people feel their own status threatened.

These realities are important for disability rights activists and independent living advocates to keep in mind now that the ADA is law. When we step out of place, by asserting our very presence (and refusal to take our presence elsewhere), when we proclaim that we are equal and deserve the same rights as the majority, we become targets for more overt acts of hate violence. Sociologists point out that economic conditions are an important factor in the emergence of racial hatred among young people. Indeed, police believed that young people were the offenders in the arson of the wheelchair ramp and the murder of the retarded man. Those who study and treat child abuse, victims of domestic violence, rape and other violent crimes are finding disabled people overrepresented as victims of these crimes compared to their numbers in the population.

Why should violent crimes against disabled people be treated as hate-motivated crimes? Bias crimes merit special attention because of their effect on an entire group of people. The entire class of persons represented by the individual recipient of the violence is likely to feel victimized. Although there are no studies on disabled people's reaction to violence directed at disabled individuals, there is a significant amount of writing by members of our community which suggests the effect is great. These crimes deserve to have the attention of the federal criminal justice system as it attempts to understand hate-motivated violence.

When disabled people are finally included in the Hate

Crimes Statistics Act, as well as enjoying the protections of other hate crime laws, people who are tempted to express their hatred toward members of the disability community will finally be on notice. Until then, however, disabled people will not have the full and equal protection of the law, and will continue to feel in danger.

May/June 1992

PRIVATE MATTERS

Public Stripping

Lisa Blumberg

*A*t a recent disability rights conference, a 30-year old woman with spina bifida described her medical experiences in a voice shaking with pain and anger. All through childhood and adolescence, Anne told us, the semi-annual orthopedic examinations her doctors required her to have took place in a large hospital room, with 20 or more doctors, residents and physical therapists looking on. After the hospital acquired videotaping equipment, the examinations were videotaped. During the sessions, Anne was permitted to wear only underpants.

When she was 12, she said, she tried to keep on her training bra. The head doctor, in order to explain something about her back to the residents, took it off without saying anything to her, but with noticeable irritation. A nurse quickly apologized — not to Anne but to the doctor.

Anne knew that when her sisters and classmates went to the doctor, they were seen by just one doctor, in a small, private room. No one ever explained to Anne why she had to be examined in front of a group. No one ever considered whether she found it embarrassing or upsetting to be viewed nearly naked by so many people. No one ever acknowledged to her that she was being used as a teaching tool. No one ever told her or her parents that she had any choice in the matter.

Anne grew up thinking that what she called "public

stripping," a crude phrase to describe a crude practice, was a periodic humiliation inflicted upon her because she was, as one young doctor called her, "significantly deformed and handicapped."

Anne's experiences are not unique. Privacy in medical examinations may be the norm for ordinary persons, but they're not the norm for disabled people — particularly not for disabled children. Doctors at hospitals and clinics which specialize in "pediatric handicapping conditions" such as spina bifida, cerebral palsy, muscular dystrophy, brittle bone disease and dwarfism have traditionally displayed their patients in front of colleagues, residents, therapists and other professionals. Although it may be slightly less extensive than a decade ago, the degrading practice continues today.

The individual is almost always examined without a hospital gown. Other procedures vary: she may be told to undress in the examining area; or he may be forced to disrobe with others in a hall.

My friend Joe, who has cerebral palsy, was repeatedly examined in an amphitheater where residents and medical students could line up to see and feel for themselves exactly how tight the muscles of a "spastic c.p." really were. Social workers, invited not for any clinical reason but just so they could feel "part of the team," looked on attentively.

The public strippings went on for Joe until he was 18, at which time he told his parents he'd never again go to any doctor for his disability. He never has.

It was only happenstance that I avoided public stripping myself. My first orthopedist, a consultant to a rehabilitation center, had both disabled and nondisabled patients, children and adults, whom he treated with equal respect and courtesy. He always examined patients in a private room, with only a parent present. Since the aim of the examination was solely to provide the patient with information, rather than to provide learning experience for other people, there was time when very little clothing removal was necessary,

My second orthopedist, associated with the esteemed Boston Children's Hospital, was a monster. He operated on me (as he did on almost all of his patients) with the result that my awkward but functional gait was turned into a snail-paced stagger. However, since Boston Children's Hospital, unlike some perhaps more egalitarian hospitals, allowed the parents to "buy" the right for their child to be examined in private — and my parents could afford to do so — public stripping was the one indignity he was unable to inflict on me. Whenever I talk to someone who has had their privacy so incredibly violated, though, my stomach churns and I feel as though it has happened to me.

Doctors seem to find it hard to understand why anyone "suffering" from something so supposedly terrible as a "lifelong handicap" would be interested in anything so trivial as modesty and privacy. To them, the examination procedures they use on disabled children seem reasonable and efficient because they facilitate teaching and the exchange of medical knowledge. Why wouldn't "the handicapped" be eager to help in the development of cures and new treatments?

What the medical profession and perhaps the larger community does not comprehend is that disabled people who seek medical advice are like anyone else seeking such advice. By and large, we want to be *provided with* a medical service — not *render* one.

Examining a patient in front of and with the participation of an audience should be regarded as bad medical practice even when considered from a purely clinical viewpoint. A person may be so upset and intimidated that he/she will not disclose all the information the doctor would need to know in order to provide effective treatment. Indeed, it is virtually impossible for a patient to develop any rapport with a medical professional in such a situation. The actual results of the examination may be influenced as well; even at 4 years old, Joe was so uptight from the experience, he says, that he believes it was not possible for anyone to determine how tight his muscles were in a typical situation — or what should be done about it.

Public stripping also presents quality-of-life concerns. People who have been required to submit to the experience repeatedly say they have been traumatized by it. The trauma stems not only from being viewed naked or nearly naked by so many people, with videotaping or photography frequently included, but also from listening to oneself being discussed — often in quite derogatory medical terms — as though one were a defective machine.

Susan, who has a form of muscular dystrophy, was driven to hysteria and nightmares by hearing a large group of people, oblivious to her views, dispassionately debate the multiple orthopedic surgeries she should have and the order in which she should have them.

Yet medical ethicists and others in the medical community who profess to be so concerned about "quality of life" when it comes to deciding whether it is worthwhile for a disabled person to live do not seem to be offended by public stripping.

Left unanswered is this question: If a person who's disabled can be subjected to medical examination procedures not designed for her benefit, can she not also be subjected to other things at the hands of doctors not to her direct benefit? Does a hospital's interest in giving practical experience to residents, for example, not play a role in recommendations for surgery?

Public stripping, of course, does not occur in isolation. Society's prejudices against disabled people are played out in medical settings in many virulent ways, ranging from indiscriminate surgery to unnecessary hospitalization to the denial of basic health care.

There are to be sure some health care professionals like my first orthopedist and my present physical therapist who will sincerely do their best for persons with disabilities who come to them for services. However, too often such individuals are found only by luck.

Both children and adults are victims of medical discrimination against disabled people. Children are the more vulnerable, though, since they lack the power to give and refuse consent. Moreover, parents who are slow to grasp the way the system works and who may be coping with their own prejudices may not always be able to act as effective advocates.

Unlike the women's movement, where health care concerns are high on the agenda, we in the disability movement spend very little time on medical issues. Our apathy in this area is amazing. We have not even begun to consider questions as basic as whether medical care given in segregated settings such as hospitals "for crippled children" can ever be equal. Not even deliberate medical murder galvanizes us into action.

As a movement, we seem to buy into the prevailing social myth that any problem a person has with the medical establishment is a personal problem — and probably the person's own fault.

However, equal access to medical care — that is, the right

to receive the same health care one would receive if one were not disabled — is as important and as vital to our interests as is equal access to transportation. Equal access to health care, like equal access to transportation, is a political issue.

Many health care issues will be difficult to resolve because they involve money and the readjustment of social priorities. We would be able to go far, though, in obtaining the right to privacy in medical examination by simply discussing the issue whenever and wherever we can. When publicly confronted with our views, doctors will find that public stripping is a practice impossible to defend.

January/February 1990

New Insights

Edward L. Hooper

"**U**h, I guess I always felt you're paralyzed, and uh, well, you have no sex life. You know — that's just part of it. Uhhh, I don't think you've gotten, uh, less *masculine* or anything. It's, uh, just something that doesn't work."

These words, coming from one of my best friends, nearly set me back on my wheely-bars. Bob's helped me more than any of my friends since my injury over a decade ago — and he was responding to some questions I'd asked several of my friends to find out what they really *did* think about the sexuality of disabled guys.

Everyone else I'd interviewed had sidestepped the issue — too personal. They wouldn't want me to know about their sex lives, they said.

Serious discussion about sexuality must be the most inhibiting topic in our culture. I knew these guys and knew they were curious about my situation — after all, I'd been in their situation before becoming disabled, but they'd never been in my situation.

They were curious. The subject was simply too intimidating. Except for Bob.

Bob said just what he thought: "It . . . just . . . doesn't . . . work."

Although was upset that one of my best friends thought of

me as sexually dead, I was sure his opinion was one most people held. Society believes that old Kenny Rogers song about Ruby, who has to "take" her "love to town" because her husband's "legs are bent and paralyzed."

Well, I wasn't about to let Bob out of my sight without telling him that it was my neck that I'd broken — not my libido. But what — and how — would I tell him? I wasn't going to verbalize some makeshift disability Kama Sutra. Still, I wanted him to know.

What had I learned myself in the decade since my accident? One thing I'd learned was that the brain — not the penis — was the cornucopia of sexuality. Neurologists weren't wrong when they called the brain "the sexiest organ in the body." It was the brain that sent and received all the messages — from fantasy to arousal. It was the brain that analyzed the body's response; the brain that provided the array of pleasure.

But before my injury, the focus of sexuality for me, like a majority of guys, was the penis. After I broke my neck I became acutely conscious that I no longer had any sensation in my penis.

I think we men learn at a young age that masculinity is measured by the erected inch — and then most of us slowly unlearn that absurdity. But to suggest to men that an erection should be unimportant is akin to asking them to agree that breathing is unimportant.

But we men can live sexually active and fulfilling lives without actually feeling penile arousal or "getting it up." When I finally got the nerve to deal with my body again after my injury I discovered that with direct stimulation I could maintain an erection — but I had no feeling whatsoever. (For men who can't sustain an erection and who feel one is important, there are penile implants and prosthetics available.) But disability can teach profound lessons, too: I discovered that by using my penis for giving pleasure — even though I was "feeling" nothing with it — I could receive pleasure nonetheless. That "sexiest organ of the body" is a most amatory sensor.

And my brain had been working the day I'd attended a peer group session on sexuality and listened to folks trying to quell the obsession with what they called "The Big O": Orgasm. It was quite possible, they were saying, for only one of the partners — or neither — to reach orgasm, as we defined it pre-disability, and still have the encounter be most fulfilling.

It's true.

My brain hasn't figured out I'm supposed to be asexual. It keeps sending erotic messages. But the focus of where I receive those messages has changed from my penis to other areas of my body where I do have feeling: my shoulders, neck, lips, ears. With intimate contact in these areas, coupled with the knowledge that I'm giving pleasure, too — by kissing, touching and embracing — my heart begins to race, my head gets warm, my mind surges, aggressively pursuing its feelings. The excitement builds to a level of intense pleasure — then subsides toward contentment.

Yes, it's like an orgasm: not with the intensity brought on by an ejaculation, though the loss of control is similar. It is in no way "merely" a mental phenomenon. Sexual pleasure now is a physical and mental meld.

I could have used this insight before my disability: that when something erotic is happening, to not force it but let both my body and mind respond. Physically it's not as pleasurably intense. But mentally, sex is better for me now than before my disability.

What do my wife and I miss? Spontaneity, for sure — since we have to plan our encounters more now. And I'll admit that sometimes we miss the old missionary position. We occasionally want to take a stroll in the woods, too — but I can't do any of those things anymore. My sexuality's become a matter of knowing what my capabilities are and fitting those into a mutually satisfying relationship with my wife. We've both adjusted to my disability. We live with it, we love with it.

Erich Fromm writes in *The Art of Loving* that "the sexual act without intimacy retains a separateness that cannot be forgotten by orgasm." Fromm's words remind me of Jack Nicholson's character in the film *Carnal Knowledge:* he had beautiful women and orgasms a sex-crazed Roman would have envied, but he never sought love and ended up as a pitiful middle-aged lecher paying a prostitute for "dirty words" and oral sex.

We all deserve the opportunity for the closeness, the intimacy, the mutually accepted pleasure of one another as sexual human beings.

I gathered my thoughts and told Bob.

His reaction? "All those years! Geez, I can't believe it! It shocks me!"

Bob said he wanted to go out and tell everyone now that he knew disabled people *were* sexual — but I doubt that he did. If he did, I doubt many people believed him anyway.

I shudder to think how much love and lovemaking has been abandoned by people with paralyzing disabilities because of the belief that "it just doesn't work." It does! We mustn't allow ourselves to be labelled "sexually dead."

November/December 1989

It's Time to Politicize Our Sexual Oppression

Barbara Faye Waxman

*I*n the September/October 1986 issue of *The Rag*, Anne Finger and I posed a question: What does the Supreme Court decision saying states can outlaw "unnatural sex acts" have to do with disability rights? Our answer: "A lot."

At the time, we called for the disability community to join other groups to "reverse the growing anti-sexual sentiment in this country and make sure that freely chosen sexual expression will no longer be criminal."

Well, it's happened. Verna Spayth, a disabled woman living in Ann Arbor, was one of 12 plaintiffs who claimed last summer that the Michigan statutes outlawing sodomy (usually defined as any sexual activity other than vagina-and-penis intercourse and including anal intercourse and mouth-genital contact) had a "chilling effect" on her behavior. Michigan was one of 24 states with such sodomy laws.

A Wayne County, MI, Circuit Court judge struck down the law, saying it "violated citizens' right to privacy under the state constitution." Privacy is a rare commodity in the lives of disabled people.

Spayth, who has a lower back condition which makes it necessary for her and her boyfriend to have the type of sex prohibited in Michigan, comments that "We're talking plain old discrimination. It strikes me as real absurd that every time we do it, we're breaking the law."

This case points to a fact of our lives: disabled people are denied sexual and reproductive freedom, as well as the liberty to establish a family in our own image. However, the disability rights movement has never addressed sexuality as a key political issue, though many of us find sexuality to be the area of our greatest oppression. We are more concerned with being loved and finding sexual fulfillment than in getting on a bus.

Public and private sector policies and practices play significant roles in keeping disabled women and men from realizing our sexual rights.

Frank and Michelle have been married for three years. Their marriage must be kept secret. Frank is quadriplegic; Michelle is non-disabled. Frank tried unsuccessfully to find a job, but found himself discriminated against because of his disability. Since he does not work, he has been a recipient of Supplemental Security Income all of his adult life. SSI, funded by federal and state funds, is the primary source of income for disabled, blind and elderly people.

Although Michelle earns about $1,000 a month as a waitress, and brings home about $800 of those earnings, Frank would find his SSI payments drastically reduced if the government learned of his marriage. Not only that, but he would jeopardize his medical and in-home service benefits which enable him to live outside an institution. In effect, it's almost illegal to be severely disabled and married.

Jane, who is in her early twenties, has cerebral palsy and uses a wheelchair. She found herself with an unplanned pregnancy. Although she is single, she decided she very much wanted to keep the child. She received no childbirth education because she was unable to find a teacher with a class in an accessible building. Overwhelmed and confused by the sensations of labor and uneducated on how to assert her needs and rights, she found herself undergoing a Caesarean. She is still not sure why.

She explained to the nurses and other medical personnel that she was always weak after surgery and that she would shortly recover her strength. Nevertheless, hospital personnel reported to child protective services that she was unable to care for her child, who was therefore in danger of being neglected.

The California county where she lived had no provision in their In-Home Supportive Services program which otherwise grants funds to hire someone to provide personal and domestic services to disabled individuals. Rather than accommodating her with supportive services, the protective agency has threatened to take custody of her child.

Rick, a 31-year-old man paralyzed seven years ago in a motorcycle accident, found that when he has intercourse, a response known as autonomic dysreflexia can set in — meaning that his blood pressure can rise to a dangerous level. Therefore his main form of sexual expression is performing oral sex on his partner. But in 24 states Rick would be subject to arrest, and in some states could be charged with a felony and face jail terms of up to 20 years for having "unnatural sex." It's even possible that the counselor at the rehabilitation center who suggested he use this method of sexual expression could find herself being prosecuted for conspiracy to commit a crime.

Carol, who has a congenital spinal cord injury, has lived in a nursing home for nearly all of her adult life. When she was 52, she met Larry, who had multiple sclerosis. They fell in love and wanted to have sexual intercourse, although at first it seemed physically impossible for them. They spoke about their dilemma to a member of the nursing staff, who arranged for them to visit a center for sexual therapy. There, with the assistance of the center staff, the couple was at last able to have intercourse.

When the director of the nursing home learned about what had happened, she was shocked and infuriated. She threatened to discharge them both if she learned they were having sex on the premises. Fearing that any nursing home would impose the same restrictions on them, Carol and Larry gave up their sexual relationship.

There is a double standard that says that those who live in institutional settings and consider these places "home" have different rights than those who live outside of them.

For five years, Max had been receiving brailled copies of *Playboy* through the National Library Service for the Blind and Handicapped. when, in the summer of 1985, Congress banned funds for its production. Congressman Chalmers P. Wylie (R. - Ohio), who introduced the measure, complained that *Playboy* contained "talk about wanton idleness, of wanton and illicit sex and so forth, and it does not seem to me as if we should be using taxpayers' money to promote this sort of thing."

Even though an outcry ultimately got *Playboy* funding

restored after that incident, blind and disabled people are more vulnerable to having what they read censored because much of their reading material is still produced through government funds. It seems the First Amendment applies only to non-disabled people.

No group in this country faces the sort of sexual and reproductive restrictions disabled people do: we are frequently prevented from marrying, bearing and/or rearing children, learning about sexuality, having sexual relationships and having access to sexual literature.

The Social Security Administration often penalizes disabled people who marry; institution administrators and staff restrict sexual activity and punish inmates if caught. Disabled gay men and lesbians receive almost no services or support; government agencies do not monitor incidence of sexual violence directed at disabled people; federally funded family planning clinics are often inaccessible and not equipped to serve disabled women and men, and, if they are, their services are too often aimed solely at keeping us from having children; we are at risk of losing custody of our children due to disability-based social service agency standards; and we live in a society which declares us sexually valueless and even dangerous.

Why hasn't our movement politicized our sexual oppression as we do transportation and attendant services? I believe we don't speak out about it because we are afraid that we are ultimately to blame for not getting laid; that it is somehow a personal inferiority. And in the majority culture this secret is a source of personal embarrassment rather than a source of communal rage against the sexual culture itself.

In a number of the responses to *The Rag's* sexuality survey (printed in the July/August 1989 issue), there seems to be some ambivalence about the source of our sexual oppression. Though respondents are providing clear, rational answers about not fitting into the sexual culture, I haven't been able to discover much rage.

In answer to the question, "Is your sex life satisfactory? Why or why not?" a woman responds with that ambivalence: "I feel somehow sexually invisible — like nobody I meet thinks of me at all in a sexual way," she writes. "So I wonder if I am communicating in some way that I'm unapproachable, or that I'm not picking up on or giving off visual cues from within me, and then how much of that is related to being blind?

"And how much are others perceiving me as asexual?"

Though other survey respondents (who may not be statistically representative of disabled people in general) said they had "very" to "somewhat" satisfying sexual lives, I decided to use this woman's quote because it accurately speaks to the sexual confusion within the disability community.

This confusion arises as a consequence of society forcing us to internalize the notion that we are sexually inferior. This conspiracy, which society manufactures by way of discriminatory social policies which lead to our sexual subjugation, is keeping us in a state of sexual self-hate.

I believe this is done tacitly to keep us from doing the thing that poses an overwhelming threat to our disability-phobic society: taking their sons and daughters as sexual and life partners, bearing their grandchildren.

If I sound full of rage to you, you're reading me correctly. I am outraged.

The source of my sexual rage and hurt are not only from my own life experience. I have worked both as a disability and sexuality educator and counselor, and as a disability and sexual rights activist for the past 15 years. During this time, I have concluded that much of the sexual loneliness, pain and abuse which I have heard about from my disabled sisters and brothers has been inflicted upon us by a culture which views us from afar with contempt and hatred.

Society holds sick and exploitative sexual values which serve no one, not even those considered to be the most sexually desirable. Consequently, we must publicize our sexual pain. Disabled people must begin to share their personal sexual oppression with one another so that the problems we think of as idiosyncratic begin to be seen as not only personal problems, but as part of a pattern of oppression we've all experienced.

It is a *fait accompli* that we are a political minority. Whether we like it or not, we are also a sexual minority. We are the Sexual Other. Verna Spayth knows this, acted on her knowlege, and, as part of a coalition with other members of sexual minorities, changed an antiquated and discriminatory law. We must follow her lead.

We must begin the work to transform policies which restrict our sexual lives just as we are working to transform the built environment and our economic and political status. We must develop a movement for sexual freedom that is broadly based. By this I mean not only one which reflects the social and ethnic diversity of our community, but one that speaks to all of our individual needs: for love, for orgasm, for being desired.

To realize our sexual freedom, our goal must be to infuse the dominant sexual culture with the richness of our own experience. We must celebrate our differences from those without disabilities. We must see that our differences in appearance and function which are the sources of our degradation also contain the seeds of our sexual liberation.

March/April 1991

It Ain't Exactly Sexy

Cheryl Marie Wade

When I read the interview with Judy Heumann on our need to have assistance using the bathroom ("The great unspoken issue of our movement": July /August 1991), I kept wondering, "Why does this article bother me so much?" Although I admire Heumann's willingness to tackle the subject at all, it bothers me that the language is so safe and careful in the discussion of what is for many of us a life necessity: the need to have the private parts of our bodies exposed and handled on a daily basis.

To put it bluntly — because this need is as blunt as it gets — we must have our asses cleaned after we shit and pee. Or we have others' fingers inserted in our rectums to assist shitting. Or we have tubes of plastic inserted inside us to assist peeing or we have re-routed anuses and pissers so we do it all into bags attached to our bodies.

These blunt, crude realties. Our daily lives. Yeah, I know it ain't exactly sexy. Not the images we're trying to get across these days.

The difference between those of us who need attendants and those who don't is the difference between those who know privacy and those who don't. We rarely talk about these things, and when we do the realities are usually disguised in generic language or gimp humor. Because, let's face it: we have great shame about this need. This need that only babies and the "broken" have.

And because this shame is so deep, and because it is perpetuated even by our own movement when we emphasize only the able-ness of our beings, we buy into that language that lies about us and becomes part of our movement, and our movement dances over the surface of our real lives by spending all its precious energy on bus access while millions of us don't get out of bed or get by with inadequate personal care. Because we don't want to say this need that shames us out loud in front of people who have no understanding of the unprivate universe we live in, even if that person is a disabled sister or brother. We don't want to say out loud a basic truth: that we have no place in our bodies (other than our imaginations) that is private.

And yes, this makes us different from you who have privacy of body. Yes, this is a profound difference. And as long as we allow our shame to silence us, it will remain a profound difference.

If we are ever to be really at home in the world and in ourselves, then we must say these things out loud. And we must say them with real language. So they are understood as the everyday necessity and struggle they are. How can we assert a right (for personal care) if we are too ashamed of the need to state it openly

And we who are on the outside, living independently, using attendants for intimate care, owe it to those of our brothers and sisters still dependent on family care or institutions to tell the truth about the pain and struggle of this life as well as the joy and freedom. Informed choice. So that the person in the institution knows that, even with this private need, you have a right to and can set boundaries on who touches you and how you are touched.

And what of the next generation? How will disabled children learn to love themselves and their bodies, how will they know they have the rights to determine their limits, if we teach them shame by our silence, by our obvious embarrassment over this most basic reality?

We don't want to say these truths because it doesn't fit the new disability mythology of "the able-disabled." It makes us seem weaker, more vulnerable.

OK. I admit it. I am weaker and more vulnerable than most

nondisabled people and many disabled people, too. So throw me out of the movement. Take away my Crip Power button. But don't make me continue the charade. I want these things to be private, too. But they're not.

On a real practical level: If I can't express openly what I need when my social worker comes to call, s/he's gonna leave it off the IHSS [California's In Home Supportive Service's program] chart and then there's no money to pay for an attendant.

And if I can't talk about the need, then I can't talk about the choices, either. And yes, even weak, vulnerable cripples have choices. But if our shame tells us that our needs lack dignity, that we lack dignity, then the next thing we hear our shame say is that it is more dignified to die than to live with these basic needs that take away our privacy and seem like such a burden.

We have an obligation to the next generation, to our isolated sisters and brothers, to stop skirting the issue. Stop contributing to our own self-hatred with silence and half-truths. Stop playing the media's game.

It wasn't Desert Storm, it was Desert Slaughter. It isn't "using the toilet," it's having someone's hands in your private hairs so you can live in the world. It's a big booger of a deal. But it's the only deal in town. And no matter how difficult, well worth it when you consider the alternatives.

If we can't say these things in *The Rag*, then where?

November/December 1991

Excavation

Kenny Fries

1. Excavation

Tonight, when I take off my shoes:
three toes on each twisted foot.

I touch the rough skin. The holes
where the pins were. The scars.

If I touch them long enough will I find
those who never touched me? or those

who did? *Freak, midget, three-toed
bastard.* Words I've always heard.

Disabled, crippled, deformed, Words
I was given. But tonight I go back

farther, want more, tear deeper into
my skin. Peeling it back I reveal

the bones at birth I wasn't given —
the place where no one speaks a word.

2. Incubator

As if from a goldfish bowl, through
small, fogged eyes. And nowhere

do I find you, even though I know
you must have been there. The hands

that turn me are the nurse's hands;
the eyes watching me are my father's.

But where is the body from which I was
born unwhole? Your body almost

died giving birth to mine. Mother,
after all these years I am asking why

you never told me. We touch through
a sheet of glass. Give me your hand —

help me find those missing bones, clear
that infant's eyes. Open them — wider.

3. X-Ray

I am eight months old and looking
for you, daddy, at the other

end of the metal table. Your eyes
told me all I need to know —

if I could just remember. I watch
the large machine rattle down its track,

feel the cold on my skin,
when all these years I wanted

the memory of your hands holding my
twisted feet in the right position.

Remembering this now I am
still that eight month old,

your son, staring into the eyes
of that machine, trying to find you

in the reflection it gives back
— nothing from the waist down.

4. Learning to Walk

There is light at the end of the narrow hall.
Enclosed in a cast, my shorter leg reaches

for the ground. My knee can't bend. Scrapes
against the plaster wall. My toes above

the carpet. If I press them to the ground,
the cast will break, my leg will crack —

If I close my eyes? If I don't look down?
The hall, narrow as the cast, held by pins,

my leg inside. No bone will hold my weight.
No arms will end my fall. Palms pressed against

the dark canal, I lift my weight. How far
is the light? With open eyes — my foot on ground.

5. Body Language

What is a scar if not the memory of a once open wound?
You press your finger between my toes, slide

the soap up the side of my leg, until you reach
the scar with the two holes, where the pins were

reinserted twenty years ago. Leaning back, I
remember how I pulled the pin from my leg, how

in a waist-high cast, I dragged myself
from my room to show my parents what I had done.

Your hand on my scar brings me back to the tub
and I want to ask you: What do you feel

when you touch me there? I want you to ask me:
What am I feeling now? But we do not speak.

You drop the soap in the water and I continue
washing, alone. Do you know my father would

bathe my feet, as you do, as if it was the most
natural thing. But up to now, I have allowed

only two pair of hands to touch me there,
to be the salve for what still feels like an open wound.

The skin has healed but the scars grow deeper —
When you touch them what do they tell you about my life?

March/April 1992

Lunch Break

Laura Hershey

Mid-afternoon, clouds have gone away,
as every July day, for a few hours,
in Nairobi.
Women all around:
in circles, singing
    the rich-rhythmed songs of tribes combined;
in groups, dancing
    bright clothes, muscled bodies flow;
in pairs, talking
    musical and articulate as all the voices of birds;
in solitude, listening,
    watching the rest
in wonder.

I'm with Sharon, my English friend, sharing
a sandwich and Pepsi.
We don't need to talk
as she holds the food to my mouth
and bends the straw
for my drinking;
so we listen
to the variegated chorus
of chant, question,
planning, laughter, song,
and stumbling translation
around us.

An American woman approaches me,
camera in hand.
I have seen her, these few days,
snapping the heads and faces
of African women who,
I've noticed,
often frown for their portraits.

Mind if I take your picture?" she asks.
"Alright," I answer.

She steps back, angles
her camera from a distance, the focus
on my wheelchair —
metal frame, shortened leg rests, torn green upholstery,
large tread tires —
then she waits.
We wait too, casually posed
under the hot sun. To Sharon she says,
"Will you give her another bite?"
"No," I snap. "Get this over with."
Her face changes, as if
I had spoken the language
of the Maribou stork.

How did this happen?
Am I a curiosity
to my own countrywoman?
So be it.

I will join the gallery
of those captured in the photographer's empty frame
and bare vision —
the Masai, Luo, Kikuyu
the Navaho, Pueblo, Sioux
the Amish
the Eskimo, the gypsy
the children
the old, the dark, the poor
the native islander, the Oriental
and "Woman" —
not born exotic,
but made so
by collectors' frozen images.

And in these frames, these photographs
of random, nameless faces,
we all know why
so many of us
are frowning.

July/August 1992

Reconciliation

Cheryl Marie Wade

I wheel my chair through Mojave sands
until I sink
There I sit
sun baking my spongy bones
so brittle
that when I stand
instead of feeling shin
push into ankle
ankle press
into heel
heel slam into a shoe of nails
my pelvic bones
snap
and I fall
slow motion
onto the warm
warm grains
I am bleached
white
nothing but a heap
of white sprigs
He comes
with his little girl
Holding her hand
he guides
her eye to the lizard

a flicker of iridescent pink
but her interest is the white twig
at her feet
She bends with a small
perfect hand
lifts what once had been
my aching finger
Look Daddy
a treasure
He leans down to admire her find
She puts it in the pocket of his plaid shirt
and the two of them walk on
My skull
opens wide
swallows the desert
and sings hosanna to the dry dry air.

January/February 1993

Reading Braille

Mary McGinnis

It wasn't my stomach that liked to read, but those socially
        acceptable parts:
the orderly hands, the thin shapely wrists, the neck with its pockets
        of deceit,
the mouth with its tiny partitions, the eyes with their flower centers;
it wasn't the nose, it wasn't the legs in their sheaths of skin,

the ankle bones that protruded — it was the head,
the brain with its secret lobes,
the spine with its little curvatures;
all of these parts read and read when I was a child,
their parts with their clear black and white English names, not

la *cabeza, o los manos o los ojos,*
o la cara o las piedras o la primavera blanca;
not the knee but the fingertips, not the thigh but the petite ear;
all of me sank into my lap where the book was;
they talked about the ambulance coming, about my great aunts
        who were sick,
my mother talked on the phone about what the hairdresser said
        about sex,
my father answered my mother in mumbled syllables over the
        blare of the television
and I sat very still on the couch so they wouldn't notice
that I hadn't gone to bed.

I read and dreamed of wild, dark places near the water,
pearl divers who dove for pearls and had seaweed on their arms;
I was not at home in my body then,
and I read until my fingers were raw, and there were

words racing through my head and I didn't have to talk
or ask too many questions.
I loved the quiet in the house when my parents were sleeping —
when I was alone with my hands.

July/August 1993

White Caps

Margaret Robison

W hite caps on the river.
        Wind all day. Hard.
You've been dead three years.
Still I write you letters in my head.
And dream some nights of us together.
Indian summer's gone.
When I crossed the river bridge at dawn
a fine powder of snow was coming down.
My aide pushed my wheelchair
while I gripped the handrail. Mother,
I'm learning to walk again.

May/June 1993

Thanksgiving Day Feast

Susan McBride

100,000 bugs for every person on Earth
and for every grain of Sahara sand,
a star.
Like a wishbone
I am tucked in the V of white bed
my arms sprouting tubes.
Television
spoons up Desert Storm battalions,
soldiers gnawing turkey;
hot gangrene tents.
In the scalpel's trough
Staphylococcus gorge at my hock.
Smart bombs slice through the Milky Way
to Baghdad.
Putrefaction is rife, an odorous conspiracy
of bugs at play; men at war
surgeries gone sour.
No windows in this room.
Under lamp glare
I imagine the sizzle of midnight stars
and suck something brown through a straw.

November/December 1993

Travelling

Katherine Simpson

Looking at shoes
In a mail order catalogue,
The Irish housewife asks me
Which I think are most stylish.
After all, I have crossed this island
And am an American.
What does she think of me—
This mother of four,
Who has never been to Dublin,
One hundred and fifty miles away.

2.

By the time I got to Cork I was sick of Ireland,
Of the drinking and stares, the lechery and religion.
I don't remember how I felt each night,
Alone or making conversation with strangers.
Though I do remember
The long 4-mile uphill grade
Into Killarney,
Where a local priest kept pace with me
Both our bicycles plodding, single geared.

And I remember the flat coast of Galway,
The long straight road to the sea,
The tiny fields and the fences of stone,
The Tower with thick walls and narrow windows,
Arrow-proof, the safest place I've been,
From which the poet William Butler Yeats
Also drew inspiration.

3.

When I go forth what do people see?
Someone to look at or not look at twice,
Or, they tell me, one whose charm or mind,
Or one whose legs in youth
Could take their sight a further step or two.
"I do not think of you as handicapped,"
They shyly or proudly say.

4.

I come from a family of judgers,
Missionaries and teachers,
Ministers. My father
Carried the Presbyterian torch
To physics and philosophy. They all
Bore the same love of knowing their own mind.

The ambasssador or missionary leaves
His home on a fixed principle,
But grows attached in his travels
To a street here, a street there,
A favorite phrase
In a difficult tongue.

How does the poet travel—Octavio Paz,
From Mexico to the Spanish Civil War,
In 1962 ambassador
To India? I imagine
The courage, the individuality
In the diplomatic courts,
The terrible cowardice,
The walls of stone.

5.

I avoid the East Bay Terminal
In San Francisco,
Since that Thanksgiving twenty years ago,
When taking the bus to family in Berkeley,
I was accosted. "If you need a job,
Join a circus. I saw a boy just like you
Back home in Mexico. He made a living,
Painting with his feet."

6.

I read Apollonaire,
In hobbling French.
I secretly believe this combination
Of the poet and his non-native reader
Produces a great reading.
His heavy bears come plodding towards the village
Pursuant to the trail of tambourines,
A place I've never been but might well be.

Sometimes the show comes home.
Our older sisters
Put on their shadow plays
In the deepest closets;
Frightened, entranced
We watch the alien plot.

In the old Sutro's at the Beach,
There were true peepholes,
And Tom Thumb's clothes,
And an entire mechanical carnival
Of toothpicks, made by prisoners
On Alcatraz.
And a Last Supper,
Life size, illuminated.

Did Tom Thumb too
Endure the stares,
The dirt, the uncomfortable beds,
The indigestible food,
For those moments at the peephole
Where to travel is to see.

Like Walking on the Moon

Nancy Scott

Snow casts unprotected streets
in dust of not known.
No curbs, no stairs, no echoes
of familiar buildings to speak
straight lines. No traffic
to plot; no cement to tap
in the rhythm that has
no excuse for staying home.
My cane makes a poor shovel
in the shuffle of this new gravity.
I stretch to catch the flakes
of white luck in my eyes.
I know the Moon is watching
and She approves.

March/April 1994

Now and Then Again

homage to James Schuyler

by Susan Hansell

1.
At 6 o'clock
I hear the boys
start up, their
hoots and
howls blow in
from basketball
courts. Whistles
clatter against
my windows, open
to Fall. A dog's
bark bounces
between the yards,
and I wonder where
the girls are.

2.
The sky is
a grey
parfait! Rain
is coming.
Rain is predicted, in fact
but the tennis
players don't mind.
Chartreuse pong
pongs, over brick-
colored courts.
Whose advantage,
as the clouds
retreat? I step
on an earthworm,
trying to make it
to the grass.

3.
Her hands, pale,
fish netted, so
lavender and chilled
the tips are tiny ice bites.
The nurse says, "roll up
your sleeve, please."
And I say, "my veins
are a green road
map, leading you
to my . . . How many
more pokes; how many
more purple bruises?"
No. I don't say
that at all, I
roll up
my sleeve.

4.
Ripe bananas sliced
into white yogurt.
He says "please
eat it."
I watch
The cat eat, and
stretch, her furrr
arching. And
I want to walk
into blue
October.
Did you ever
notice how sleep comes
in ninety minute
intervals?
The clock
unwinds, and sometimes
the phone rings.

5.
Night shuts quickly
down. Almost November so
light all the lights.
Today I thought:
I could ride my bike
to the ocean, and at
the top of the peak
let go
the brakes.
See my body
toss, or sink.
"It's not death you
want, but release," Robin said.
In my kitchen, my refrigerator
gurgles. Its long
black cord just reaches
the wall.

6.
It's raining
now. The skylight
pours in dark
blues, and from
the window I watch
the pear tree suffer,
its orange veined leaves
run to brown and
finally drop.
What a relief
to wake up
to rain.
Hard weather
I will not want
to go out in, but
I wish for
your voice
calling.

March/April 1994

Trajectories

Brian Hartshorn

I remember the moment of impact,
the swift, clean fall, the certainty
that all was changed, all that I
had thought I was about,
put in abeyance.
No real pain, just certainty
of broken bone, I sat in wonder
on the wet pavement, considering
the skewed bone of my arm, fingers
trapped within those of my other
hand, my snapped leg stretched
before me.
Men who knew me from the local pub
stopped to see if they could help,
an ambulance was called, the wheels
of the machineries of mercy
set in motion.
I shared a room with sixteen
other men. "I hope to God,"
moaned one, as they made him use
the walker, "You never have pain
like this." Another late at night
would say, "On nights like this,
I ask myself, what is the state
of the North Sea fleet,
and how are the men?"
That was the summer that men first walked

the moon. At night we asked the nurses,
pointing to the antiquated orange
globes that lit the room, "Please turn off
the bleeding moon."
The day they landed on the bleeding moon,
a man across the room was seized
with savage snoring, and only stopped
by ceasing breathing. "A small step for man,"
into the airlessness of the
Sea of Tranquillity.
"A giant step for mankind," he
declined the help which came in answer
to his nurse's call, and when they'd closed
the curtains round about the ward, he did
his disappearing act, into the
alien sunlight, leaving the tracks
no wind would erase.

July/August 1994

Becoming Beautiful

Nancy Bigelow Clark

I saw a man in a wheelchair once
who survived his high wire act
without the wire. It was a sort of
genocide; the nice guy purging himself
in ways only the football grind em into dust
hero would recognize or accept accolades for,
but the poet more interested in
other gentlemanly poets than cheerleaders
or drinks at Joe's, the make your parents
proud even if it kills you kind of guy
had to lose himself in order to find
that center of the known universe
from which all balls flow perfectly spiraled
into hands at peace with weights or
similar flesh. An honest pen could live there,
telling it all, if first he didn't tell it to air
like a bad pass or a goal line stance
that fails to part when commanded.
Legs tell a sorry tale when mixed with cement.
Bones corrode when secrets told are told to air
too thin to hold them. So he fell,
the linear definition of flesh stretched,
pulled apart, somehow made whole by going
backwards through that kiss, becoming
a frog prince with a story to tell.

July/August 1994

THE PITY PLOY

. . . And the Greatest of These Is Charity

Anne Finger

Doesn't Jerry look great? Doesn't he? It's two minutes into the Jerry Lewis Telethon, and Ed McMahon's just said, "He-ee-eere's Jerry!" and Jerry's doing one of his silly walks across the stage. You know the one I mean: bent knees as if he's sitting down, turning his face out toward the audience, rolling those marvelous double-jointed eyes of his, and quacking like a duck. This man is fun*ny*. The audience is going nuts. They love this man. They're on their feet. They love him.

Jerry, instead of holding up his hands like stop signals, is gesturing toward himself, saying, "Come on, more. I love it. I love it." What a funny man.

Danny Thomas got into the charity field early, and naturally grabbed the best disease left after they went and cured polio: leukemia. *Leuk,* in case you didn't know, is Greek for pale, colorless or still. Those pallid young children wasting slowly into death. No ugly protruding tumors. No convulsions, no spasms, no missing limbs. Danny got himself in on the ground floor, hooked himself up with St. Jude. Could there be a better combo: Danny, the all-American man with his family show, fading children, a saint?

Muscular dystrophy is the next best thing. Since no one knows what it is, there are no unpleasant associations. No, Jerry does not do telethons for epilepsy or colitis or sexually transmitted diseases.

Doesn't the man look great? He is pushing 70 (do you think he uses Grecian Formula?) and he's out there on stage acting like a 3-year-old.

"Here we are in Las Vegas," he sing-songs. "Las Vegas. Caesar's Palace. I want to extend a great big thank-you, thank-you to all the folks at the wonderful, wonderful Del-Webb Corporation; they have really, really put themselves out for us, my kids, my staff . . ." Jerry bursts into a song which he *actually* wrote himself: "Unless we hear those telephones ring . . . we just can't do without you." Comedian, humanitarian, lyricist.

"OK," Jerry says. "Ed."

We switch over to Ed McMahon, who says, "Can we have a timpani roll, please, maestro." The drums roll, and the camera pulls back to reveal the electronic scoreboard: $1,670,924.

"That's a lot of money, Ed," Jerry says.

"It sure is."

"It's a lot of money, but we're going to need a lot more. So please. There are phone numbers appearing at the bottom of your screen. Call up and make a pledge. If you can only afford to give five dollars, give five dollars. Ten dollars, that's OK, too. Whatever you can afford to give. Please," Jerry says.

"Do it for my kids. Because we're doing this thing out of love. We really are. Despite what some of the dissidents might think. We really are doing this out of love. . . . And to all of you who've donated to my kids, I want to say, I love you, and Jerry's kids love you, too." Jerry turns his face away from the camera, the way he always does when he's looking humble.

"OK," Jerry says. "There's a hero worship going both ways between the gentleman I'm going to introduce next and myself. Let's welcome Tony Orlando." As Tony sashays onto the stage, the orchestra strikes up (of course) "Tie a Yellow Ribbon . . ." Then it's "Sweet Gypsy Rose," and this fellow knows how to work an audience. He jumps off the stage and is down there with them, getting them to wave to the folks at home and sing along.

Tony's not somber, but he's definitely serious when he gets back on stage. He's doing a tribute to a great artist who is no longer with us. "Oh the shark, babe, has such teeth, dear, and he keeps them pearly white . . ." Bertolt Brecht? "Splish-splash, I was taking a bath, 'long about Saturday night . . ." Bobby Darin, of course. "Bing-bang, I saw the whole gang, dancing on my living room rug."

Tony says, "You know, when I was starting out in show business, there were two people who I definitely considered to be my professors: Jerry Lewis and Bobby Darin. Jerry, I want to tell you, I think you are a great-great man."

"Thank you, Tony," Jerry says, turning his head away from the camera, the way he always does when he's feeling humble.

Now Jerry is telling us that not all of his kids are children, and we see a film of people saying, "I'm 57 years old and I'm one of Jerry's kids." "I'm 34 years old and I'm one of Jerry's kids."

"OK." Jerry says. "Let's switch over to Chad Everett. Chad."

"Thank you, Jerry. I'm going to be letting the folks at home know something about the great-wonderful job that the 22,000 member National Association of Convenience Stores has done in raising money for Jerry's kids."

Chad makes eye contact with the red light on the camera. "Convenience stores," he intones. "Those are the little store down on the corner: some of them are mom-and-pop grocery stores, and some of them are part of larger chains, but they all offer you friendly service and shopping ease. And the National Association of Convenience Stores has again this year done a super-tremendous job of helping out Jerry's kids. They have pledged themselves to raising over $3 million for Jerry's kids."

"They're wonderful people, aren't they, Chad?"

"They sure are, Jerry."

"Convenience stores are wonderful places," Jerry says. "You don't have to hang around in those long lines. You run in, you get what you came for. You don't have to hunt around the aisles, you know; what you're looking for isn't over on aisle 17-B, it's right there . . . OK. We're in the corporate-sponsor part of our program now, and we're going to bring out the president of General Foods. General Foods is a wonderful, wonderful company; and this year they've pledged themselves to raising $1 million for my kids."

The president of General Foods comes out: he shakes Jerry's hand and says, "You know, Jerry, I want to remind you that while convenience stores are wonderful places, many of our fine General Foods are sold through supermarkets and we think supermarkets are wonderful places, too."

Jerry couldn't agree more. "Supermarkets are wonderful

places, too," he says.

"I'd like to show you a short film now about the fine people who work for General Foods." Cut to the GF logo. The voice-over says, "General Foods' people work in offices, factories and distribution centers. This year, General Foods has put together a special promotion with Sanka Brand Decaffeinated Coffee to raise money for Jerry's kids." The film shows coupons being pulled off along a dotted line: as each coupon disappears, we see more and more of a poster of Jerry, looking sad, holding a little girl with braces who looks even sadder.

"You know," Jerry says, "this film only tells part of the story. Last year, General Foods donated $1 million to my kids — but they spent $7 million — yep, $7 million — printing posters and coupons and letting folks know about the fine work that they're doing for my kids. I think that's super-terrific. What do you folks think?"

The studio audience thinks it's super-terrific, too.

We switch to local fundraising in San Francisco; then back to Vegas; then to Atlantic City, where Sammy Davis and Ol' Blue Eyes are going to perform for us.

Sammy is glittering. He's not just wearing a medallion around his neck that catches the stage lights and tosses them right back; he's wearing three thick gold chains, three bracelets and five rings. Sammy sings for us. Then we get a split screen: Sammy on one side, Jerry on the other.

"That was beautiful, Sam." Jerry says. Beau-ti-ful. Beau-ti-ful. It really was. Beautiful. We love you," Jerry says.

"That's a two-way street," Sammy says. "And I mean it, Jerry. I don't say that just because I'm on the air."

Sammy and Jerry start goofing. Jerry tells Sammy he's got a lot of rhythm. Sammy asks Jerry to sing along with him, then peps up the beat till it's totally frantic. Jerry says, "I can't do that. I'm white."

Then Sammy and Jerry start pretending to kiss each other, bringing their lips to either edge of the split screen. It's the funniest thing you've ever seen. The audience is cracking up.

We're back in Los Angeles with the Senior Vice President of 7-Up.

"It takes a lot of guts to follow Sammy," Jerry says. "A lot of guts." Here's a film about everything the fine folks at 7-Up have done for the Muscular Dystrophy Association. Here's the

Executive Vice President of Electronic Realty Associates. He is presenting a check for $354,000 on behalf of the 30,000 Associates of Electronic Realty Associates.

"Say that for me again," Jerry says.

"$354,000."

"That's beautiful. You know, that's a lot of love. A lot of love."

Now, representing the 500 Hickory Farms stores, this is for the kids: $225,000 from Hickory Farms.

Kentucky Fried Chicken. Anheuser-Busch. The Mall Marketing Association.

Tammy Wynette sings, "Stand By Your Man."

The Jaycees present their check, "I'd like to tell you a little bit about the Jaycees and what we stand for," the presenter says. "We believe that the brotherhood of man can transcend the sovereignty of nations . . . that free men can best express themselves through free enterprise . . ."

We cut to a film about a disabled woman artist. "I found that I could no longer do the sort of paintings I used to do. I used to have such beautiful hands. I really loved them . . . Now my paintings work more through line and color, the longing for movement . . ."

Chad is choked up. He really is. He has to swallow hard before he can say, "The National Association of Convenience Stores has a membership of over 22,000 . . ."

September/October 1987

A Test of Wills
Jerry Lewis, Jerry's Orphans and the Telethon

Mary Johnson

"The very human desire for cures . . . can never justify a television show that reinforces a stigma against disabled people." It was 11 years ago when those lines appeared on the opinion page of the New York Times — September 3, 1981. Labor Day. On the tube, the annual Jerry Lewis Labor Day Telethon was in full swing. The article was by Evan J. Kemp, Jr., now chairman of the U.S. Equal Employment Opportunity Commission. At the time Kemp was Director of the Ralph Nader-inspired Disability Rights Center. "Aiding the Disabled: No Pity, Please," read its headline.

Evan J. Kemp, a man with one of the neuromuscular diseases the Muscular Dystrophy Association said it was fighting to cure, was criticizing its star-studded fundraiser. Kemp was also criticizing MDA's star and savior, comedian Jerry Lewis.

Society, Kemp charged, saw disabled people as "childlike, helpless, hopeless, nonfunctioning and noncontributing members of society." And, he charged, "the Jerry Lewis Muscular Dystrophy Association Telethon with its pity approach to fund raising, has contributed to these prejudices."

Kemp contended that such prejudices "create vast frustration and anger" among disabled Americans, then numbered at 36 million. Kemp charged that disabled people suffered far more from lack of jobs, housing — lack of access to society — than from the diseases MDA sought to cure. He accused the Telethon's "pity approach . . . with its emphasis on 'poster children' and 'Jerry's Kids' " — of creating prejudice. He called upon the Telethon to reform; to portray disabled people "in the light of our very real accomplishments, capabilities and rights." The Telethon, he insisted, "must inform the public of the great waste of money and human life that comes from policies promoting dependence rather than independence."

Kemp took out ads in daily *Variety,* the entertainment newspaper. "Color Us Useful," they read. They called upon Lewis to reform his telethon.

The following year, Kemp was invited onto the MDA Telethon. His on-air pitch was mild: "Your pledge to this Telethon can help create meaningful, productive lives for many. It can also help save the lives of others. I urge you to phone in your pledge right now."

After that, Telethon criticism died down. Other telethons — the Easter Seals', United Cerebral Palsy's — changed somewhat, adding more disabled adults and offering more segments on things like "independent living" which those in the disability rights movement had urged.

MDA briefly hired a disabled man, Steve Lockman, in an effort to deflect criticism that they had no one on staff with the disease they were seeking to cure. But Lockman stayed on the job only a short time, quitting in disgust and accusing MDA of lacking any intention of reforming.

And Jerry Lewis kept on being Jerry.

Perhaps MDA had simply hired a new ghostwriter for the annual pap piece that ran each Labor Day weekend in *Parade* magazine under Lewis's byline. But the 1990 one, published in the September 2 issue of *Parade* magazine, took a new twist: "What if the twist of fate that we hear so much about really happened? What if, when the gifts and the pains were being handed out, I was in the wrong line?" Lewis began . "What if I had Muscular Dystrophy?" was its title.

"I decided after 41 years of battling this curse that attacks children of all ages, I would put myself in that chair, that steel imprisonment that long has been deemed the dystrophic child's plight," he continued.

"I know the courage it takes to get on the court with other

cripples and play wheelchair basketball, but I'm not as fortunate as they are," Lewis wrote, halfway into the piece. He had so far managed to include nearly every term or concept offensive to disability rights advocates, and his next sentences would work in the others: "I'd like to play basketball like normal, healthy, vital and energetic people. I really don't want the substitute. I just can't half-do anything. When I sit back and think a little more rationally," he continued, "I realize my life *is* half, so I must learn to do things halfway. I just have to learn to try to be good at being half a person."

The article outraged disability rights activists nationwide — in a way little else has. *The Rag* received countless copies of the article for our "We wish we wouldn't see . . . " pages. In Chicago, Cris Matthews and Mike Ervin, a brother and sister who both had forms of Muscular Dystrophy and had been MDA poster children in 1961 and who had been active in ADAPT actions and had started a group called AccessAbility Associates, decided to do something about it.

Two months before the 1991 Telethon, Matthews wrote to Robert Ross, Executive Director of the Association, a deceptively simple letter. "The wheels are in motion to begin the campaign to remove Jerry Lewis from your Telethon," she told him, by way of introduction. "We intend to keep at it until he is no longer associated with MDA, and the negative, degrading nature of the Telethon is changed to reflect the truth about life with muscular dystrophy and disability in general."

The Association, she charged, was "expert in exploiting the worst side of disability and, with the eager assistance of Lewis, has made us out to be nothing more than pathetic burdens to society, whose only desire is to walk. Much attention is given to the kids who may not live to adulthood, but for those of us who do live on, not one word or one dime is devoted to the concept of independence." Lewis's *Parade* article, "full of the condescending paternalism the Association foists on the viewing public, is an outrage and an insult," she told Ross.

"No one is negating research or the individual's desire to be cured," she wrote. What they objected to was the paternalism, "the attitude that stresses that, no matter what one does, life is meaningless in a wheelchair."

Ervin went further. In an October letter to Ross, he threw down the gauntlet. "[Jerry Lewis] is never going to change his stripes. He will continue to be a liability to you as long as you keep him around."

Jerry Lewis must go, Ervin said; there would be no negotiating the point.

In announcing the kickoff of their fight against MDA, Matthews and Ervin, who had dubbed themselves "Jerry's Orphans," listed the group's demands: MDA would have to "enter into negotiations with a group of consumers with disabilities of our choosing to determine how or if the Telethon can be restructured so that it does not continue to sabotage the hard work of those in disability rights"; the charity would have to stop using "the archaic and degrading word 'patient' to describe those it serves" and replace it with "something more dignified, like 'client' or 'consumer' "; it would have to provide services for its clients' "more immediate needs, including advocating for their rights" and it would have to put people with disabilities into "meaningful positions of power" within the organization. This included putting disability rights advocates onto its board.

"We are not necessarily out to put the Telethon — or MDA — out of business," he wrote, 'but we are definitely out to put Jerry Lewis out of the disability business."

Whether putting Lewis "out of the disability business" would cause the demise of the Telethon or MDA, Ervin told Ross, "is totally up to MDA. We wish to avoid it as much as you do, but we will do our battle on whatever field you choose.

"As long as you cling to Jerry and your charity-laden fashion of depicting the disability struggle, the fight will continue," Ervin wrote.

Though Kemp had fired the first fusillade, now the battle would start in earnest. It was a battle that "would continue to grow," Ervin warned Ross. "We will challenge you in greater numbers; we will protest in your local offices. We will pressure your corporate sponsors to pressure you. We will make Jerry Lewis and the pity pitch as much a liability for you as he is for the rest of the community of disability," Ervin warned.

"You can choose to doubt our ability to win this fight," Ervin continued; " but we have been in bigger fights than this."

Matthews, as it happened, was on the list to receive a motorized wheelchair from MDA. That fact would be publicized relentlessly by MDA to smear her reputation; Matthews says MDA got information from medical records of a Chicago-area physician with neither her knowledge nor her consent.

The Muscular Dystrophy Association is one of the nation's largest charities — and considered one of the best-run (last December, *Money* magazine cited it as one of the ten best-managed large charities in the U.S.). Since its start in 1950, its focus has been on medical research, its goal the cure of neuro-muscular diseases. Criticism of its fundraising tactics by Kemp a decade ago irritated the group, but it's safe to say its manage-ment has never truly understood the reasons for Kemp's criti-cism. The new critisms also took them unawares.

In Denver, former MDA poster child Laura Hershey orga-nized a protest of the 1991 Labor Day Telethon, using the name "Tune Jerry Out." Her protests, and those of groups in Los Angeles and Las Vegas, garnered national publicity. Hershey was invited onto the nationally syndicated Gil Gross radio talk show originating on WOR radio in New York City.

The show aired on September 3. Callers branded Hershey "ungrateful" and a dissident." MDA circulated a transcript of the talk show and urged that letters be written to Hershey. Hershey says she received over 50 hate letters.

"Your entire interview was a bitter, negative slam against MDA and the Jerry Lewis Telethon," wrote David A. Sheffield, an assistant district attorney from Kountze, TX, who has muscular dystrophy and who would later serve on MDA's Task Force on Public Awareness, a group set up to counter the demonstrators. Sheffield accused Hershey of perpetuating "the false, age-old stereotype of disabled people as angry, deeply embittered, negative persons."

"The MDA has not been founded for the purpose of making you look good," wrote Shelley C. Obrand, who signed herself "one of 'Jerry's Kids.' It is not Jerry Lewis's or MDA's responsibility to fight for disabled rights. . . . You are a selfish, negative person,"she wrote.

Hershey began dutifully replying to the letters. "My basic objection to the telethon is that it encourages us to mourn again and again; that it reinforces the message that being disabled is not okay; that it implies that disabled people should get what they need through charity, not as a matter of right; and that it discourages us as a society from accepting disability and seeking to accommodate it permanently into our social fabric," she wrote.

"The disability rights approach views disability as a natural phenomenon which occurs in every generation, and always will," Hershey wrote to her critics. " It recognizes people with disabilities as a distinct minority group, subject at times to discrimination and segregation . . . but also capable of taking our rightful place in society. From this perspective, people with disabilities have rights, which society must guarantee . . . the right to health care, full integration and opportunities for . . . . non-institutional living. Instead of begging, we are expected to participate fully in the community."

By this time, the Association had moved on to other methods of discrediting protestors.

In October, MDA Director of Research and Patient Services Administration, Ronald J. Schenkenberger, put out the word to selected people associated with MDA in and around the Chicago area that "developments relating to initiatives undertaken by Chicago-area residents Cris Matthews and Mike Ervin . . . have sufficiently hurt our fundraising programs in your area" that the Association would "regretfully" have to "enforce a regulation of many years' standing" to limit admissions to MDA camps.

Lest anyone believe this was simply following policy, Schenkenberger made it clear that this cutback was all Matthews' and Ervin's fault. "Action of the nature undertaken by Cris and Mike can only serve to impair our ability to raise funds and thus have a negative impact on the Association's ability to provide a full range of services."

He urged writing to Matthews and Ervin directly, and provided addresses. He also pointed out that Matthews "will shortly be the recipient of an MDA-purchased power wheelchair costing over $8,600."

MDA disputed Matthews's and Ervin's claims that they themselves had been MDA poster children. When columnist Dianne Piastro referred to the brother and sister as former MDA poster children, she received a swift letter from MDA Director of Field Operations Gerald Weinberg insisting that Piastro verify the fact. Other letterwriters, both to Piastro and Matthews, disputed the claim also. Only when Matthews was able to dig up a February 1962 newsletter of the Greater Chicago MDA chapters proclaiming the smiling brother and sister "muscular dystrophy poster children for 1961," did the questioning stop.

Even more direct was the attack on Hershey from Mike

Gault, MDA's Director of Community Services. "This Association has received a considerable amount of negative publicity as a result of your Tune Jerry Out campaign," he wrote Hershey late last October. "Your campaign is a factor in what appears to be a serious financial drop in Association income this year. As a result, it will be necessary to curtail — or eliminate entirely — certain of MDA's programs."

Gault enclosed a newspaper clipping about Rhondi Geist, "a 38-year-old Friedreich's ataxia patient [sic]" in a Colorado nursing home who had recently been the recipient of a wheelchair from MDA. Gault told Hershey that a thank-you note from the man (which Gault also enclosed) had "started me wondering how much longer MDA will be able to provide the kind of help this young patient received. The thought struck me that this is a matter you'd like to think about."

Hershey says she was "shocked by both the content and the tone" of Gault's letter. "If your attitude is representative of the Muscular Dystrophy Association as a whole," she wrote him, "then I must conclude that the Association's problems go much deeper than just the offensiveness of the Telethon." Hershey told Gault she thought he might be exaggerating the drop in funds to make her feel guilty, but said she was even more disturbed by MDA's response to the drop. "You seem very willing — even eager — to cut client programs. . . Has the Association considered administrative salary cuts instead? Or is this part of the budget considered sacred?" she asked.

In 1990, MDA had spent $34.6 million on salaries and benefits; its executive Robert Ross received nearly $285,000, making him one of the top paid of all the nation's charity executives.

As to Geist's situation, Hershey wrote to Gault, "It seems to me that MDA has condoned, and even participated in, the widespread institutionalization of people with disabilities in this nation. . . . MDA, with its medical-model approach, has done little to provide independent living services and supports or to free its clients from the confinement of nursing homes.

"I do not want my views or actions to punish Rhondi Geist and other disabled people," Hershey told Gault, "but the fact is that if Mr. Geist were living independently, outside of a nursing home, he would most likely be eligible for Medicaid — which, in Colorado, would enable him to obtain not only the high-tech wheelchair he needed, but also home health care services and other equipment he required to stay independent and healthy."

If Gault intended his letter to make Hershey back off, it did not work. "Protests against the Jerry Lewis Telethon will continue, and probably increase, until the Muscular Dystrophy Association changes its approach to fund-raising, as well as its attitudes toward clients," she wrote. "As long as MDA's organizational and service philosophy values charity over independence, it will continue to be in conflict with the goals of equality and empowerment of people with disabilities."

If MDA's threats last fall were efforts to instill guilt, by early 1992 they had become more serious. Matthews began to be harassed by MDA officials demanding copies of Jerry's Orphan's nonprofit status and tax exemption, evidently not realizing at first was that Jerry's Orphans was merely a name, not an organization. Later, they began hassling Matthew's about AccessAbility Associates, which was a non-profit corporation — which Ervin reports they were continuing as this story went to press.

A January 14 registered letter from attorney Bruce S. Wolff of the law firm McDermott, Will & Embry warned Matthews that MDA had hired his firm to "advise the Association on an ongoing basis concerning its rights to hold you legally accountable for any damages it may incur as a result of your efforts.

"Our firm intends to monitor — from our offices in Chicago, New York, Washington, DC, Boston, Miami and Los Angeles — the activities which you . . . may engage in." Any activities "which have the effect of disrupting or interfering with, or which are intended to disrupt or damage, the Association's relations with existing and prospective sponsors and/or Telethon stations will provoke a swift and substantial reaction."

"I don't know what they could do to us," Matthews laughed. "We have no money; we have nothing to lose."

Matthews says she thinks MDA targeted Evan Kemp because they realized they could win nothing by fighting Jerry's Orphans. Kemp was a bigger target; his dismissal from the Bush Administration would be a win for MDA. But they lost that gamble, too. He was renominated by the White House in June.

Few reporters have had the interest — or the guts, maybe — to take on the Muscular Dystrophy Association. One who tried was Dianne Piastro, disability columnist of the syndicated "Living with a Disability" column. Piastro wrote a six-column series on the issue, starting by outlining the protest, giving readers the opportunity to contact Matthews and Ervin, and ending with an unflattering look at MDA finances. MDA stonewalled when Piastro sought financial information from them. "In light of the obvious bias that so extensively characterizes your apparent ongoing assault upon MDA, I believe it would be decidedly counter-productive to the interests of those served by the Association to participate in any interview with you," wrote MDA Director of Finance Robert Linder in response to Piastro's verbal, then written, questions about expenditures on the group's IRS annual tax forms. Piastro finally obtained the forms from the Illinois Attorney General; she had to file a complaint with the IRS about MDA's refusal to release them.

Despite their refusal to set the record straight before her article ran, MDA seemed outraged when her column hit the papers. They had the accounting firm Ernst and Young scrutinize every financial allegation in her column, and used it to send a four-page, typeset point-by-point rebuttal to newspapers that had run her column, characterizing her facts as "uninformed and misleading," "out of context" and "grossly incomplete," which seems particularly unfair given MDA's refusal to answer questions she had asked.

Miami Herald reporter Marjorie Valbrun was contacted by MDA folks to do a story on Jerry when he came to Miami. When they learned Valbrun had contacted Kemp for his side of the story, MDA's offer of an interview with Jerry dried up. Valbrun told MDA she couldn't do a story with just one side — and the story was never done.

Jerry's Orphans vowed to Ross to "pressure your corporate sponsors." ADAPT's Mike Auberger, with the allusion to South Africa not unintended, calls it pressure for "a divestment plan."

The divestment plan is simple: Don't give money on the Telethon. That was what Matthews began asking major Telethon contributors last year. With ADAPT behind it, the campaign has picked up this summer. Protesters targeted United Airlines, Southland Corporation, which runs the 7-Eleven convenience stores, Gannett Outdoor Advertising, Service Merchandise and TCI, the nation's largest cable TV operator.

Protesters did not ask corporations to reduce their contributions to MDA. They merely asked that the contributions not be made to the Telethon itself, and that contributors not appear at the Labor Day event. "This way, the Telethon is neutralized," says Auberger, "while MDA's fundraising efforts are unharmed."

ADAPT and others point out that the bulk of money shown as being raised during the Telethon is actually raised months before. As major corporations' gifts are announced on the Telethon, the amount on the tote board rises; but that money has in reality been raised in preceding months. The appearances by corporation heads like Service Merchandise's Raymond Zimmerman are a form of free advertising for the corporate giants, and, in a way, their contributions can be seen as advertising fees — because they believe the good publicity generated by appearing on a Telethon for a worthy cause that isn't controversial can only help them in the eyes of customers.

ADAPT's Diane Coleman calls it "advertising at our expense." She was among the activists who met with Zimmerman earlier this summer to ask him to stay off the Telethon; he refused. Activists from Denver reported better results with TCI.

As Telethon time rolls around again, MDA's Task Force and Telethon officials appear to be making attempts to defuse what they fear may be mass protests in Las Vegas, where the Telethon takes place. In May, MDA officials traveled to Denver to meet with ADAPT; in July, members of the Task Force tried to arrange a meeting with ADAPT activists in Texas in an effort ADAPT says they characterized as "building bridges."

ADAPT's Bob Kafka said a Task Force member had called him to try to set up a meeting with Regional MDA folks; the conversation, with a man Kafka had known in disability circles years ago, he said, brought home to him why he had always been "anti-MDA."

It was two things, he said: "The Jerry's Kids image — that's paternalism — and their 'patient services' approach — that's the medical model.

"Those are the two things the Muscular Dystrophy Association has interjected into Americana," he continued. "They are the two things which are the antithesis of what we stand for."

Though MDA tries to convince the public that its detractors are simply jealous of the fundraising group's success, says

Kafka, activists' real anger, he thinks, is at the group's success in projecting images into mainstream America — images activists hate.

Lewis told the *Los Angeles Times's* Charles Champlin in 1990 that his telethon pulled in 120 million viewers, a figure he claims is just below the Super Bowl and the Miss America Pageant in audience size.

It's precisely because they have such an impact on public perception, says Kafka, that the MDA is the target of activist criticism. "MDA is Americana," says Kafka. Because they have made such a pervasive image, he says, "they have a higher responsibility to project an image of disability that is real."

September/October 1992

Time to Grow Up

Julie Shaw Cole and Mary Johnson

*T*he line protesters use so frequently — "Jerry, we're not kids anymore!" — is truer than intended. When protesters use it, they're generally thinking of chronological age: they're adults. But where it's really most true is in a psychological sense. It pertains not just to disabled people but to the disability rights movement. To a psychologist looking at this issue, it's clear why the telethon issue was destined to be the next "burning" issue that would command the soul of the community that fought successfully to pass a major civil rights law.

During the 1980s, activists in disability rights grew tired of serving as the collective recipient of society's negative projections. The activism was a sign of our collective growing up; the accomplishments of that activism — from lifts on buses to passage of the Americans with Disabilities Act — hastened the change in self image that had begun in us because of the activist actions we were taking. Pride and self-awareness were growing. We were growing up, not just chronologically, but psychologically. We have been maturing as a movement. And today, as a result of that activism, many disability activists are different psychologically than we were just a decade ago. We are less likely now to incorporate those projections; we are less likely to accept the identities others wish to thrust upon us.

A major psychological shift like this in a culture shakes

everyone up. This is even more true when it occurs with no fanfare; no warning. As with most changes occurring within disabled people, like major changes that have happened to society as a result of disability rights activism, it's taken society unawares. No newspaper articles chronicle it. No reporter outside the movement has yet homed in on what's really behind these Jerry's Orphans and Tune Jerry Out protests that grow each Labor Day, in little pockets all across the country — much less figured it for the important sociological passage it portends.

But what's happening is that a sector of the "downtrodden" in society — disabled people — is throwing off society's own projection. And the projection they're throwing off is one society very desperately wants to remain on disabled people.

Whenever a projection is discarded, there's great resistance. Anyone who's been in therapy knows this. Here the psychology of an entire nation is undergoing change. Resistance is fierce. Whenever a set of society's "Others" makes a movement to move out from under society's projection, it stirs up all kinds of energy as the culture looks around for some other group they can foist their projections onto — and they highly resent those who refuse to serve that role any longer. They're also angry at having to cope with the strengths of the newly-emerged group they've wanted to ignore — in this case, people with disabilities.

A great change is occurring in the relationship between disabled and nondisabled people; one neither of them fully understands the reasons for; one that many are afraid of, one that many are fighting hard to resist.

When such psychological upheavals occur, either in an individual or in a society, there's an effort to keep the old roles. This happens in individual therapy: old ways are comfortable, and people resist growth when it comes, for it's painful. When a society is undergoing similar change, both the society doing the projecting, and the people serving as that projection, will often fight to retain the old roles, because, tired as they are, the old roles are familiar. Yet others will at the same time be struggling mightily to cast off the projection. Thus we have disabled people fighting against the telethon, wanting to cast off that projection, locked in battle with disabled people who are afraid of the new and more comfortable in the old roles. Nondisabled people line up on either side of the battle, too — and the result is confusing to participants and observers alike.

Many disability charities hold telethons; yet Jerry Lewis's telethon has always been the target of disabled people's ire. Why his, and not the others? It's the same reason MDA is the most successful of all the telethons: focus.

MDA has either been savvy or has simply stumbled onto the truth: a hero, one larger-than-life individual, draws people like no mere cause ever does. MDA latched onto this hero in Jerry Lewis. No other telethon has had such a larger-than-life hero.

Lewis has served MDA well because of his great ego; but MDA has helped Lewis, too: it gave him an image, a persona, greater than anything he could have ever attained as a comedian. In a way, MDA saved Lewis — something that becomes clear from a look at published accounts of Lewis's life.

The image Lewis would assume is an image that forms a deep and powerful myth: "hero to children." It's an archetype of enormous psychological energy, as anyone who's read any of Joseph Campbell's work on myth will know.

Batman, Superman and Captain America are all children's heroes. They all use their superhuman powers to right wrongs done to the powerless. This hero archetype gives children a way to fantasize about their own strengths, even as seemingly powerless children. It gives them a guide to use in completing their own hero journey which is a part of all growing up. (Readers may want to read Joseph Campbell on hero journeys).

But the hero image is one of limited staying power. When children grow up, they no longer need such heroes; the hero has served his purpose for them.

MDA, in creating a hero for disabled children in Jerry Lewis, in a way poised itself for the problem it's now facing.

It exacerbated it, too, by attempting to cut off the process such a hero serves in myth: though it gave disabled children a hero, the Association evidently did not understand that in such myths, children in the end always complete their own hero journeys. Despite MDA's attempt to stop the myth in midstream, it has, as myths do, followed its own course, and the disabled children did grow up. Passage of the ADA made disabled people their own heroes.

Whether MDA has intended it or not, its refusal to dismiss Lewis has had the effect of appearing to be an attempt to thwart the psychological growing up of an entire generation of disabled people. It is this that Jerry's Orphans perceive so acutely on a gut level. By insisting that Jerry be always there to intercede eternally for his "Kids," MDA truncates the process of development that all people seek in growing up. By refusing to let Jerry go, MDA is in a sense commanding that growth not occur.

This is dangerous, on two fronts: What will happen when there's no longer a Jerry (for we all pass on, sooner or later)? And what happens when kids grow up and no longer need a hero?

The second question is the one we're being forced to examine in the wake of Jerry's Orphans protests. The question is all the more shocking because it's taken society unawares.

Despite civil rights advances and "public awareness" campaigns that have made the point over and over, society has simply not, on any deep level, taken in and digested the truth that disabled people might be anything other than infantile, immature beings — "kids." Society really does view all disabled people as kind of perpetual children — still, despite laws, despite all the talk, despite all the "awareness." Evan Kemp perceives this; all telethon protesters do.

Telethons did not create the image of the disabled person as perpetual child; it's been society's view of disabled people for as long as anyone can remember — and it's powerful. The Telethon's creators merely observed (probably unconsciously) what role it could play in raising money, appropriated it, honed it, focused it, and burned the image ever deeper into our national consciousness.

Only in the last decade has this image been questioned. Even now, it's questioned by relatively few people. The stigma of being the perpetual child is one that even many disabled people, though they deny it, still accept. It is society's negative projection that they are accepting.

Vulnerability, lack of capability, immature abilities — these are traits that we, as a society, want to deny in ourselves — that we seek to project onto others. Who better to project them onto than disabled people? And that's what society's been doing. It's a lot easier to project one's vulnerability onto someone else — a disabled person — than to have to face it personally.

For many disabled people, too, it has been easier to accept this negative projection of society, and live with it, than to throw it off and find one's own internal, neglected personal power. Yet that's what activists have begun to do. They have at last begun to claim their own power. This has energized them like nothing else. They are casting off society's negative projection. And they are seeking to stop it at its source.

Giving to Jerry's Kids allows a non-disabled person to fend off her own fears of vulnerability, powerlessness and mortality. Being a Jerry's Kid allows a disabled person to avoid facing one's own strengths and power.

Looking at the situation through yet another myth, we can see that MDA has set Lewis up as a king. (Sir James Fraser wrote about this in his classic book, *The Golden Bough*). And it is no exaggeration to say that Jerry's kids, grown up now, are out to symbolically kill off that king. Consider the cultural phenomenon of a society killing off its king when he no longer historically suits the needs of the people. You see it at work here also.

MDA can continue to insist that this is all the fault of protesters; that if they'd just go away and leave well enough alone, things could return to normal. But MDA would only be fooling itself with this delusion. It's precisely because they set Lewis up as hero and king that this is now occurring. It's a developmental process that was bound to occur as disabled people grew up psychologically — the only way it could have kept from happening would have been if disabled people had remained eternal children. For people who truly believed that's what disabled people were, the current events are no doubt shocking and inexplicable. To those who knew that disabled people would claim their power, it was an inevitable next stage.

It is due in large part to the disability rights movement that many disabled people have experienced the psychological growth that now threatens MDA's status quo. That, perhaps, explains the source of MDA's very real frustration, confusion and rage: they honestly don't comprehend that disabled adults are no longer children psychologically — and though they suspect that disability rights has something to do with it, they don't understand precisely what that is.

But quite apart from protesters, MDA has created its own problems by putting all its eggs into the Jerry Lewis basket. For what will happen to MDA when Lewis dies? By setting him up as the sole symbol of why people give to MDA, the organization has not only put him in a personally difficult position, but has endangered the organization's future potential for support.

Protesters who fight for Lewis to leave are in a way doing

MDA a service. They are forcing the organization to confront the problems reliance on one larger-than-life individual can create. MDA would be wise — and would do Lewis a big favor — by working to move its fundraising focus away from him and toward the issue of a just society; toward making life good for disabled people while it continues to seek cures and treatments for neuromuscular diseases. This is precisely what the movement is urging MDA to do. The Association would be wise to listen.

September/October 1992

On the Barricades with ADAPT

Mary Johnson

"*I* am tired of rules and regulations. And them telling me what you have to do. None of them has worked for me as good as being at home. In nursing homes, they put you on sleeping pills to keep you from getting aggravated with what will occur.

"You can't pay — you don't have any money to pay an attendant at night, when you're on SSI. All of these things they're constantly cutting. I haven't been in a nursing home for 15 years — and I don't plan to go."

It's Saturday night in Chicago. Nearly 300 ADAPT members have gathered in a meeting room in Chicago's Bismarck hotel, getting ready for the group's May 1992 assault on the Windy City. People are telling their stories. Many are there because there was a nursing home in their past — or they don't want one in their future.

The next day the group will swoop down on the University of Chicago's commencement exercises. U.S. Department of Health and Human Services Secretary Louis Sullivan is speaking, and some in the group can't believe their late-breaking good fortune at getting another shot at hassling the Secretary who has steadfastly refused to meet with them to discuss redirecting Medicaid funds to in-home attendant services. A planned Mother's Day March to a graveyard — to symbolize how this nation kills its mothers in nursing homes — is cancelled. "I was never for that dead stuff anyway," ADAPT organizer Mike Auberger says.

The week's events are debated. Somebody wants to know why they see police taking photos of them whenever there's an ADAPT action. There's an attorney available for people who get arrested, the group is told; they're given his name, as well as ADAPT organizers to contact if they get arrested.

"I'm telling you — and it's the most important thing I'm gonna say," Auberger warns the group, "have your medications with you if you're going to get arrested. Have 'em labelled. No pill boxes; bottles. Make sure it has your name on it — nobody else's. Make sure there's no illegal substances on you; no weapons. 'Cos this is going to follow us down the road."

As it turned out, Chicago was mild compared to Orlando's confrontations last fall, in which nearly all ADAPT activists were thrown in jail — some in solitary confinement — for the week. In Chicago, only ten people would be cited and fined in Monday's confrontation at the HHS regional offices in downtown Chicago, and only four police-tagged "leaders" arrested the next day at American Medical Association headquarters; all were released at day's end. Perhaps the national outrage in the wake of the Rodney King beating acquittal in Los Angeles a few weeks before had made Chicago police, considered to be some of the most brutal, cautious.

The University of Chicago graduation turns out to be a beautiful Chicago spring day. Police and Secret Service are allowing ADAPT members into the auditorium without any hassle. Later, though, Jim Parker is asked to leave. He protests loudly as police haul him out a side door: "Why am I the only one being asked to leave?" About that time Tim Carver of Tennessee simply rolls off into the men's room, unnoticed, to wait out the sweep.

Several ADAPT members unfurl a large FREE OUR PEOPLE banner over the wall below their seats, off in the "handicapped section" where the Secret Service have relegated them. Big burly Secret Service men with their walkie-talkies run over quickly and reach down to pull it up. Bob Kafka and Allen Haines are as determined that they won't succeed. A kind of arm wrestling match ensues, with Kafka and Haines holding firmly to the banner to keep it hanging over the wall where it forms a backdrop to the stage area where Sullivan will be speaking. The Secret Service have the advantage of leverage; they're taller. One especially burly guy finally wrests the pole with its banner away from them and, with a contemptuous jerk, flings it high into the bleachers behind them. "Clear 'em out," mutters an all-business police captain. Four cops to a chair seems to be the agreed-on method of removal. Paulette Patterson of Chicago is removed this way. Over on the side, Anita Cameron and Jim Parker, back in and out of his wheelchair, and Frank Lozano, minus dog Frazier, are scooting down the steps on a side tier, trying to make it down to where Sullivan will speak, but they're caught and removed, too.

"Get as close to the doors as possible," says Bob Kafka to the other activists who have now been ejected from the back of the building. With police blocking doors, clots of ADAPT move to every entrance. Well, almost every one. Jean Stewart and Eleanor Smith use Stewart's crutches to pound on the metal doors, trying to create a disturbance inside, as the graduation ceremonies begin. Inside, though, the noise is barely audible.

Nancy Moulton of Atlanta is sitting quietly on the ground, leaning on a door, with her guide dog Nan beside her. "Get up," says a blue shirted Chicago cop. Moulton doesn't move. Nan rests her head on Moulton's leg and rolls her eyes up at the cop towering over them.

Now there are four Chicago cops and one guy who must be from the Secret Service hanging over Moulton and her dog. "If you don't move, we'll have to grab you, and the dog will attack," the cop persists. Still Moulton sits. "If you're concerned about the dog, move!" the cop barks.

Moulton gets up, worried that the cops will hurt Nan.

While some block doors, others pass out leaflets to late-comers. The chants of "hey hey, ho, ho, nursing homes have got to go!" change to "We want Sullivan!" The police have barricaded the exit with blue sawhorses that read "police line." A pickup truck from the University's facilities management is unloading yellow university police barricades.

A lady inside the back of the auditorium, hearing the faint chanting coming from outside, mutters, "they're not making friends." She's with the university.

The University of Chicago is so large that commencement

is held in two shifts; a morning one and an afternoon one. Sullivan has finished speaking and the crowd is emerging from the pavilion. They walk down the long fence of police barricades, while ADAPT chants and hands them leaflets: "Wanted: Sullivan. For crimes against disabled people."

It's lunch. ADAPT always feeds its activists. Today it's Burger King. Attendants and other walkies pass out cokes and burgers. Nan, Moulton's dog, gets some much welcomed ice cubes from the big bag under the tree, put into the little folding plastic water bowl Moulton carries with her. A new crowd is coming to the arena. They, too, get leaflets and chants. Tim Craven has been ejected when police found him inside, but not before he and the other two who had hidden themselves in the press box get off a few good chants in Sullivan's direction.

A reporter for *Habilitation,* a disability magazine out of Seattle, has marched up to Sullivan, she reports, and asked him the questions ADAPT has so long wanted to ask him. To every single question, she says, he has responded, "It's a very nice day."

Most of the students don't want to talk to a reporter. They have no comment. Some think that it's wrong of ADAPT to spoil their special day. Others think the group has a right to make itself heard — just not here, not now. One woman who has read the flyers says that "they don't want to be prisoners in nursing homes." A man, who hasn't read one, says he doesn't know what they're protesting about but he thinks they have a right to do it. His daughter is graduating today — with a degree in special education.

Each ADAPT contingent blocking an entrance has its contingent of cops. The two groups joke with each other and pass the time in small talk. It's a lot like a chess game, says Haines, this trying to puzzle out where Sullivan's going to exit.

Just about the time it occurs to several of the organizers, who have been trying to psych out from which exit Sullivan will be spirited away, that the one exit that has no guards on it is the parking lot entrance, a police car comes screaming down the street, makes an abrupt U-turn, and, at that moment, Sullivan's car, driven by Secret Service, shoots out of the entrance. Several ADAPT wheelers are on his tail in a flash, but it's too late.

Sullivan again escapes — but the point, say the activists, has been well made to the over 10,000 people who have attended. Thousands of flyers have been passed out.

ADAPT makes no effort to block the streets surrounding the Pavilion. Monday's a different story. By 11 a.m., both State and Adams Streets are blocked. Downtown Chicago is taking the flyers as fast as they're being passed out. Many of them are surprisingly in agreement with ADAPT's call for 25% of the current Medicaid money to be redirected to in-home services. One businessman engages Bob Kafka in a long and intense discussion over the merits of attendant services. He has buddies who were in Vietnam, he says, and want the same thing Kafka does. He gives Kafka his card. Many other people are giving ADAPT members their cards, too; they are interested in the issue. Nobody, they say, has brought it up before.

Certainly not the *Chicago Tribune*, which, instead of covering the baccalaureate brouhaha, runs a feature story on a college camp-out.

"What I'm looking for is a reasonable atmosphere to address the issues." Delilah Brummet Flaum, HHS's Region V Director, would have to shout to make herself heard over downtown Chicago traffic and hundreds of milling demonstrators. And she's not shouting. She has come down, along with Chester Stroyny, Regional Director of the Health Care Financing Administration, and HCFA official David DuPre, in response to ADAPT demands. They want to meet with "officials"; they've blockaded the Region V HHS headquarters and aren't letting anyone in — or out — unless they're willing to climb and crawl over protesters. About 20 activists have gotten all the way up to the HHS offices on the 15th floor, and have a bunch of police in there with them.

It's lunchtime by the time Flaum, Stroyny and DuPre are trotted out to Karen Tamley, Bob Kafka and Teresa Monroe and the others in the middle of Adams Street.

ADAPT wants them to call Sullivan, to make him come back to Chicago and meet with them. Flaum can't do that. "I am willing to do anything else you want us to do, to try to get this resolved," she's saying. But she wants the group to be "more reasonable." She tells Tamley that she is "well aware" of ADAPT's concerns, and that "the Bush Administration is working on non-institutional care options." Anna Stonum asks more questions. People in the crowd are starting to yell that they can't hear.

Flaum is telling Kafka that "shutting down a building" is not the way to get a meeting with Sullivan. Kafka responds that they've sent at least four letters to Sullivan and he's never responded to a single one. "You know as well as I do that the Secretary sets the tone for the discussion," Kafka lectures her.

Kafka and DuPre engage in a debate about facts and figures. They can't trip Kafka up; he seems to know as much if not more about the issue than these folks do. At times the officials even seem to agree with him. Not, however, when he charges that "nothing the Secretary has said or done" changes anything "because he's in the pocket of the nursing home industry."

"We disagree with that," say all three officials simultaneously. "We do favor the de-institutionalization model."

"The damn Secretary has not said one thing — ever — has not even said the word 'attendant services' publicly," Kafka yells, and swears that ADAPT will continue to hold the building.

"This is not being positive," says Flaum.

"These are people's lives you're talking about," Kafka retorts.

"You don't know what it's like," Monroe shouts at the officials when Kafka's done. "I want to talk to Sullivan. You get him here. He has no idea. Don't tell me Sullivan knows." Monroe's point, which she makes to Flaum, is that the money should go directly to the disabled person "because no person knows better what they need than the disabled person. Let us have our dignity." She argues with Stroyny over nursing home inspections.

Mark Johnson accuses Sullivan of "being in the pocket of the nursing homes." And meetings like this, he charges, aren't worth a thing "unless there's a commitment."

The group, hearing Johnson, takes the cue: "We want a commitment!"

One of the workers in the HHS office has come out for lunch and now finds she cannot get back in over the demonstrators. Still, she thinks what they're doing is "positive." She's a volunteer in a nursing home herself, she says. "And I know they're the pits. People who don't frequent them don't know. These people who are walking around here" — she gestures to lunch-hour Chicagoans moving up and down the street — "they could become victims of nursing homes, too. I look at these people here" — and now she means ADAPT — "and I know I wouldn't want to be jailed up in a nursing home."

But then, she believes in protesting, she says. "I think protests are fine. I'm in tune with them. I was with Martin Luther King back in the '60s," she says.

"I was in jail with Dr. King. I was 14 years old. That was just what you did; you went to jail. Some of our young people don't understand.

"This is how to explain it," she continues, warming to her subject. "These people want to get heard. We couldn't get heard in Birmingham, either. That's why we marched on Washington." She won't identify herself, though, but will only say she's a spectator. But she works upstairs in the HHS office, she says.

"And they got time to listen to that TV stuff — people come in talking about that, they make a big deal about the stuff they see on TV. And they got these people out here and they don't want to pay attention. When I was upstairs, they were callin' 'em 'beasts' and 'vultures.'"

It is a measure of the erosion of belief in the system that has become the trademark of ADAPT that, when an EMS ambulance pulls up to the door and the word goes out that police are bringing down a man who's had a heart attack, the thought passes among the group that this is yet another ploy. They think the stretcher rolled into the lobby and up on the elevator may be a ruse to make them move away from the door, which they nonetheless do, not wanting it to be said that they cared not for another disabled person who might be in danger. And when the man is brought down on the stretcher, there is more speculation: wasn't he one of the officials out here earlier? Did the confrontation and excitement give him a heart attack? Is he faking? Is it really a medical emergency, or just a move to get someone out of the building who has an important meeting to attend and doesn't want it stopped by cripples?

No one remembers the man in the stretcher more than a few minutes after the ambulance pulls away, lights rotating, into the Chicago traffic.

Jane Garza from El Hogar del Nino is with the protesters, blocking a door by leaning against it. She's part of the protest, she says; disabled herself, though she knows she doesn't look it. She works in early childhood education.

Some of the signs protesters are carrying were made by the children at her center, she says. "It's a way to bring them into it," she points out.

The parents of the disabled kids at the center "are all reasonable people," she says. "So they understand my being at an activity like this." If she gets arrested, she says, she has an understanding with her agency: they will bail her out. She's been arrested with ADAPT before, she says; that was in Montreal. She's been with ADAPT protests in Washington — the one to get the ADA passed; and one in St. Louis.

"No one wants to see their child in a nursing home. People can really relate to that." She says the group at her door has been talking to passersby all day about the issue.

"I was on the verge of going into a nursing home myself, back in '82," says this woman who doesn't look disabled. When she had her aneurism and was in rehabilitation, she says, the Illinois Department of Rehabilitation Services gave her money with which she was able to pay two people — one for the morning, and one for the evening. "I just needed help getting up and then getting to bed. I was so weak. I just needed minimal assistance, somebody there to help me get dressed. But without that program, they would have put me in a nursing home."

Illinois Gov. Jim Edgar's budget cuts have forced the Department of Rehabilitation Services to extend a freeze on intakes in that program through the end of 1993, and Edgar, Chicago ADAPT charges, is trying to eliminate a yearly cost-of-living adjustment for attendants.

"After I got stronger, I was able to manage on my own. But look at how many people are in my shoes!" she says. "I worked; I had money. I was a social worker back then; one who had to apply for public aid just so I could get assistance."

The philosophy and tactic of door-blocking: Let people go in and out, if they're willing to climb over you and your chair to do it. Arrest is not the objective here; inconveniencing people is. "We want them to see what it's like for us," says one who has engaged in many door blockings.

Tuesday morning's *Chicago Tribune,* instead of covering

ADAPT's HHS confrontation, reports on stepped-up security measures at the downtown State of Illinois building where, the *Tribune* reports, in error, ADAPT was "supposed" to be demonstrating Monday. ADAPT, it says, changed its mind. In fact, ADAPT planned to hit state offices on Wednesday. Speculation abounds as to who fed the paper the false information, the effect of which is to make ADAPT look disorganized. It later becomes apparent that state officials have had a hand in it. There is nothing in the *Tribune* about the people who stopped along State Street and asked questions, about Flaum, about any of it. The *Sun-Times* carries a photo, inside.

At the corner of State and Grant, a baby-blue police wrecker, the same blue as the cars, as the barricades, has blocked a curb ramp. ADAPT has blocked four intersections adjacent to the American Medical Association. Wheelchairs are stretched across 16 streets.

At the intersection of Wabash and Grand, in the back, Paulette Patterson is hassling the policemen, mouthing off and chasing them with her motorized chair. It seems she is trying to get arrested.

The police are being friendly enough. It won't be until noon that things will get rough. The cops will barricade the main entrances to the glass-walled fortress; many ADAPT members will take that as their cue to launch themselves out of their wheelchairs onto the high-curbed stoop around the building, crawling up to bang and hammer on the wooden barricades. A few find satisfaction in pounding on the glass walls.

This will happen, though, only after the confrontation—the confrontation that resulted in Jerry Eubanks of Chicago being dropped from his wheelchair; picked up — by his neck, it seems to other protesters, who holler for an "Ambulance! Now!"; the confrontation that causes Patterson to roll from her wheelchair and shriek at the top of her lungs, kicking her legs wildly as police try to pick her up. The police back off; when they come at her again, her screams again drive them back. Finally, Patterson is left alone, and, once more in her wheelchair, rolls off to the side, where she admits slyly and with her trademark smile that she enjoys discomfiting police. "They don't wanna mess with me," she says proudly.

Suddenly they are all there again, surging at the entrance,

trying to get up the high curb. Stephanie Thomas and Diane Coleman and others are wedging themselves in next to the Chicago Transit Authority paratransit vehicles that are a sure sign of arrests: it's the only way police can haul off a wheelchair to the hoosegow. Allen Leegant is diving under a barricade trying to get up to the entrance. Chris Hronis and Arthur Campbell are trying to follow; they are caught by police. Campbell is carried, spread-eagle, by four cops, directly to a CTA van.

Cameras are everywhere; TV crews have materialized out of nowhere. Campbell has been arrested. Mike Auberger has been arrested. Campbell and Auberger are each put into his own van. The police have their eye on Mike Ervin. When you catch a snatch of cop-to-cop talk, you learn they're trying to pick off those they figure to be the leaders.

"What the cops never understand is why the demonstration continues after they've hauled off the folks they think are leaders," says someone who is blocking a street. "They can't figure out that arresting leaders doesn't work; that as soon as they arrest someone, somebody else just moves in."

Susan Nussbaum, blocking a side door, answers questions about whether the movement will ever see violence. "There's always the potential for violence," she is saying. "But it would be good if that could be understood in the context of a larger issue.

"I am not in favor of getting my head beaten in."

At 3:15 the building starts to empty out. ADAPT has managed to block all the exits, so AMA workers and officials alike are subjected to a gauntlet of taunts as they trot, under tight police protection, down the ramp to the alley and across to the parking garage. The taunts seem mostly to be of the "AMA Shame On You" variety.

When ADAPT members arrived at AMA headquarters in the morning, they found tables set up with water coolers and cups of refreshing water awaiting them. Later, the AMA's Department of Geriatric Health would confirm for a reporter that the AMA had done this so the disabled people wouldn't get overheated and get sick.

Many protesters were wary of the water. Some suspected it had been spiked with Valium; others thought it a ploy to get them to have to pee later on, adding to their discomfort and hopefully ending the demonstration early. Much of the water was left untouched.

Water was also running through hoses into the sprinkling system of the AMA's lawns. This had the added effect of keeping protesters off the grassy knolls fronting the building. Shortly after ADAPT arrived, one demonstrator had parked his chair on the hose while others moved across the area to block doors. Later, the water was simply turned off.

The AMA's flak, Arnold Collins, was standing around with the TV and radio reporters most of the day. The AMA had issued a statement insisting it "supports the home care objectives of ADAPT." Dr. Joanne Schwartzberg, Director of the AMA's Department of Geriatric Health, said in the news release that a meeting the previous Thursday with ADAPT had been "productive" and that the two groups had "considerable common ground."

Campbell, who attended the meeting, had a different analysis. He said he believed Schwartzberg truly had no understanding what ADAPT wanted; that some of their ideas had been totally inconceivable to her.

Schwartzberg said ADAPT was the first group she had ever met with and felt "hostility." "It was a great shock," she said. "I always thought of myself as being a great advocate. But I wasn't an advocate enough for them." Schwartzberg said that ADAPT didn't understand that there were "really frail people in nursing homes — a kind of frailty that these disabled don't have.

"I was really scared that the demonstrators might get harmed, the way they throw themselves out of their chairs," she went on. "They're very courageous; I think they're a little reckless. Luckily, nobody's gotten seriously hurt."

"Do you think she really believes the things she says, or do you think it's just a pose?" a filmmaker wondered.

The AMA had issued "a guideline for medical management of homecare patients," she said, and they were putting on eight seminars for doctors "in managing home care." She knew ADAPT wanted AMA members to divest themselves of their financial interest in nursing homes and cut nursing home admissions. But the AMA couldn't do that, she explained patiently. "We are a voluntary body, not a regulatory body."

"They couldn't understand why we couldn't do more," she said.

The *Chicago Tribune* was still concerned about the State of Illinois building. Every day *Tribune* stories had chronicled the increasing security at the site. On Tuesday, Paulette Patterson and another disabled woman filed suit in U.S. District Court alleging denial of access due to increased security. Though a temporary restraining order was not granted, Patterson's attorney, Matthew Cohen, said filing the suit had had the desired effect. The *Tribune* covered the suit.

Finally, on Wednesday, ADAPT obliged the *Tribune* and state officials by staging a protest at the building, drawing attention to state policies that were cutting people off from attendant services in Illinois.

On Thursday, the *Tribune* ran a long story on ADAPT. Calling them "a group of vociferous activists savvy in street action," it quoted a miffed Chicago official who refused to be named saying that "one of the strongest points in their civil disobedience is making themselves look as pathetic as possible." "The group's history is rife with attention-grabbing acts of protest," said the *Tribune,* which compared them to ACT-UP and Earth First! protest groups. "Though some may question their tactics, none can doubt they have impact," said the *Tribune.*

July/August 1992

Wade Blank's Liberated Community

Laura Hershey

*T*he death of Reverend Wade Blank on February 15, 1993, left a profound emptiness in the hearts of many people who loved and respected him. But any void in the disability rights movement is only momentary, for Blank left behind a wealth of humane values, a keen analysis — and scores of skilled, committed leaders ready to carry the movement forward.

American Disabled for Attendant Programs Today, or ADAPT, and its "mother," the Atlantis Community in Denver, both embody the spiritual, organizational, and strategic lessons Blank carried over from the 1960s black civil rights movement. He had been a Presbyterian minister, a War on Poverty field organizer, and a disciple of Dr. Martin Luther King, Jr., before becoming an orderly, then an assistant administrator, in a Denver nursing home.

Early in his career as a iconoclastic minister and civil rights worker, Blank developed the concept of a "liberated community" — a society where human beings could live in equality and develop the power to effect change. When, at the Heritage House nursing home, he found himself in the midst of a "community" of people with severe disabilities, whose only community structure was one of oppression — the confines of the institution — he took on the challenge of making the "liberated community" a reality.

It all started when Blank came to Denver seeking a change. "The nursing home industry in Denver recruited its nursing home administrators from the ranks of ex-ministers," he recalled recently. The industry had built too many nursing homes in Denver, he explained. There weren't enough old people, and the state institutions were dumping disabled people out, so the nursing home industry decided they would get them. A nursing home executive called Blank. "They said, 'You're young. You're hip. Could you start a youth wing for us?' So I started a youth wing."

Hired by Heritage House in December 1971, Blank went to visit the residents the evening before he began his new job. "I remember for dinner that night, we had baked potatoes, applesauce, and scrambled eggs, and this was near Christmas. The place was like a morgue. The food was cold." Blank chatted with severely disabled individuals, some of whom would later become ADAPT organizers. "Little did I know," Blank recalled, "that I was to enter the most important moment of my life.

"I had 60 young people I recruited. Every morning at 7:30, they'd get dressed and get on a school bus, and go to a workshop and count fish hooks. Called it [a] work activities program."

At council meetings of the young people, the residents made simple requests, and an idealistic Blank tried to implement them. "I let them evaluate the nurses," he said. "They wanted co-ed living. They wanted to have pets. They wanted to have rock 'n' roll bands. So three years into this experiment, this nursing home is just like a college dorm on a crazy weekend all the time.

"I still was trying to change it from inside, and I didn't understand the monster I worked for," he recalled.

In 1975, Blank proposed "that we move a few of them out into apartments, and we let the aides and orderlies punch in at the nursing home, then go to the apartment and give them service." That idea got Blank fired. "The nursing home saw where I was going, and they couldn't let me go in that direction."

Once Blank was fired, the nursing home erased all his reforms. "They came in and they took all the stereos and TVs out of everybody's rooms, had the dog pound come by and get all the animals, and in one day it went from everything I'd built for four years — to that."

But Blank wasn't about to give up. Thinking to himself that

he'd "recruited all these people to this hell," he decided simply to move them out "and do the care myself.

"You think marriage is a serious commitment, you try moving eight people who are severely disabled out into their own apartments and be responsible for dressing them, feeding them, bowel programs, bathing them," he added. Had he given it much thought, he probably wouldn't have done it, he continued. "But within the first six months, I'd moved 18 severely disabled people out. So now I was wed to the concept. You know, I couldn't walk away from it."

That exodus laid the foundations for the Atlantis Community and its political-action offshoot, ADAPT. "We began to learn about power and what empowerment is, and how to use it," Blank said. While Atlantis was liberating people from nursing homes, ADAPT (which then stood for American Disabled for Accessible Public Transit) took on discrimination in Denver's, and then the nation's, bus systems. Using nonviolent, direct-action tactics similar to King's movement, ADAPTers made bold demands and achieved extraordinary results.

Blank found himself at the center of another civil rights campaign, similar to the one he had seen African Americans wage. "All the issues are the same," Blank asserted. "The black movement wanted to ride the buses equally. The black movement wanted to eat at the Woolworth counters. The black movement wanted the right to vote. The black movement wanted the right to keep their families together. The black movement wanted the right to be integrated into the school system. That's what the disability rights movement wants, exactly."

ADAPT, appearing in the time and place it did, was "a strange breed of cat." It wasn't connected to the independent living movement simultaneously emerging in Berkeley and elsewhere. "Denver is sort of sitting out in the middle of the prairie, isolated from the rest of the country," Blank explained. "A very radical disabilities rights movement grew in a very apolitical city."

That isolation continued even as ADAPT spread throughout the nation. ADAPT's priorities and approaches always set it apart from mainstream disability-rights organizations.

That was fine with Blank. "All those well-intentioned Carter Administration things came nowhere near what I was doing — I mean, in the sense that I was freeing the slaves," Blank said in describing the situation in the 1970s. "While they were talking about equal employment and stuff like that, that didn't apply to my group.

"The ADA doesn't even affect people in nursing homes — other than to make the building accessible," he continued. "You've had 504 and all that around, but it in no way affected people that were locked up in institutions. It didn't guarantee them anything."

While not dismissing other efforts — "I don't want to take anything away from that [independent living] movement. It gave us a lot of momentum to do what we have to do now," he said — Blank was clear about the differences. "The independent living movement is into meetings and lobbying and socials," he said. "My members are into confrontation. We'll tell somebody what we want, and we'll talk about it once or twice, but that's it. Then we deal with you. Either we'll shut you down or whatever."

Confrontation worked, Blank believed, because it took society's fears — those fears we're always trying to dispel in disability awareness workshops — and turned them to a new use. He described how he learned this strategy. In the late 1960s, Blank helped a Midwestern black community obtain water and sewage services from an indifferent government. The black leaders, who wanted to get along and avoid making waves, refused to challenge the responsible authorities. So Blank went to the local pool hall and recruited several dozen black teenagers. He outfitted them in dark sunglasses and leather jackets. "They looked bad," he recalled. They piled in a van and paid a visit to their U.S. senator. The action brought almost immediate results, in the form of a federal project to construct the needed reservoir. "All that was," Blank expounded, "was taking their blackness and making it even more mysterious and threatening to a white person, and going up and intimidating a senator."

Years later, Blank remembered the technique and applied it in a new way: "So I said, 'Well, if that's true, then people being in wheelchairs has that same mystique to it, so let's take 25 wheelchairs and go out and surround a bus and hold it, and see what happens.' Bam! Just like magic. It worked. Total power. Police couldn't move the wheelchairs, because they were afraid. The mayor said, 'Don't arrest disabled people.' We win."

Direct action was not only effective, Blank said, it was also empowering. "This was very therapeutic, blocking buses. I mean, it's like giving the finger to the white man." Anger wasn't a dirty word to Blank; it was a powerful force, which ADAPT actions harnessed as a force for change. "Anger is the root of advocacy movements," he said once. "Oppression breeds anger."

While many disability-rights advocates were emphasizing employment issues, Blank encouraged people to take advantage of their low-income status. Individuals receiving SSI do most of ADAPT's organizing work, supplementing their benefits with small monthly stipends. Blank himself collected unemployment for a year while setting up the Atlantis community. Even as co-director he never paid himself more than $18,000. Some critics accused him of perpetuating a "culture of poverty" with this approach. But Blank saw it as a matter of pragmatism. "Let's be professional organizers," he told his apprentice revolutionaries. "Let the government pay your salary, and you go out and organize."

Blank's focus on fundamental human rights, and on the most impoverished members of the disability community, distanced him from more affluent groups. In this, too, he emulated Martin Luther King. "King involved the poorest in the community," Blank said, "and a movement cannot really change things unless they address the poorest, the least. When King was shot, he was beginning to attack the ghettos." For Blank, "our ghettos are the nursing homes, and we need to address the ghetto.

"The Ed Robertses and the Judy Heumanns don't deal with nursing homes. They've never been in one. They don't understand them," said Blank, using as examples two leaders of the independent living movement. Blank was often critical of the independent living movement's elitism. "If it doesn't address the people that don't have any money," he contended, "you don't really represent the movement."

Blank attacked not only the mainstream disability movement's economic hierarchy, but also its disability hierarchy. "You go around to independent living centers and you'll see a lot of post-polios and a lot of spinal cord injuries," he said. "But you won't see people that slobber and can't speak clearly like you do here." These are the people often excluded or left behind by more "respectable" advocacy organizations, he pointed out.

Despite these strong opinions, Blank rarely bore malice toward his rivals within the disability community. And despite his enthusiasm for civil disobedience, he was personally uncomfortable with conflict. But he understood the value of debate and disagreement. "The way we measure a movement is not only the feeling of energy and charisma, but also the in-fighting," he pointed out. The conflict, he felt, was healthy. "Usually what in-fighting reflects is the growling and creaking of growth. You know, one group saying this and one group saying that. Over the years, ADAPT has been wrong on a lot of issues; but that's how a movement grows."

Critics remain, but Blank's commitment, personal devotion, and success rate turned many skeptics into supporters. Justin Dart, Chair of the President's Committee on Employment of People with Disabilities, once warned Blank that he wouldn't get anywhere using such confrontational tactics. Yet Dart became a solid backer of ADAPT, and frequently credited Blank with driving the ADA through Congressional obstacles. Dart, a wealthy, disabled Republican, was no doubt charmed by Blank's essential idealism. As Blank himself declared, "The greatest compliment to a democracy is organizing, because it assumes that the government will change."

Other opponents accused Blank of stifling democracy within ADAPT, and of suppressing leadership. ADAPT leadership feels the inaccuracy of this view will likely become apparent in coming months.

Blank actively cultivated leadership among Atlantis and ADAPT members. He helped train activists throughout the country who have now formed dozens of local ADAPT chapters. Besides participating in the semi-annual national ADAPT actions, these chapters also do independent actions throughout the year.

Blank found leadership qualities in people who had never before thought of being leaders: former nursing home residents, people with speech impairments, people labelled retarded and others typically disenfranchised both by society at large and by traditional disability organizations. Blank had little patience for people who put their own egos or their own careers above the movement.

But more people were and are being empowered every year to free Americans with disabilities from institutions. All are encouraged to help plan protests, identify issues and targets, hold press conferences, and become a part of the "liberated community."

Blank made a point of keeping himself humble and honest. "I never do any public speaking without a disabled person with me," he said. "I have to do the attendant work when I'm on the road myself. I don't take an attendant to do it. I do it myself. I may want to be a star in front of the crowd, but then I have to go upstairs and give the guy a bath."

Blank's unpretentious leadership style and courageous example helped teach and inspire a host of grass-roots disability rights leaders. These individuals — Mike Auberger, Karen Tambley, Tom Olin, Robin Stephens, Stephanie Thomas, Bob Kafka, Mark Johnson, Diane Coleman, and hundreds of others — took their protests to Washington, D.C. this past May, demonstrating at the Capitol and the American Health Care Association to push for a national attendant services program. For the first time, the Secretary of Health and Human Services met with the group. Sec. Donna Shalala promised the group a response to their demands for redirection of a fourth of the Medicaid budget from nursing home to in-home services.

Blank is gone, but his spirit lives on.

July/August 1993

The Power of One Person

Mary Johnson

The Americans with Disabilities Act may be ushering in a new era of access. But for well over a year already a man in Rhode Island and a woman n Maryland have each singlehandedly gotten scores of agencies and programs to provide access. How? They are forcing them to start obeying laws that have been on the books for nearly two decades. They are using Section 504 of the 1973 Rehabilitation Act and their states' human rights laws. And neither has yet lost a battle for access.

In Rhode Island, Gregory Solas, a former ironworker, has in the last two years filed complaints with the Rhode Island Department of Education's Civil Rights Office on 30 of the 37 public school districts in the state. He's taken complaints out on private and parochial schools as well; he just won a complaint against Salve Regina University. In his hometown of Warwick, RI, he used the 1984 Voting Accessibility for the Elderly and Handicapped Act to force access to his formerly inaccessible polling site.

Solas has used the Fair Housing Amendments Act to win a battle against realtors who were steering him away from houses he wanted to rent and now, with the encouragement of the Rhode Island Governor's Commission on the Handicapped, he's pushing to ensure that the state's open meetings law, which gives disabled people access to public meetings, is enforced.

Last summer, after three years of fighting, Marilynn Phillips of Westminster, MD, won her case against the Maryland State Arts Council — which had insisted it didn't discriminate — and for the first time in history, the National Endowment for the Arts took away a state arts agency's federal funding. The arts group soon came into compilance, installing a lift to its historic rowhouse headquarters and making the restroom accessible. Phillips, a professor at Morgan State University, now says she's determined to see that the hundreds of programs the state arts group funds become accessible, too.

Though it was her biggest victory, Phillips has had others. She filed a complaint against the Baltimore-Washington International Airport for failing to have restrooms she could use. She's filed complaints against Caldor's discount store, Sears, Paul Harris Stores, Casual Corner and Macy's — for not having accessible dressing rooms. Using the state's human rights law, she's filed complaints against the Leisure Health Spa, Western Maryland College and Westminster High School for "discriminating against wheelchair users." Some are still under investigation, but she hasn't lost a case yet, either.

Together, these two people are changing the meaning of access in two states.

How do other disabled people feel about lone wolves like these?

"If we had a Greg Solas in every county in this country," says Bob Cooper, director of the Rhode Island Governor's Commission and a fan of Solas's, "we would live in a country which would not have needed Congress to enact an Americans with Disabilities Act. Most states have similar statutes. But the vast majority [of disabled people] are unwilling to challenge authority. Solas is. He has yet to lose a complaint. He does his homework."

His statement was echoed by Maryland Commission on Human Relations' Deputy Director Henry Ford, speaking of Phillips. More things are becoming accessible "thanks to Dr. Phillips" and others like her, says Ford. He thinks the attention Phillips has brought to the issue has been healthy. "Within the last year we've gotten a flood of complaints" about access, he said, and he expects to get more after the ADA takes effect. "It's like the Clarence Thomas-Anita Hill hearings. That law [forbidding sexual harassment] has been in place for years too, but it seems something has to happen to bring it to public attention."

People like Solas and Phillips make many of us uneasy.

William Anderson, who has a disabled child, told the Providence (RI) *Sunday Journal* last summer he disagreed with Solas, and that access laws were too stringent. "To just spend money indiscriminately to do all this stuff, I just can't see it."

Though they are only pushing for what is their right by law, they are seen as "bad cripples," to use Marilynn Phillips's term. But it cannot be denied that they have made access occur where it has never occurred before.

"It's amazing how much more willing folks are now to recognize that there are problems still to be dealt with and to plan ways to overcome them than there was before [Solas's] publicity," says Cooper.

Solas takes a straighforward view of all this. "I've been hitting home runs right along," he says.

Ironically, Solas and Phillips are people for whom the ADA will make little difference. They have found that current laws work fine — when used.

That's the problem, say activists concerned over the ADA's impact. Disabled people are simply afraid to use the laws. "All the ADA has done is create expectations that are going to be dashed come January 27," says Cooper. "It's created great expectations among people with disabilities that somebody else will take care of the problems for them."

Many, perhaps, take the view of Marian Vessels, director of the Maryland Governor's Committee on Employment of People with Disabilities, who insists that "using the legal system should not be the first step." The first move should be a "willingness to negotiate." Others, though, find in this attitude just more proof that we don't take our own rights seriously, are willing to agree to less access than we are even conceded by law.

To say that Vessels and Phillips don't see eye to eye is putting it mildly. Phillips says she encountered Vessels when she first started to look into filing complaints and was steered "in the wrong direction."

"Filing complaints is the keystone of the ADA," says Cooper. "On an intellectual basis" disabled people know this, he says; "but on an emotional basis, they expect somebody else will take care of it. That's certainly been the problem with 504."

"You only get the rights if you're willing to push for them," he continues. "We may have freed the slaves — but all we did was take the chains off. We've left them on the plantation to become sharecroppers. Only those who are willing to insist that what was written on a piece of paper in a law — who are willing to exercise their rights — have gotten them."

Solas and Phillips are unusual among disabled people: They believe, without question, that they have rights. They know there are laws on the books that guarantee them access. And they use those laws skillfully. They see it as fighting for what is rightfully theirs — and all other disabled people's.

"Nobody should be intimidated by the law," argues Solas. "The laws were designed for people to use. He likens them to "opening up a door. They're there," he says. Just like we should be able to use doors into businesses, "we should be able to use the door of justice as well.

"I just can't tolerate anyone getting ripped off of their freedoms," he continues. "We pay taxes like everybody else and we should have the same entitlements."

What amazes Solas, come lately to disability rights, is that more people don't use the law. "It's just incredible," he says.

"I just consider myself a regular guy who wants to get something done that's right." The former welder minces few words. "I've taken on an issue that happens to be very important to a lot of people," he says.

"Everybody has the potential to get out there and do this stuff," he points out. "Just one thing, just one curb cut. Or get one telephone pole removed out of a curb cut. Or just address one little issue. It's incredible what we'd get done" if each of us just did that, he insists.

He doesn't pretend that change comes easy: "Just go try to get a curb cut changed. It's not the easiest thing to get done. But it can be done." That's his message: one person *can* do it. "And it's nice when you get something," he says.

Despite what his critics believe, Solas says he likes to address issues "like a gentleman, without friction. But if it comes to where you have to file a complaint, and use the force of law, so be it."

Like many who know their rights, he takes the long view of opponents. "If they're having a hard time with it, then they're having a hard time with it. But down the road they'll convert and understand that this was right. They'll realize they didn't understand it."

If that attitude has not enabled Solas to move mountains, it has certainly enabled him to get barriers removed. Solas's polling site wasn't accessible. "They think, 'well, they can vote in their car,'" said Solas, ever wise to the ways of injustice. "I went through that once, but I'm not going through it again.

"It didn't take much," he continued. "I got on the radio and voiced my opinion. A day later they're out there banging away with their hammers and nails. They knew they had to get their thing in order."

Both Solas and Phillips find it almost unbelievable that people don't use the laws.

"I didn't think it was fair for people to tell me go to the bathroom before I came to a meeting. In other words, 'Why do you need a water fountain? We'll get a drink for you.' Or, 'Why do you need a phone? We'll make the phone call for you.' 'Why do you need the fire alarms lowered? We can pull the alarms for you.' I mean, these are just people's attitudes!

"What a world disabled people have been living in! This is incredible! Until you get disabled, you don't really know the score.

"I mean, this stuff is not hard to see. It's all over the place."

Phillips and Solas stress that it's important to know the laws well — to do your research. And to be persistent.

"Once you take the mystery out of the law, it's not that difficult," says Solas. " Step one, two, three, four, and you get to the end. There's a pattern to these things." Like Phillips, who tells of being put off the trail by various disability "advocates," Solas points out that the dedicated disability activist must "get past all the smokescreens and distracting opinions and baloney, where they try to try to steer you off or distract you to where you get disgusted." Over the years, he says, "people got worn down, disgusted, and left the issue."

"All the 'no's' you get when you first call about an access issue can turn to 'yes's' with persistence," counsels Phillips. The Maryland Commission on Human Relations, charged with enforcing the state human rights law that forbids discrimination on the basis of disability, was resistant to interpreting it "in terms of accessibility" at first, she adds — "they didn't think they could do it." The problem was "the same Catch-22 we see everywhere": the law requires "reasonable accommodation" — but not if it involves "undue hardship," as Ford put it.

Phillips used that law to gain access to places many advocates would have given up on "by persistence and kind of continuing to argue the logic of it — which is basically what I did."

The bottom line was that neither would take "no" for an answer.

"I kept on arguing the logic of things," explains Phillips. "I used evey kind of analogy I could: to racism, to sexism. I had very interesting intellectual debates with them. They had never had been pushed to the point where they had to be 'insightful' about the law. My impression is that every time someone had called up and said 'I've been denied access,' they said, 'Well that's a shame, but we can't help you.' Nobody ever got past that.

"I got past that," she said, even though "it took three years."

"Finally, about 18 months ago," she continued, "they finally said, 'Ah, I see!' It's kind of like with students I teach. With students, after you keep pounding things in over and over, they 'see.'"

Phillips wants it made clear that the Commission didn't "bend any law." They just "kept looking" at it. "You have to push them to do that," she said.

Though similar in their approach, Solas and Phillips couldn't be more different in background. Solas comes to disability in mid-life, after years as an ironworker. He says his background made him aware of access, and good at solving problems. "I knew about building codes. I used to weld the rails, the handrails, you know, for the ramps. I was with Local 37 and I went all over the state. So I had this background already."

Part of it, too, he says, "is just being a wise consumer. If you buy a product, I always say, you should look at it and see if it works. I was always an interesting guy to talk to at coffee break.

"It's hard work being an ironworker. You take chances with your life. I was used to that. Get up on the girders and stuff. I always knew I might be disabled," Solas insists. "You don't play peek-a-boo with life." Because of Solas's working-class background, says Cooper, "the more blue-collar folks with disabilities are cheering him along. One of them is pushing the system."

Phillips, in contrast, is an academic. She thinks that has helped her. She talks of having been "intellectually isolated from disability" growing up, which led to "emotional isolation" — a problem she has since explored in her research. "I did my dissertation on oral histories of disabled people. It opened up my eyes to the fact that we have the same experience — we all have the same experience. The intellectual side of that was very important. It made me confident."

Both arrived at the same point: We have rights.

For Phillips, this sometimes means that "you have to be willing to embarrass yourself. I had to be willing to call everybody, and maybe get somebody who'd say, 'Hey, you're going too far; you don't know what you're talking about; don't you know this doesn't apply to you?' It helps," says Phillips, to know that "I've done my homework."

"A lot of people are afraid of change," says Solas. "We're in a tough situation in this country right now; we're in a recession. And when people think 'money,' they panic." But, he points out, "you can't segregate black people anymore — and you can't segregate disabled people. It's parallel."

There's another parallel Solas sees, too: "The blacks were physically beat on in the '50s and '60s. Disabled people have been beat on psychologically. And they're in a situation where they've really suffered.

"And we shouldn't have to suffer," he adds.

What would Solas tell the average disabled person? "Go enjoy your life. It's your life; it's not their life. Make sure you get what's yours. You're not asking for anything more; you're asking for the minimum of what everybody else has."

Why aren't there more Phillipses and Solases out there being "bad cripples" and causing headlines? Solas is not as given to introspection as is Phillips. He doesn't talk about the "disability community." He says he was invited to speak at a high school but hasn't done it yet; he was on the cable TV show produced by Cooper's group recently, talking about how it's done. But the sense is that he's not a joiner; a lone wolf. He likes what he does; he likes getting results. When questioned about other disabled people whom he's worked with, he moves the conversation around to other things.

"I don't really picture myself parading down Main Street at night with a lit candle singing, 'We shall overcome.' That's not my style. I'm not gonna plead with people to do their jobs; I'm gonna make sure it gets done. There's no pleading. I'm as equal as anybody else. And I'm not going to have my self-esteem banged around — or that of any of my peers or any of my friends."

If Solas has a theme, it's this: "Anybody can do what I'm doing. It just takes somebody to do it."

He knows that "people are afraid of retaliation — or they may feel uncomfortable." Or, he says, they may feel they or their kids won't get a fair chance if they speak up — something he disputes. "When you do speak up, you do gain respect, and you do get equal services," Solas believes.

That belief informs his style: "I give people a chance to get things done." When they don't, Solas doesn't waste time filing a complaint. "When they come to me, they come to a final stop sign of 'no, the discrimination is not gonna continue; yes, you are going to abide by the law.'"

"The white collar disability community is appalled by him," says Cooper. "He is not playing the game; he is not a nice, kind, quiet, polite kind of fellow." Some professionals with disabilities "are very upset that he has rocked the boat, that he hasn't backed off, that he files a complaint and then, if he doesn't get a positive reaction, immediately goes to the press." Others, Cooper says, "defend his results but want to keep his tactics at arm's length, which is unfortunate."

Phillips is keenly aware that she's considered "the maladjusted cripple." "I'm the sort of individual who finds it difficult to use all my energy in meetings," she says, preferring to work alone. Is she unusual? "I hope it's not unusual to believe that I'm equal to everyone else." She finds that many members of disability groups are "afraid and uncomfortable. They don't want to be 'the bad cripple.'"

Other disabled people sometimes see her name in the paper and call her, wanting her to "fight their cause." And "sometimes it's such a little tiny thing — they could do it snap, snap, snap! but they're terrified." This terror would make sense, she says, if they were going to lose their job. "But we're talking about being afraid to file a complaint because they can't go to a performance — I mean, that's not going to hurt their job! They're afraid of being typed a 'maladjusted cripple.' That's the bottom line. That's the fear we have to get over."

Phillips says she remembers having that fear herself once. "I don't know why I've become so obnoxious — maybe it's age," she laughs. She really thinks it's her research, though. "I have evidence coming out of the woodwork that I'm right."

"We have to fight for now," Phillips insists. "We have to recognize that we can't put off making these claims."

Neither intends to stop what they're doing. "I said to myself, 'OK, Marilynn, you can go to meetings, or you can file complaints.'" But, she warns, "We have to have the balls to be publicly crucified, too."

"I've never felt better," says Solas. "Maybe my life is programmed to be this way. Who knows? Everything becomes relative. Maybe whatever you suffer in your life there's a reason for it. If you search for an answer, you find it. I'm a very optimistic person.

"I don't consider this 'work,'" he says. He considers himself "pretty effective. I can cut through a lot of red tape. I make them come to the bargaining table.

"But I am not the only one who's capable of doing things," Solas is quick to add. "I'm just another person who's come along and said 'no.' I feel better now that these things are being addressed."

By the time you read this, you'll be living in a country that says it's illegal to keep you from attending any meeting, going to any shop, applying to work in any but the smallest business, ride anywhere — because of your disability.

Time moves quickly, say these activists. Like the Nike commercial says, "just do it" — even if it's something small. "You can't be afraid to speak up," Solas would tell you. "It may sound like the most difficult thing to do at times, but the rewards far outweigh the negatives. You become a much better person for doing it."

Phillips and Solas have taken laws like the ADA and used them. They've learned how to do it. They say it's simple. They outline how to do it.

Now: What are you going to do about it in your community?

January/February 1992

ARE WE BEING SERVED?

The Do-gooder

Billy Golfus

When I say Do-gooder I don't just mean the counselors, staff, vocational (do you really need four syllables to say "work"?) personnel and assorted "helpers." I mean the agencies, programs, or what they call "care providers." The term Do-gooder appears to suggest the kind of neighbor that brings over chicken soup when you're sick — and once in a while somebody'll even do that. But that's not what I mean. I guess, for the most part, I'm talking about the professionals.

After my accident I started to have my eyes opened very slowly. It took me years, like they say, to process what had happened. While the physical disabilities and the brain damage that I have are inconvenient, a drag even, they're not as bad as the treatment by my friends, social systems and especially the Do-gooders. These people are "professionals," for God's sake

To hang the word "helping" on "professional" gives the connotation of humanity, generosity and compassion. As if their reasons for acting came out of a sense of community and personal beliefs. Give me a break! Obviously the Do-gooders don't go into that line of work for the money — although they are making a better living than the people they "serve" — and even though the words are about supporting and serving, they're basically trying to fill their own neeeds, to use the jargon.

The most reprinted essay in the English language (in case you're ever on a quiz program) is George Orwell's "Politics and the English Language." He talks about the use of language to hide meanings. I used to be a "closed head injured client" instead of brain damaged. Do-gooders call kids "at risk" that we used to call delinquents when I was one. The phrase "at risk" sets up a relationship between the Do-gooders and the kids. Alright, for ten points: who does that phrase suggest knows what's going on? Whose values does that phrase validate?

Do you see it now? Do you see how the language works with disabled people? Do "clients" and "professionals" and "service providers" make the Do-gooders have more in common with doctors or with patients?

Language is always political. How could it be otherwise? It's got to do with power and the distribution of goods and services.

Chris Ringer is a therapist who does seminars on co-dependency for the helping professions. Minnesota — land of 10,000 treatment centers — is the alcoholism/chemical dependency state. Our Governor has tried to sell alky treatment as Minnesota's new growth industry, so it only makes sense that Ringer would do "co-dependency" seminars for the helping professions. (If it sounds like I'm making fun of Chris Ringer's perspective, I'm not. The guy's very interesting, smart, well-read and concerned.)

Chris Ringer points out that it's an interesting comment on American mores that the Do-gooders make so much more money than those they allegedly do good for. "The culture says that it's virtuous and commendable to be a helper," Ringer says. "But [on] the other side, those who need help are [thought] probably responsible for their own misfortune. Who knows, it may be God punishing them, so the very fact that people are helpers is 'proof' of their virtue . . . The underbelly of that is that we live in a culture in which suffering is [thought to be] optional. That having problems is optional. Or worse, that suffering is God punishing you for being human. Some people say that it is a revision of the Puritan ethic. You know, I'm wealthy and healthy because God loves me. And you're not because you didn't do it right, and this is what you get for it.

"And that's a very dangerous model."

Human kind cannot bear very much reality.
- T.S. Eliot, *Murder in the Cathedral*

Ringer says "People get into the 'helping' professions for personal reasons. If they're going to stay in the professions and do a good job for their customers, their orientation must change," he says. "They have to become aware of what personal needs that they [are] trying to meet in becoming a 'helper.' And, make sure that their personal needs are not in conflict with their customers' needs. This is central."

Actually, I think the mistake that Chris Ringer is making is in believing that the customers are the persons "served." The customers are the ones who pay for the service: the agencies and programs and "service providers." You know, like when you go to the hospital the nurses who want you to fill out the three forms before you get the chicken soup. They know who pays their salary. The patients are not the customers; the "third party reimbursers" are the customers. The hospitals pay the nurses. You want to understand motivation, just trace the money.

Probably the place where it's easiest to see the adversary role of the alleged Do-gooders and those served is in the Social Security System. Most of the nondisabled (how do you like that term?) have the fantasy that "you'll always be taken care of" and "nobody goes hungry" in this country. For those of us who live in the opulence and plenty that the Social Security cornucopia provides, we have a different feeling about the bounty of America. We've had to give up that fantasy.

The Social Security system won't tell you who you're dealing with or who made the decision. You're supposed to get the feeling that Social Security is a monolith; a person didn't do this. In fact, the idea with all these social-system Do-gooders is not to mention their names.

In Minnesota, it's wrapped in the Minnesota-Nice style: be nice and don't use real names. It's non-personal. Individuals are not responsible "It's the SYSTEM." 'Course all Do-gooders and their agencies use that come-on. You know, they've got their "guidelines" and "I vas only followink whorders." No one is responsible; it's just "policy."

Down that alley, when I got a cost-of-living increase last year from $411 a month ("and don't spend it all in one place") to $430 a month it knocked me off medical assistance because I now

make "too much money." I've got to admit that living on $430 a
month IS too much money, and I've considered hiring financial
planners to decide how to invest all that money.

Janie, who was just mangled by a car, loves to tell me that
she was in a coma longer than the whole time I was in the hospital.
Janie gets $388, so like I say there's no fairness or logic to it.
"You're lucky to get anything at all."

Of course it's not fair or even logical. If you make "too
much" money, Social Security will take away your benefits. Some
of us have wanted to know how much money you can make without
losing your benefits. Dig this! Social Security WON'T TELL YOU.
In fact, when I called Washington and asked how much I could
make and maintain my benefits, they told me, "We can't tell you."

As it happens, I'm an award-winning journalist and I'm
skilled at getting answers. The Social Security people, like other
government employees, are skilled at dodging questions. My
mom was a big deal in business. Traffic Manager of 20 corporations. She called her Congressman and she couldn't find out how
much you could make on top of your benefits.

Dr. Professor George Shapiro teaches at the University, has
been a consultant to business and government. He called his
Congressman. Same brick wall.

Michael Nedenfer, a financial planner, tried. Made 15
phone calls. Same dead end.

So far I haven't been able to find out.

Sometimes it can look like sadism.

It doesn't just look like it. Sometimes it is sadism.

What is the point of keeping the "clients" away from the
information? And why do they behave like this?

Everybody has their own personal list of jerks. (Interesting that some of the jerks are the same from list to list.)

In part, it is personal. That's the reason that I think it's
real important to say their names at every possible opportunity.
It names their behavior. And it's the beginning of holding them
responsible.

When you're disabled and these Do-gooders pull their shit
there is allegedly nothing that you can do. I know. I've suffered
years of the Do-gooders' afflictions. Their game is about wanting
to be in control of other people's lives. You need some help, you
had better be willing to give up your dignity and autonomy. And
show some gratitude.

Don't it make sense that Chris Ringer and social psychiatrist Thomas Szasz are talking about "helpers" with "high control needs"? Do you see the connection of "high control needs" with "helpers" that puts you over a barrel? Different kinds of people seem attracted to the "helping professions." Some of them seem to have high control needs. With those high control needs there may or may not be empathy.

"Right!" says Chris Ringer.

The behavior and motivation of the "helpers" come out of how they grew up, just like anybody else. Chris Ringer feels that a lot of them came out of a family where something was wrong. "Dysfunctional families" is the trendy phrase. The helping pros of course say that we all come from "Dysfunctional families" rife with multiple dependencies, alcoholism, abuse, love and eating disorders. The kind of dreadful spooky obstacles that need troops of "professionals" to overcome them. Dealing with human misery is not a gig likely to go wanting for work.

Ringer says that many of them came out of these families where they had to "take care" of the adults in different ways. He says, "If you're a child and you're good at caretaking, what will happen is people will say, 'Gee, you know, you're really mature for your age. You're just a little adult. You're a wonderful person.' You know, 'You're so kind, you're so decent.' Well, as you get older, if you're good at this, it's second nature to turn pro and go into the helping professions."

I don't think the Do-gooders are consciously vicious. They think that they're nice people. And probably a lot of them are, if you were going to have lunch with them or something like that. If Chris Ringer's perspective of the Do-gooder is right, and I think it is, a lot of them are really unconscious and unaware of what they're doing. I hate to generalize, but their behavior does seem instinctive and involuntary to me. There is something about these beliefs that reminds me of cult thinking. Something very like Eric Hoffer's The True Believer. Certain "truths" accepted without question.

I want to beat this point into the ground so you don't miss it: some people working as Do-gooders learned to do things as kids for people to get their own needs met. They learned manipulation for survival. But, however they learned it, manipulation by any other name is still manipulation for the purpose of control.

"I think it was the Buddha that said — how many centuries ago? — the most deadly of all human impulses is the impulse to control." Chris Ringer targets the core. "And so the [self-appointed] saint has no choice. It's their God-given duty to stick their nose into other people's business. And, there's another piece to it which is: not only is it their God-given duty to control or change or fix other people — but the only way they can get their personal needs met is while doing that. So, in effect, the equation is: 'I need you to need me. I will take care of you whether you need it or not.'"

What attracts them, beyond a conscious awareness of wanting to do good, is this "control need" that Chris Ringer and Thomas Szasz talk about. Szasz values autonomy, the control of one's own life. Independence. Chris Ringer points to the difference between "autonomous" and "heteronomous," to be controlled from the outside.

"But, all these things I'm saying here assume and presume a value in autonomy," Ringer goes on. "There are people who believe that people are not responsible for themselves and should be controlled from the outside.

"It's hard to believe in a system that supports autonomy when you've been developed and trained in a system that operates on the basis of coercion," Chris Ringer says. "Szasz talks about this a great deal . . . that a lot of helpers are really developed and trained in a system that's intrinsically coercive. [Professional helpers are] people who were early on put into the priest function that began to disappear in our culture well over a hundred years ago.

"And that's very dangerous because they believe in a notion that somebody outside of you should control you. Whereas I'm talking about a point of view that says that you should be in charge of your own life to the degree that you can be. This does not mean that if you're having trouble we let you fall through the cracks. But we interfere with you as little as possible."

Falling through the cracks? Like, my Department of Rehabilitation Services (DRS) counselor Mary Hiemenz is a good counselor, already. One of the best, and I'm damn lucky to have here. But you can't reach her. I mean, you really can't reach her. One the one hand, she's got two hundred clients — does that give you a hint of the priority that the disabled are in the grand scheme of things?

On the other hand, I have to live and run my life on the basis of things that go through her and her office. I have had to go through an unbelievable amount of uncertainty about my future and my life — just plain worry and uptightness — because of her inability to answer phones or return calls. Every time she doesn't return a phone call, she's disconfirming me — she's giving me the message, "You don't exist."

As horseshit as Mary's communication skills are — and they suck, believe me — she's many times better than her colleagues.

Like, say I'm trying to register for a class and Mary's got to authorize "funds" for it (thank god they don't have to waste real money on me) — only she can't use the phone. So, I call and leave messages and am worried the class might close — only she never answers. Like I say, it's not her thing. So, I drive downtown and go to her office — not that easy; I'm a little gimped out — and leave a message. Only she never answers. The next day I call again and again she doesn't call back. So, I go, one more time, to her office, all the time worried that the class might close, only she's not there.

There was a point where I thought that Mary was going to get a new job, and I went into a deep, almost suicidal depression because I knew how bad anybody else might be in that job. In fact, Jane, at the bookstore, says that Mary's authorization is the only one she'll take over the phone because the other counselors "just don't follow through."

Or, like I'm teaching computer use to Janie and you should see the junk I have to go through to get paid. You have to call and call and ask for the money — for work that's already been done — and sometimes I just get the feeling that I'm supposed to be really grateful to get paid. Begging and humiliation keep the gimp in his place.

Not that I feel somebody's trying to do me in. It's their system, and nobody's supposed to be responsible for that. With their systems and stuff the Do-gooders operate in a world of powerlessness. Like, they're not making decisions, day vas only followink whorders. They are never responsible, And, nobody ever says, "The Buick stops here."

Every humiliation, every unreturned call, every unanswered Social Security question is a microcosm of systems all over the country — state, city and county and the big Federal government. Some departments are worse than others, but all the time they're patting themselves on the back for how they're helping "the clients" and how they're professionals and quack quack.

This is so you should know you're not the only one who feels that way.

July/August 1990

Why the Nation Doesn't Have Attendant Services

Mary Johnson

S ay the words "attendant services" to someone not intimately involved in disability rights issues.

You'll get a blank stare. "Attendant services?" It's the term our disability rights movement's been using for years (although until recently we called it "attendant care") to describe the kinds of services severely disabled people need to live in their own homes: assistance getting dressed, getting bathed, getting into one's wheelchair, eating. Things our society used to call "nursing care."

There's nothing medical about it. "Services delivered to us are seen as medical services rather than simply the support we need to live in our own homes," says ADAPT.

The reason these kinds of services aren't delivered in homes, but predominately in nursing homes, is "because of the influence of the American Health Care Association and other lobbying groups," they continue.

Disabled people have little chance of getting out of institutions "because the dollars flow to the institutions — not to where we want to live."

The independent living program, such a bright idea in the late '70s, talked about providing services to allow severely disabled people to live in their homes. Today, the Rehabilitation Services Administration provides a measly $26 million to fund

all the "independent living" programs in the United States —
while the bulk of its money contines to flow to state "vocational
rehabilitation" agencies to provide questionable services that
allegedly help people get jobs — yet the number of unemployed,
working-age disabled people has remained steady at 66 percent
for years. "Vocational rehabilitation" offices make no dent in
that figure.

"Independent living programs," while full of much promise, have often been unable to follow through on the promise to
help disabled people live in their communities because there
was no money available for the programs disabled people needed.
The primary thing severely disabled people need is attendant
services.

The United States has no national policy for a non-medical,
"user-driven" community-based attendant services program
that will allow disabled people to live in their own homes, says
ADAPT.

The need for assistance in one's home, to help one get out
of bed, get washed, get dressed, is basic. When people like Ed
Roberts started the first independent living center in Berkeley
in the late 1970s, they knew having an attendant was basic.

Those pioneers were readier than many of us proved to be
to cobble together pots of personal benefits and find somebody
to work for them. Even then it was very difficult. And California,
where independent living was born, has more social programs,
more benefits, than any state. Yet even there, attendant services
are today an iffy thing.

Disabled California activists eventually got the state to
fund an In Home Support Services program that's considered the
best in the nation. But every year it goes on the chopping block
— and no other state has yet been able to set up an attendant
program even to match its fragile benefits? Why not?

A lot of reasons are given, but it boils down to this: the
state won't take its Medicaid money away from the nursing
homes, who, through their state Health Care Associations,
have a stranglehold on Medicaid. Even Medicaid rules — Title
XIX of the Social Security Act — require states to offer nursing
homes to people on Medicaid. It does not require states to offer
in-home, consumer-controlled attendant services. Why not?
Because a change in law like that would take money from
nursing homes. So the American Health Care Association fights

any move in this direction swiftly and silently.

One of the biggest weapons AHCA uses is "quality of care," a lot of bunk about the need for "professional" "nursing" care for people who need nothing more than someone to help them get in and out of bed, wash their body and use the bathroom. There's not a lot of medical skill needed for that, but since AHCA has been holding court, and the disability movement's been mostly polite and silent about it, the public for the most part — and the media — has never questioned it.

When cost-cutting moves to reduce institutional stays were put into effect several years ago over the howls of the medical establishment, the nursing home industry was quick to appropriate the "home health care" field, too — making sure the term used was "home *health* care." The disability rights movement missed its opportunity at that time to wrest a powerhold away from the nursing home lobby. Now nursing home operators are often the same folks who run the community's "home health care" agency.

Moves to allow Medicare and Medicaid money to be spent on "home health care" — again as a cost-saving step — were pushed by this same nursing home lobby. If any noises were heard at all about "consumer-controlled" attendant services (and if Congress heard of it, few members remember the issue clearly), they were drowned out with the "quality of care" argument. The World Institute on Disability's talked for several years about getting legislation on a national attendant program introduced, but no Congressperson's done it yet.

States that several years ago had begun to listen to disabled people and offer programs, under Medicaid waivers, that allowed disabled people to hire their own attendants, have quietly changed the rules: many programs that started out as "consumer-controlled" have had regulations imposed in the last few years that required the money go to a "home health care" agency — at about three times the cost, usually. Why did this happen? The state's Health Care Association was usually to be found somewhere behind the scenes.

None of this has anything to do with "quality of care." It has everything to do with money. Nursing home operators, home health care agencies, want it: they don't want to let it go. It's as simple as that.

Unfortunately, the independent living programs in this

country have never had the inclination or foresight to attack the root of the biggest problem their clients face: finding reliable attendant services. They've tried to help set up state programs; some work with home health care agencies. Many see nothing wrong with home health care agencies.

The independent living dream was this: that a disabled person, once introduced to the independent living philosophy, would attain the skills to find, hire and be employer to one or more people who would work for her in her home.

The reality was never that simple. Besides the problem of even finding someone who'd work for the abysmally low wages most disabled people, even with state financial help, could pay, many disabled people felt they didn't have the skills to manage their own attendants. The attendants left — or worse, abused them and took their money.

Disabled people who'd lived their lives in institutions or under their parents' protective wings were afraid to set out on their own to be an employer. A lot of us weren't good at it, weren't ready to practice to become good. A lot of us, it turned out, wanted "home health agencies" to hire people for us — or at least preferred that alternative to the one we were being offered: responsibility and the possibility of being left low and wet when our attendant failed to show.

We put up with the restrictions the agencies imposed because we didn't have any choice. And the restrictions are degrading: wait until the agency decides you should get up; which day you should wash your hair. Get an attendant (the agency calls them "aides," or, not infrequently, "nurse's aides" when there's absolutely no "nursing" going on) for two hours in the morning, two again in the evening. Go to bed at 6 p. m., because that's when the agency says to; that's when they'll send the aide. What kind of a life is that?

A lot of disabled people know exactly what kind of a life it is: it's the life we have to live if we don't want to go into a nursing home, they say.

Independent living, the promise that it was, with its measly funding, was never able to make much more than a dent in the system this country has set up for providing "services" to disabled people.

Now ADAPT comes along and says it wants radical change. It wants to "dismantle" the nursing home system itself. It wants to take the nursing home's pot of money.

ADAPT takes a radical stance because it believes that's how change occurs. It's never in the past been afraid to name the Enemy. Now it's named the American Health Care Association and the Health Care Financing Administration, the arm of Social Security that funds nursing homes.

Once again, no doubt, some in our movement will bristle at ADAPT's all-or-nothing approach. People will say ADAPT should "work within the system" to bring change. But the history of our movement shows that working within the system usually gets us the crumbs.

ADAPT wants more than the crumbs. "We are being treated like commodities by a corporate nursing home industry more concerned about profit than need," reads their literature. "The medical community has too much influence over how our services are delivered."

ADAPT wants money taken from the nursing homes. And, as in the past, ADAPT intends to fight the nursing home industry till it gets what it wants.

January/February 1991

Auschwitz on Sesame Street

Lucy Gwin

*T*he last this insurance company heard, their policyholder was in a coma. Once he was discharged from the hospital to a rehabilitation facility, the bills began to pour in. He was receiving Recreational Therapy, billed at $110 per hour, five hours a day seven days a week — this in addition to the $1,100 day rate being charged for his care.

That's where an MD I know — let's call her Dr. Donna — came in. This insurance company hired her to fly in and take a look.

Donna, disabled herself, noted Telltale Sign #1 as soon as she arrived on the rehab center's grounds: a mob of clients sitting at picnic tables outside the center's back door. Some crouched together in groups, smoking cigarettes, talking among themselves about how their lives used to be, before.

Was this the $110 per hour recreational therapy? Donna wondered.

She was met by a tour guide who, Donna says, "was a woman of exceptional stupidity. Plus she had no idea who I was." Who Donna was: the only MD who raised early warnings about rehab to the media, to congressional subcommittees, to teaching hospitals and state departments of health. Dr. Donna herself had run a hospital's in-patient rehab. She'd first heard disturbing rumors, and later got the word from families themselves about the horrors going on in the name of rehabilitation.

This center's tour guide rushed Dr. Donna past the crowded picnic tables and into the facility. First stop was the gym. Telltale Sign #2 was all too obvious: the gym was gleaming but empty. Dr. Donna wondered aloud if its emptiness was due to the fact that, this being a major holiday, many of the clients were at home with their families.

"Oh, no," the tour guide told her, "we don't let them go home on holiday. That would cost the company money."

At that point Dr. Donna noted Telltale Sign #3: equipment in this gym was perfect. Not a scratch on the shaft of the rowing machine, not a chip in the paint of a dumbbell, not a sign to betray the gym's use. "This must be new equipment," Donna commented. "Oh, no," the tour guide answered, "it's the same equipment we've been using since we took over the center from New Medico a year and a half ago."

Someone with a keen or cynical eye for these things might conclude that the gym sees use only as a tour stop.

Then the tour guide was paged away to take a telephone call. Dr. Donna scooted back outside to talk with the folks at the picnic tables. She approached a woman who uses a wheelchair to ask what's the story here. This woman's story: she'd had her first exacerbation after being diagnosed with multiple sclerosis. The hospital released her not to her home but to this rehab center. She had been there for a year and a half. "It's like being in a prison," the woman told Donna.

Why didn't the woman just go home? Her home was in another state, more than a thousand miles away. "And the therapists here tell my family I have MS dementia. I don't think I'll ever get home." According to Dr. Donna, this woman had about as much MS dementia as you do.

Those were Telltale Signs #4 and #5: people with disabilities being sent far from home for rehabilitation and then being at the mercy of therapists' communiqués to their families. "He has behavior problems. You couldn't manage him by yourselves." "She requires a highly structured setting." "He perseverates."

"Perseveration" is a widely-used rehab term for perseverance. As when an a G.I. prisoner of war perseveres in striving to escape. In rehab land, this is not a healthy sign of recovery, it's a symptom.

A few years back I lectured an amphitheater full of professionals on the subject of patients' rights in rehab. Follow-

ing the lecture, a rehabilitation professional took me aside to set
me straight. She told me about a client who had been at her
facility for several years of rehabilitation. "At first she was
constantly perseverating about going home. But now when she
says it she hits! her! head! on the sink! You can't tell me we should
let that woman go home."

Rehab centers are not licensed as hospitals, are not for the
most part run by MD's, do not for the most part have MD's on staff,
are not held to standards set by state or federal boards, are not
required to furnish you with a statement of your right to go home.

Rehab centers, with very rare exceptions, are licensed as
nursing homes. They are surveyed by state departments of health
according to nursing home standards.

As in nursing facilities, you will not be going home. It is
not in anyone's interest but your own to go home. You are a second
class citizen now. Your interests are unimportant to the outcome
of this business transaction. Should you attempt to check out of
one of these roach motels, you will be told that your precipitous
discharge will put a stop to further third-party funding for your
rehabilitation. That may be true.

Insurance companies, who have long been aware of negli-
gence, abuse, and fraud in rehabilitation centers, would still
rather send off one check per month to a phony rehabilitation
center than sort through the mangy pile of bills for your out-
patient P.T., cab receipts for your trips to those sessions,
contractor's bills for ramps and remodeling to widen your
bathroom door, receipts for shower chairs or guide dog training
or alphabet boards — the messy everyday etceteras of genuine
rehabilitation.

The rehab center's interest is in your continued rehabilitation and its continued funding. Your personal injury lawyer's
interest is in your continued rehabilitation. (Personal injury
rule of thumb: the court will award 2-1/2 times the amount spent
on rehabilitation. Your attorney thus wins a larger prize in his
40% of your settlement.) Your own family's interest is to get you
back fully rehabilitated — which is to say cured, intact, and just
like your old self: nondisabled.

Back in the '70s, when Medicaid and then private insurance put caps on hospital stays (e.g., two days for an appendec-
tomy), no one thought to put caps on rehab. As an MD who works

as a congressional aide told me, "Traditionally, any bill with the word 'rehabilitation' in it gets a nod from Congress. Congress believes in rehabilitation. If you're fighting that, you're swimming upstream."

With the capping of reimbursements for hospital stays, the smart money moved into the rehabilitation business. Nursing home operators smelled money and changed their signs from "Willowcreek Nursing Home" to "Willowcreek Rehabilitation." They rolled out oriental rugs in the anterooms, put silver tea sets on display in the dining rooms and draped the commons room in designer fabrics. They invented scientific-sounding terms such as "cognitive therapy," "infant coma stimulation," "community re-entry" and listed these therapies on their newly-minted billing forms.

These changes to nursing home façades made the real change, the billings change, possible: nursing home per diem rates rose overnight from $100 per bed to $900 for rehabilitation beds. Today those fees max out at about $1,800 per day for private insurance beds, $1,100 per day for Medicaid beds.

"Patients will be released from the hospitals quicker and sicker," says Abe Gosman, chairman of Mediplex, a chain of 41 nursing homes with more than 4,000 beds. Gosman, owner of "Octopussy," the world's fastest yacht, recently sold Mediplex to Sun Healthcare Group Systems for $320 million. The chairman of Sun Healthcare, Andrew L. Turner, told *The New York Times* that "In ten years we will be in the hospital business. But it will be called something different than that."

Those words are your cue to get cold chills.

A schoolteacher in her 50s who had founded a Mensa chapter in her home town was hit by a car while crossing a street. The accident left her comatose, then quadriplegic. She was released from the hospital to an out-of-state rehabilitation center with a reputation for excellence. (Its director is chairman of the Ethics Committee of the National Head Injury Foundation.) For two and a half years, a visitor tells me, she was "marooned next to a nurses station, strapped upright in a wheelchair, taken back to her room if she said she wanted anything."

The rehabilitation center depleted her insurance funding, her personal injury settlement, and proceeds from the sale of her house given over by the family that wanted her back as good as new. When all funding sources were exhausted, she was discharged. To a nursing home.

"It's much better here," she tells me. "At least they read to me sometimes."

None of the funding supplied to the rehabilitation center was spent to purchase a ramp for the woman's home, a page-turning device, or even a power wheelchair. The center's administrators knew what her family did not: that she was never going home.

A 26-year-old Massachusetts man who survived a broken back is now in his tenth year of rehabilitation by The Greenery Rehabilitation Group. (The Greenery Group was recently purchased by Horizon Healthcare Corporation for $350 million, giving Horizon just under 9,000 beds.) When I asked him why he didn't just up and leave, this man responded "They won't let me." After further conversation about his human and constitutional rights, he reverted to his convoluted complaints about certain therapists, fellow clients and aides. Academics have a name for his malady: socialization to institutional life. In lay terms, his world has shrunk.

A young girl lay in a coma at a rehabilitation facility for some months. (A good question at this point might be, How do you rehabilitate someone who's in a coma?) Her mother, an RN back in their home state, saved up and flew out to see her. Mother whisked past the Sesame Street characters painted on the walls of Pediatric Rehab Reception. As usual, she found her daughter feverish and wan in twisted grey sheets and a soiled nightgown. As she undertook the daughter's personal care, she saw to her horror that her daughter's vagina was full of excrement. The girl had been raped so brutally that her perineum was torn.

A postman who survived a broken back — he'd been admitted for rehabilitation two years before — showed an investigative reporter the fuzzy green mold growing on the inside of a plastic G-tube which had been implanted in his stomach so that he could receive nourishment while in coma. He was chowing down on a pizza when he hauled up his shirt to show off this tube. The reporter wanted to know why it was still stuck in his stomach. "They just haven't gotten around to taking it out," the postman said.

What the postman probably didn't realize was that the facility was able to bill $200 more per day to the third-party payer because of that G-tube.

A woman in her 30s who is daughter of the founders of the National Head Injury Foundation, was, when last heard from, undergoing her seventeenth year of rehabilitation in a Learning Services Corporation facility in North Carolina.

A note from real life: You prepare bread dough and pop it in the oven. At some point the bread is done and you pull it out of the oven to cool. Your family swoons over its fragrant, golden perfection. Unlike homemade bread, the recipient of rehabilitation is never done.

A mother found her daughter, who was being rehabilitated after an episode of depression, lying in her bed enduring repeated grand mal seizures. This seizure state is known as *status epilepticus* and causes serious brain damage. The mother called the charge nurse who called the rehabilitation company's headquarters which called a doctor whose message service couldn't reach him. *Status epilepticus* went on for a day and a half until a second MD arrived to order a dose of Dilantin. The severity of the seizures did not noticeably decrease. The doctor did not reappear to up the dosage. Several days later, with the frantic mother still beside her bed, the daughter died.

She had not been admitted to a hospital. The Medicaid-paid day rate would have been lost to the rehabilitation center and paid to the hospital instead. That's not good business.

A mother was told that the facility had been required to move her 30-year-old son, a brain injury survivor, to the Behavior Unit because of a recurrent problem with what the therapist called "acting out." The mother, a person not easily put off by professionalese, arrived at the center next morning. "It was one of my pop inspections. And there was quite a to-do," she told me, "about whether they could risk my safety by allowing me to go on the Unit. They wanted to bring Eric down to me in the room where they've got all those oriental rugs and fancy cabinets. But they didn't even want to do that because I'd be 'interrupting his therapy.'" This tough mother pushed past the administrators and caught an elevator to the Behavior Unit on her own.

She calls the place where she found her son "a vertical coffin." It was one of several plywood boxes bolted to the wall. Inside the box her son was seated on a wooden shelf, held there by four-point restraints. His schedule, posted on the outside of the box, called for him to spend twelve hours a day in that box.

Rows of boys in boxes — what will they think of next?

If the people of whom I speak seem like born victims, easy to push around, you must remember that in rehabilitation the name of the game is Keep Away. Every kid has played this game and dreaded the moment when she must be It. One friend tosses the ball over your head to another friend who tosses it back to the first. The object of the game is to keep the ball away from you.

As I noticed during my own rehabilitation at New Medico's Community Re-Entry Systems of Cortland, NY, none of the clients were consulted or even informed about the cost of our rehabilitation and certainly not about the number of hours we were putatively receiving for putative therapies. New Medico sailed the bills over our heads to the insurance company. The insurance company sailed its checks back to New Medico. Far overhead, therapists called my family to report that I was a Behavior Problem. My faraway family called the therapists for updates on my progress under the therapists' care.

I was It. For one long week I knocked on administrators doors, only to be told that "whoever signed you in has to sign you out." And who had signed me in? "I don't know. Ask Dr. Brown." "Ask Dr. Green." "Ask Dr. Blue." I gave up on signing myself out officially and awaited a chance to escape. That was a long shot. I had not a dime in my pocket. I was 150 miles from home in a town where no one knew me. Then my old friend Frank came to see me.

During the half hour it took to pack up my bags and get out, the aide on duty called the Boston office for instructions on how to stop me — seeing as Frank was bigger and meaner-looking than New Medico's "behavioral health technician." The Boston office called back and asked to speak with Frank. They told him he'd have to sign a form taking responsibility for me and for all of my actions for the rest of my life. Where many an escape engineer might back off, Franco signed on the line.

The Boston office called again to tell him I was a danger to myself and others. Where many a friend would have thought twice, Frank said, "I've known her for 16 years and she's no more dangerous than she's ever been."

The Boston office called once more to tell him that if he took me off the premises, he would be arrested and hauled to jail. Where other friends would have thrown in the towel, Frank threw me into his truck and we got away quick.

If Frank had not persevered, I would still be locked up, banging my head, or some therapist's, on the sink.

A page from the New Medico employee manual made it into the U.S. Congressional Record. It says: "The Program Case Manager serves a vital role to maintain facility census and maximize client length of stay. Facility census and client rates/length of stay directly affect facility/corporate revenues."

Business is business. As many a therapist and aide told me during my three weeks at New Medico, "There's no crime in making a profit."

Dr. Donna's tour continued through the Computer Room, the Counseling Room, the Neuropsychological Testing Room. All were well-appointed, well-equipped, and empty of clients.

The tour concluded when the tour guide led Dr. Donna to a large, dimly-lit room where the client she'd come to see about was receiving therapy.

Around the room's perimeter clients were strapped up-right in wheelchairs or strapped prone on gurneys. All of them, according to Dr. Donna, were "in coma or in vegetative state. Whatever you want to call it, they were out like a light." There was no therapist in the room, no orderly, no aide. Over in one corner, however, a TV-VCR played tapes of Sesame Street.

"And this!" the tour guide announced, "Is Recreational Therapy! And right here is the client you came to see! Richard, say hello to Dr. Donna. Come on Richard, be nice and say hello . . ."

July/August 1994

LIFE AND DEATH

Unanswered Questions

Mary Johnson

*T*his is a story in which the subject refuses to be interviewed. Or maybe is kept from being interviewed. It's hard to tell.

It's a story about a group of people — a father, an attorney or two, a reporter, and some disabled people with some opinions. It's a story about how difficult it is going to be to break through to any understanding of why more and more severely disabled people are petitioning the courts for the right to die.

The story begins with a May 23 [1990] report in the *Las Vegas Sun* by Jeff German. A 31-year-old man, Kenneth Bergstedt, was petitioning the Las Vegas courts for permission to "end his 'painful' existence."

Bergstedt, the article said, "was a 31-year-old quadriplegic hooked to a respirator for more than 20 years" for whom "life is no longer worth living."

Bergstedt's attempt to get a court to condone his effort at assisted suicide was depressingly familiar.

Bergstedt was "mentally alert and can speak," German wrote. He "wants to be given a sedative, have his life-support system turned off, and be allowed to die in peace." According to a court affidavit, German reported, Bergstedt "has no happy or encouraging expectations to look for from life, receives no enjoyment from life, lives with constant fears and apprehensions and is tired of suffering."

The next day's story quoted Las Vegas psychiatrist Jack A. Jurasky, who German wrote had been "a psychiatrist for 34 years." Jurasky told German things like "he's not a vegetable" and "he's alert and intelligent."

The issue had to do with "quality of life," as Jurasky put it. "The quality of life for this man is very poor, moderated only by momentary distraction, *but forever profaned by a future which offers no relief.*" German says Jurasky told the court in an affidavit — I added the italics.

Jurasky's affidavit went on. He had found Ken Bergstedt competent. "Intelligence is estimated as superior. Awareness and insight into his situation appears realistic and judgment is estimated as good and uninfluenced by impulse or emotion."

Even in these cases, which are becoming regrettably familiar, such prejudice — believing that suicidal judgment on the part of a quadriplegic is not influenced by emotion but is, rather, completely rational — is startling.

Disability psychologist Carol Gill believes such prejudice, specifically on the part of the counseling professions, fuels such cases which are springing up with more and more frequency.

She writes, "In the vast majority of cases, when a severely disabled person persists in wanting to die, there is an identifiable problem in the support system. All too often, they are surrounded by people who accept their desire to die as understandable. All too rarely is that desire adequately examined."

She deplores what she calls an "absolute absence" of examination in these cases by professionals with adequate background in disability. "They don't even use rehabilitation psychologists!" she told us; it's as though the courts have no understanding that there could even be such a thing as prejudice at work, she says. "And there are far too few of us working in the clinical field," she says, referring to psychologists and psychiatrists who are themselves from the disability culture.

By June 9, Las Vegas district Judge Donald Mosley would rule, much as a Georgia court ruled last year in the case of Larry McAfee, that Kenneth Bergstedt had the right to be given a sedative and taken off his respirator. By some feat of tortuous reasoning, he concluded that Bergstedt's death in this manner would not be suicide; Bergstedt would merely be regulating his own medical care. Therefore, anyone who helped him die would not be breaking any law.

And like Georgia Judge Edward H. Johnson had done, Mosley too ordered the case appealed to the state Supreme Court so that it would set a precedent.

Sources close to the case have indicated that Bergstedt's attorney, Jack Cherry, would very much like to see a precedent set and suggest he took the case much for that reason. Bergstedt's father had contacted several attorneys before he found Cherry to take the case. Cherry said, in an interview with German, that Bergstedt's ventilator "only prolongs an agonizing existence."

The pattern was emerging again: The man who wanted to end his life; the family who wanted to help him — in this case his father — the attorney who seemed all too eager to help, the psychiatrist who seemed to have no questions as to the psychological appropriateness of a disabled person's desire to die (when, I suspected, they would have many questions about that appropriateness were the person a nondisabled, working, white middle-class male). I also noted the zealousness of *Las Vegas Sun* reporter Jeff German.

By the time German wrote his June 9 story on Mosley's decision, he had already provided *Sun* readers with three other stories, in which he told readers that Jurasky was "a respected Las Vegas psychiatrist." He told readers — and this apparently before he'd ever seen Bergstedt ("I haven't had the privilege of meeting the Bergstedts," he wrote in that same column) — that "throughout his day, Bergstedt lies on a gurney, breaking the monotony by reading, watching television and writing poetry on a computer by blowing into a special device."

His articles did not examine how Bergstedt had gotten the computer, nor why; why Bergstedt spent his day watching television; or, in fact, what life for a person with Bergstedt's disability could potentially be, were he not living in isolation with an elderly father cut off from any contact with a disability community. German had not asked questions about Bergstedt and any disability community.

Instead, he wrote that "love was working overtime at the Bergstedt home"; that "Kenneth's wish to die, and Robert's willingness to help him fulfill that wish, probably are the greatest gifts of love either man could give the other."

"They sound at peace with each other," he wrote. To me,

they sound isolated, cut off from any contact with a disability community and involved in an unhealthy depression that was feeding on itself — and I felt I was at least as qualified as German in making that assessment. German had talked to an attorney and a psychiatrist; I had, over the years, talked to hundreds of disabled people — and read their writings, heard their thinking, sat in meetings with them as they discussed emotions, fear and, at times, suicide. I'd heard them talk about the effects of oppression, isolation and negative self image. I had heard them talk about the saving grace of a disability community.

Nowhere in any of German's four stories had any questions been raised as to why institutionalization would be inevitable with the elder Bergstedt's demise; nor any question about the fact that Kenneth Bergstedt had never appeared in court but had in all instances been spoken for by his father.

Neither Bergstedt nor his father would talk to anyone but their attorney, I learned. Bergstedt hadn't even appeared at his own court hearing — his 65-year-old "adopted" father (German's words) had appeared in his stead, toting a five-page affidavit that the court accepted as being the son's words — a statement that said he "had no encouraging expectations to look forward to from life, receives no enjoyment from life, lives with constant fears and apprehensions and is tired of suffering."

Mosley had in fact given the go-ahead on Bergstedt's suicide without ever even meeting the man.

I couldn't help wondering how many of those words had been inspired by his isolated existence with a father who was quick to tell everyone that he had lost a leg in an industrial accident himself, has high blood pressure "and other physical ailments."

What did Bergstedt really want, I wondered. How much of this was orchestrated by his father? I tried to find out.

I called attorney Jack Cherry. "He won't talk to you," Cherry snapped at me. They'll only talk to Jeff German, he said. Cherry repeated that Bergstedt was living an "agonizing existence" and "was not stable."

I called German. He had just gotten an "exclusive" interview, he said.

No, he said peevishly, in answer to my question, he had not asked if Kenneth had considered any options other than a nursing home. No, he hadn't discussed whether Kenneth had been involved with disabled people. He was covering the legal issues of the case, he pointed out. He sounded to me like a man in a hurry.

German's exclusive interview ran July 29, by which time Bergstedt's existence had transmogrified to "hellish." The interview with Bergstedt and his "ailing father" turned up no new facts other than German's observation that Kenneth's body "periodically went into convulsions and he had trouble breathing and talking because phlegm was building up in his throat as the result of being hooked to a breathing device."

I found that odd. In subsequent interviews with over a dozen people who used respirators (none of them used the term "hooked to"), as well as with rehabilitation physicians, none described life on a respirator as being as horrific as this. I had asked one man specifically about phlegm build-up. "Sure," he had said, nonchalantly. "It happens sometimes. You clear your throat some and that takes care of it; if you have a cold you might need to have your attendant suction you out every now and then, but it's no big deal."

But the man I talked to had an attendant. Bergstedt had only his "ailing father."

Nowhere in this interview was there any discussion of the serious need for Bergstedt to have someone other than his father help him. That he could obtain no competent assistance was evidently accepted fact — and the solution suicide.

I called Paul Longmore. Longmore, visiting assistant professor of history at Stanford University, uses a respirator. In recent years, he's been increasingly vocal in opposing the court-sanctioned assisted suicide cases he sees cropping up with what he calls "alarming frequency" today.

When Larry McAfee made news with his suicide plea, Longmore went head-to-head with McAfee's attorney on *Nightline*.

"People don't choose suicide rationally," says Longmore. "They choose it when they have absolutely no hope.

"Why do ventilator-using quads feel they have no hope?" he presses. "I would contend it is not fundamentally because of their disability; it's because of their social situation. If we have learned anything in our society we should have learned by now that there is nothing inevitable about the social isolation and the deprivation of self determination of even the most severely disabled people."

Even with Kenneth Bergstedt evidently present at German's exclusive interview, it was the elder Bergstedt, it seemed, who told the reporter Kenneth's wishes. "'I'm 65 years old, and he [Ken] doesn't know whether I'm going to fall asleep and have a heart attack or stroke and not wake up,' Robert Bergstedt said. 'He's afraid that he'll be all by himself on the machine and drown. It'll take him four to six hours to die. It will be a painful process.'" Still no explanation from German as to why it was Bergstedt's father, rather than Bergstedt, saying this — nor any discussion of what Bergstedt might need other than suicide.

"'It's very tiring,'" Robert Bergstedt continued to tell German (who seemed to report it without question). "'We have been so dependent on so many different people for years. Let's face it. He's been in jail for 21 years and I've been his keeper.'"

How true that was, I thought — though not, surely, in the way Bergstedt or German meant it.

Accompanying the interview was a German column: it seemed so unfair, he wrote, that the state Supreme Court was dawdling with its decision; he urged the judges to "show a human side" and hurry up with the decision that Kenneth could kill himself and no one be blamed.

German reported that the Bergstedts "told me they can no longer wait for the Supreme Court to act."

When I talked to Robert Bergstedt a week later, they were still waiting — for the Court to act, the elder Bergstedt told me.

Robert Bergstedt answered the phone when I called the Bergstedt residence. His was a quiet voice, but, as it turned out, a voice determined that I would not speak to Ken. Not angry, but protective. I had sort of suspected I would find as much.

"That would be very difficult, really," Robert Bergstedt replied when I asked if I could speak to his son. His voice was low, but insistent. It was a sentence meant to brook no interference. Nonetheless, I persisted. Why would it be difficult to talk with him, I wanted to know. He was in the other room, "on a respirator," he explained, as though that should explain everything.

But I know plenty of people on respirators who didn't let that stop them from talking on the phone. So I pressed the issue, suspecting that at any minute Robert Bergstedt might hang up the phone. They would talk to no reporters, after all, I'd been told, except German. But the elder Bergstedt didn't hang up on me — he simply reiterated that Ken wouldn't come to the phone. "I do most of the talking," said his father. "I've done most of that. He insists that's the way he wants it."

I suspected that was true. But I couldn't help thinking of the hundreds of disabled people I'd known over the years who, almost always in anger, told about parents, spouses, children speaking for them, telling them to be quiet, that they'd handle it for them. I know that more than a few of these disabled people had said that for a long time they'd felt they shouldn't speak but let someone else do it for them. That they were embarrassed.

I asked if Ken used an iron lung; thinking the term might be the one the man used; thinking perhaps the phone didn't reach into the room. "Oh, no, he's on a portable respirator," Bergstedt was quick to correct me.

"Those who haven't met Kenneth might find it difficult to imagine why he wants to give up on life," German intoned in his July 29 commentary. "Those who have met him have no trouble understanding."

Longmore snorts at this thought.

"Yeah. Those who have met him — who don't know anything about disabled people — have no trouble understanding him," he sneers.

"Carol [Gill] got the same thing from the guy that did David Rivlin in. He and Gill were on a radio show. He said, 'Dr. Gill has never met David Rivlin. I have.'

"He met him a couple of times — and then he killed him. They think that makes them experts?"

The same thing happened with Larry McAfee, said Longmore.

"McAfee's lawyer said that [Atlanta area disability activist] Mark Johnson and I and 'other people like us'" — meaning disabled people — "don't know Larry McAfee since we've never met.

"The lawyer had never met a disabled person in his life — he was an aviation lawyer, for God's sake! — who, after a few conversations with Larry McAfee, understood him better than we disabled people did!

"So what happens to him over the next couple of months?" Longmore asks rhetorically. "He gets the right to die.

"Then some people that know about disability get to him; they start talking to him about some of the possibilities, and the next thing you know Larry McAfee changes his mind."

As Longmore says this, I recall a phrase dropped innocuously into German's exclusive. Even though the lower court had ruled, Bergstedt wasn't in any hurry to end his life, German reported. Might it be, I wondered, that Bergstedt would like to have an option to allow him to continue living? German certainly wasn't exploring it.

I wanted to talk to some other people who'd used respirators to see if life on a respirator was the hell the court documents had made it out to be. Of course I'd talked to sex educator and Los Angeles disability activist Barbara Faye Waxman a number of times in the past — and she'd never indicated life had been hell for her; nor had Ed Roberts, head of the World Institute on Disability. They were both "on respirators."

"The whole thing is outrageous," said Roberts, who knew about the case. "I am getting angrier and angrier about these cases. They feed on each other. The attorneys, the courts, the judges, they don't know anything. They see somebody like Bergstedt, they say, 'of course he wants to die.'

"What's happening is we're killing disabled people in this country and then act like we're doing them a favor. It's outrageous!"

I thought back to German's columns and thought that Roberts had expressed my thoughts better than I had.

"I've been on a respirator for 26 years," the MacArthur "genius" fellowship award winner continued, "and I watch these people's cases — they're just as dependent on a respirator as I am; the major difference is they know they're going to be forced to live in a nursing home — or they're already there — and I'm leading a quality life.

"That's the only difference. It's not the respirator. It's the money."

Not once did "money" appear in any of German's writings on the case.

"We're supposed to be able to get a nurse for 40 hours a week," Robert Bergstedt told me. The nurse, he said, was to be paid for by Medicare. "But we can't ever seem to get anybody for 40 hours."

Despite what Roberts said, and what I wanted to believe, I knew I shouldn't compare people. I knew that in the final analysis everyone's decision is his own. I knew I could not —

should not — judge from remarks made by one gimp about his life that another gimp's life would be equally valid to him.

Linda Knipp agreed with that. Also a respirator user, Knipp is chair of the Personal Assistance Committee of the California Association of the Physically Handicapped and serves as chair of Los Angeles County's In Home Supportive Service's advisory committee.

To her, it's an issue of privacy. "I'm probably a renegade in the disability community because I do believe it's a matter of individual choice; that if somebody chooses to turn off their respirator they should be allowed to do that."

But, she added, they should be given adequate psychological and social care before such a decision was made. She understood Longmore's argument that more services for living independently should be allocated so people on ventilators were not "needlessly incarcerated," she said.

"If those resources were available, it's less likely that disabled people would choose suicide," she agreed. "But the reality is that those resources are not available right now.

"Even California, one of the best states in the nation" for providing disabled people with money for hiring attendant care services, she continued, provided only enough to pay an attendant minimum wages for little more than eight hours a day.

"It's painful, it's wrong that people have to make such choices," she went on, referring to people like herself who are dependent on respirators. "It's wrong that social and medical services are set up so that the state will pay up to $2000 a day for someone in a hospital but, if you try to live at home," you're only eligible for a fraction of that amount.

"That's the basic problem," she reiterated. "The state pays for care in an institution -- if you can find one. It doesn't pay for adequate care on the outside."

What made her angry, she said, was the lack of exposure of the financial issues in news accounts of people like Bergstedt. "Most people don't have any idea of the financial constraints placed on people who use ventilators," she said. "They're so amazed that we're even alive that they don't even bother to look at how we manage to stay alive financially."

Even though every disabled person I talked to believed one could live a productive life even if one were using a respirator, perhaps their disabilities weren't the same as Ken's. So I talked to Dr. Stephen Wills, MD at the National Rehabilitation Hospital in Washington, DC, who knew specifically about medical conditions of people who've had injuries to the cervical vertebrae, C-1 and C-2 — like Ken Bergstedt. I asked him a lot of questions. I asked him about the blood pressure specifically — because Ken's father said he couldn't sit up because of blood pressure problems. What about that, I asked Wills. Could people like that sit up? Yes, he said; they would need to be worked with to learn how to do it, but they could.

I asked about a host of other medical problems that I'd been told could occur; Wills answered each question. In the final analysis, he said, there was no medical reason someone with the condition I'd described couldn't live on their own, go about in the community — provided it was accessible — or even hold a job.

So I knew it was probable that people who wanted to end their lives weren't having problems so much with their actual disabilities — though I know they often represented their problems that way, because that was how they appeared even to them — but with other things. Lack of resources. No money — not to purchase the kind of therapy Dr. Willis was talking about, not to hire attendant services. Depression was bound to result.

I knew from German's articles that the elder Bergstedt had been talking about dying a lot — to the attorney, to the court, to German. If Ken lived alone with his dad — as the papers, over and over, stressed — if he was kept isolated with an elderly man focused on his own death, wouldn't it stand to reason that a son would also begin thinking of death.? If a son were told his only option was a nursing home; if a son had been cared for for five years only by a father who described himself as "ailing," wouldn't it stand to reason that a son's thoughts would be bent, as it were, toward ending it? Toward seeing no options?

How different might it be if Ken knew of options, or wanted them! To my knowledge, Ken had no contact with other disabled people, nor wanted any. I decided to call back again — knowing I might be hung up on.

Once again I asked to speak to Ken. Robert Bergstedt knew who I was — I was the woman who put out a newsletter for handicapped people. Maybe he didn't consider me a reporter; anyhow, he continued to talk to me.

But he did not let Ken on the line. He was resting, I was told.

When I pressed it, Bergstedt got exasperated. "He doesn't like the way he sounds, OK?"

I wondered if Ken could sound any worse than the others I'd talked to who used respirators, whose talking was puffed and labored, punctuated with pauses and the slow, steady hiss of breathing apparatus in the background. What difference should that make? Between those I'd talked to, leaders in the disability rights movement, and Ken, though, there stretched an entire world.

Did Ken ever go out? I asked

"Well, he can't," Bergstedt said slowly. "There ain't nothin' he . . . he . . . just can't do anything when he goes out," Bergstedt offered by way of explanation. "See, we used to travel all over, and . . ." Here Bergstedt paused, as if remembering. He seemed by voice and phrasing to be a man resigned to sadness: "Ken wasn't always this weak. He's gone downhill in the last two, three years, Very much so."

Was it all physical? Or was it partly emotional? When I asked, though, all I got was another recitation of Ken's physical condition.

"We used to go out," Bergstedt said. And Ken had friends, he said. But it seemed an iffy thing. "They come over and he's not feeling good and they feel guilty and then they don't show up anymore."

Bergstedt forgave them their behavior, though. "He's in pain quite a bit of the time, see?" When I asked what the pain was caused by, I was told, "Oh, everything."

I wondered if any disabled people had called him since news of his interest in dying had surfaced. Had he been in contact with any disabled people, or groups, I asked? "No." The elder Bergstedt was emphatic. "He doesn't want to be."

I tried to learn about what kind of options they'd considered. But Robert was taciturn with me. They'd had a "nurse," he said; from what I was able to learn was a home health agency. But they'd never been able to get her for the 40 hours they were supposed to, he said; he never did really explain why.

The picture being painted as I talked to the elder Bergstedt was, unfortunately, as depressing as I'd imagined it.

Vernon Cox, an advocate specialist at the Marin (CA) County independent living center, had told me, "One of the problems you ought to look at is, are there any underlying causes for him feeling like he can't deal with life.

"In that Bouvia case [Elizabeth Bouvia, who in the early 1980's petitioned a California court for assistance in committing suicide] they said, 'Oh, that poor lady, she's upset because she's handicapped.'

"The lady'd already lost her husband, lost her job, had her kids taken away from her — of course she's upset! But all they could say was 'Of course, she wants to die; she's handicapped!'"

Cox told me that Bergstedt's alleged fear of being on a respirator without someone present to attend him constantly "well may be a psychological feeling — or it may be a rational, real feeling — but it may not have any validity.

"You've got to find out what he knows versus what he's been told," Cox insisted.

Cox wasn't a therapist, he stressed, though he did have some background in psychology. He had, he said, counseled many disabled people who had had feelings of wanting to die. "I always approach these situations with the idea that there are some valid rationales that only the person with the disability can know, but that there are also some what I call 'suppositions' — they think something is going to happen. They think, 'Oh, I can't be left alone because I will X [die, suffocate, fall off my gurney].' Well, it's not necessarily true that these things would happen. But they think they will happen.

"What I try to do is find out what they base their assumption on. Like, they'll say, 'I'll strangle if I'm left alone ten minutes!' I'll ask, 'Well, why do you say that?' I don't say it's not true; I just want them to tell me why it is true.

"And then, as we talk about it — 'I'm afraid of this, I'm afraid of that' — I might ask, 'Well, have you ever tried it?'

"In other words, give them a goal toward some more rational way of believing. The way to lead a person is to get them talking about 'it' — whatever 'it' is. Having to defend it, fight you about it, you talk about it. And as you talk about it you may find that the wind may blow the fog away and you may see that it's a straw bull, not really a very big bull at all."

Has Cox seen any patterns in the counseling he's done? Yes, he says. "When in isolation, any person feels desperation." It's almost a poem. But then, I've noticed, Cox talks in a kind of poetic way.

I was supposed to use Cox's approach if I ever got Ken on the line. But I never got Ken on the line.

"As soon as I can get the right stuff [meaning, German had written, the Seconal sedative they were seeking], I want to do it right away." That's what German had reported Ken as saying.

Robert Bergstedt had told me, "I think he is going to continue to put pressure on the Supreme Court for us." Bergstedt hadn't directly asked German to do this, he told me, but that he thought German "just thinks it's the thing to do.

"He wants my son to have his wishes — to do what he wants to do — he should have the right to do what he wants to do.

"He's very human, you know what I mean?" Bergstedt said admiringly, referring to German. "A very nice man."

I knew that even before this story was printed the chances would be that Ken would have ended his life.

I was curious that no one other than me, it seemed, had contacted Bergstedt. Oh, there had been other media attempting it, for sure. "Yeah, we've refused them all," Robert Bergstedt told me. "Peter Jennings, *Good Morning America,* and all that. We won't talk to any of them — they want to come in, take a bunch of pictures, and yak, and we're not really interested in that."

But there hadn't, if Bergstedt was telling me right, been any calls from disabled people. Maybe, I thought, precisely because it hadn't been on TV.

Or maybe because disabled people were reluctant to get involved.

I'd talked before starting on this story with several people in California who gave me names of others they thought were "working on the case." But the leads proved false. I was unable to find a single disabled person or disability group who'd written any letters, made any phone calls, or sought through the Nevada attorney general's office to file any legal briefs in the case.

I called the Nevada Association for the Handicapped in Las Vegas, who were listed as having an independent living program. In another article in the *Sun,* this one by reporter Mary Manning, Madge Lange, vice president of the National Association of Pro-Life Nurses, had told Manning that Bergstedt "was referred to the Nevada Association of the Handicapped" but that "apparently his mind was made up."

So I talked to Association director Vince Trigg. "We're not really involved in the case at all," he told me, right off. There had been no recent referral that he knew of, he said; he thought, if memory served, that several years back the Bergstedts had contacted the group's independent living program about some equipment — "he needed some assistance getting some equipment; he's on life support, you know," Trigg added. But Trigg emphasized that "I don't really have any details" about the Bergstedts' current situation.

"We have a peer support group that meets here regularly," Trigg went on. "We've kind of talked about it. With the disabled people we work with, the consensus we're getting is that he should have that right [to end his life]. There really hasn't been a strong indication from any of the people we've talked with that he's doing anything other than requesting the right to die with dignity."

Trigg paused. "Now, the deeper questions, like, 'Does he have some emotional problems that need to be addressed, would he be able to be more functioning if he were able to have some counseling, be more interested in pursuing life?' — I don't know.

"Those are questions that I don't know if you ever get the answers to."

Longmore, when I contacted him, wanted to know what "the disabled community in Nevada" was doing to help Bergstedt. I reported Trigg's comments.

Longmore's response was unequivocal. "I'm really getting fed up with this bullshit stuff from the disability community," he told me, "about this, this spurious 'autonomy' we're supposed to be able to exercise. It's as dumb as what the libertarians are saying — those Hemlock Society people!"

I told him they seemed to see the issue as "freedom of choice."

"God, what kind of freedom of choice does an oppressed person have?" He shot back at me. "When will we get it through our heads that people don't make these choices because of their disabilities but because of their oppression?"

I suggested that perhaps the people I'd talked to hadn't figured that out yet.

"I don't think a lot of people in the disability community have figured it out yet," he added. "And what this indicates to me," he continued, "is a gross naiveté and denial on the part of a lot of disabled people — really a lot of the people in the movement — of the reality of the depths of oppression of disabled people."

Trigg did not bring up the attendant services issue, so I did. There was an attendant program in Nevada, he said; but they didn't administer it; United Cerebral Palsy of Southern Nevada did. He gave me their number.

"That's one of the principal aims of the program, I know that," he volunteered after a moment. "It's to keep people from being institutionalized."

When I contacted UCP, I learned that while UCP had indeed been administering the program for the last two years, the Nevada Association for the Handicapped had managed it prior to UCP. Strange, I thought.

It was clear, though, that if Kenneth Bergstedt would pursue this avenue he'd run only into a dead end: The program, passed by the legislature a few years back, and funded by the state to the tune of a measly $500,000, can serve about 45 people. The program provides a maximum of 28 hours of services a week.

Right.

I have continued to wonder what Ken Bergstedt's life was like. I find myself, in the absence of any way to ascertain the reality, inventing fantasies of his life. I know this is dangerous; yet for me it is also, perhaps, instructive.

I invent a room with a man lying on a "gurney"; that's what German's reports have told me. I imagine a man whose sole conversations are with a father who always tells reporters that he himself has had a leg amputated; who offers the tidbit that his wife died of cancer; who most recently has told German that he thinks he has cancer but hasn't gotten it diagnosed because he fears hospitalization himself; and then who would care for his son?

I think of this as I recall Dr. Wills's comments that people with C-1 and C-2 quadriplegia, who must use respirators, can indeed go out and about in the community; absolutely; that there is no medical reason they can't even hold down a job if the workplace is modified; that, yes, they might need an attendant every 30 minutes or so; but nonetheless they can live a life. I think of Vernon Cox's instructions: "You've got to find out what he knows versus what he's been told."

And: "Give them a goal toward some more rational way of believing."

I think of Ed Roberts's anger: "The only difference between them and me is money."

I remember attorney Jack Cherry telling me that his client "is not very stable, medically." I think of Robert Bergstedt, pointing out, as a way of explaining why his son can not go out, that if he sits up in his wheelchair "his blood pressure goes down to 60 over 30." I remember asking Dr. Wills about this very thing, and being told that people learn to live with such low blood pressure; in rehab, they work with them to adjust to that, he says; they can get wheelchairs that tilt; that people with such conditions can — I hear it over and over — live full lives.

And yes, I know that every case is different, and that I'm no doctor and shouldn't judge Bergstedt's physical condition. But then I didn't think I needed to judge it to see that there was a lot of evidence piling up that Ken Bergstedt was, very indirectly and kindly, being led to a belief that there was no way out.

I think of all these medical things, and I think of Robert Bergstedt's seeming fixation on them — and the attorney's, and the journalist's. And I figure that Ken's trapped in a medical nightmare of the people around him, with no way out.

Still, I know that McAfee got help — he's living in a small group home of five people now, Mark Johnson's told me. Not the best situation, admittedly, but it seems there's been some forward motion — it seems if the Kens of the world would start lashing out at what their problems with attendant services are, as ADAPT wants to start doing, if he goes on *Good Morning America* and says I want to die because I can't get decent attendant services" — as I hear Mark Johnson say McAfee might almost be ready to do — then maybe, just maybe, things would start to move forward — and Ken Bergstedt would still be alive.

In my mind, I see Ken Bergstedt trapped inside his dark room, inside the dark room of other people's minds; other people who see his death as some sort of a release.

A release, I wonder, for whom?

September/October 1990

Suicide
Political or Personal?

Julie Reiskin

*E*very crip in the movement seems to have formulated an opinion about the politically correct way to die. We have the self-righteous crips: many of them have stable, non-progressive disabilities, or injuries rather than diseases or illnesses. Some of these folks have decided that they have the answer, and it is they who can shed light on what life is like for all people in all circumstances with all disabilities.

They assertively maintain that having a disability is fine and dandy. They angrily denounce people with disabilities who are suicidal. They wisely avow that if society were only accessible, and if government support services were adequate, no crip would want or have to die . . . ever!

Then we have the crips who choose public suicide. They go to the press, appearing on national television to demand their right to die, with assistance if need be. They have convinced one doctor so thoroughly that life with disability is not worth living that he developed a machine to assist people with suicide.

These folks are clear that they do not want to live the life of a crip. They proclaim suicide as a valid, if not preferable, option for dealing with illness or severe disability.

The rest of us voice our opinions mainly by debating among ourselves which type of crip is more wrong, and why.

Whether we want to admit it or not, all of us who have

severe disabilities have dealt with life-and-death issues. Our bodies are not as capable, and cannot weather as much trauma or interference as can the bodies of non-disabled people. Many crips have their line. The line (just so you nondisabled readers will know; all crips know what this line is) is the level of disability at which you believe you could not continue living.

Three years ago my line lay at not being able to run. Then it moved, to: not being able to climb the stairs. It moved again, to: not being able to walk, then to: not being able to drive. . . . Seeing as how I am writing this and I can no longer do any of these things, it's clear I've changed my line again.

A few years ago, a woman I knew killed herself ten days after learning she had multiple sclerosis, the disease I have. I was clearly in the category of the self-righteous crip who thought this woman was wrong and was making the movement look bad. I angrily wrote an article, which I sent to *The Rag* but then withdrew. In that article, I wrote, "To her, being one of us was unthinkable."

As my disease progressed, I got to the point where I myself saw suicide as my only valid option. As I saw myself getting weaker, and as I lost abilities, I saw a not-too-pretty picture of my future.

I saw what others had gone through in attempting to end their lives. I also saw what I belived to be the reality for severely disabled crips without resources, which was confinement of some sort — probably to a nursing home. I began to set up legal safeguards: I wrote and signed a living will. I had a legal document drafted to ensure that, if I developed an infection of some sort, I would not be hospitalized and a feeding tube inserted.

As I got near the point of acceptance of death, knowing that my illness was getting worse and yet feeling comfortable with my choice to end my life when the level of disability got unbearable, the magic words "experimental treatment" were spoken to me.

This was the first time my doctor had ever used the words "multiple sclerosis" and "treatment" in the same sentence. From the day I went for the initial interview in Boston, I made up my mind to undergo the treatment. Within a week I had convinced myself it would work and that I'd have several more "good" years. I felt stronger than I had in a while; the old anger and militancy about issues that have always informed my life returned.

I underwent the treatment. Nothing miraculous happened, but I hoped for improvement. Then I became very depressed — and didn't know why. I underwent the treatment again; this time the results weren't so ambiguous. It was clear it wasn't going to work.

I became very ill and didn't know if I was going to live. I felt very close to death, then; others around me also thought I was close to death. I felt a strange mixture of calmness and fear. I literally hung on — afraid of the unknown, afraid of more loss.

When I got slightly better, I figured it out: neither the quality nor the quantity of my life has any certainty. I have no ability line anymore.

I can no longer say that, when such-and-such happens, I will commit suicide.

But neither can I say that I will fight to live, no matter what the level of my disability. I am no longer willing to make a personal or political commitment to stay alive, and those close to me have to realize this. I intend to keep my high-strung job working with an AIDS coalition; it is important to me.

I have always been a person who is more comfortable with political issues than emotional and spiritual ones. I would love to make death and dying the new political issue of the 1990s; I could get right into it. I would choose a side and get good and righteous about it. I'd write legislation; I'd go to public hearings. I'd write letters to the editor and organize protests. I'd gossip about those who didn't agree with my side. I'd probably even think up a catchy campaign slogan for the issue.

The problem is that death and dying is a spiritual and emotional — and very personal — issue.

Because so much of our oppression as crips is political, and the oppression hurts us on a very personal basis, it's understandable that many crips are today trying to politicize this dying thing. For too long we didn't see the political implications in much of the oppression we faced — we saw our problems as merely personal in nature. Now that those of us in the movement have finally begun to see the political nature of our oppression, perhaps we have become too insistent that everything about our lives is basically political.

And part of this issue of death and dying may indeed be

political. But there's another part of it that certainly isn't.

What we're dealing with is not about whether suicide is right or wrong. We're not dealing with the need to come up with some sort of a value statement on our lives. Nor are we really grappling with what I would do if I were in so-and-so's shoes — or chair.

This is about each individual. Where am I in my life? Do I have options? Am I sick, in pain, do I have people around me? Have I done my job in life? Do I still need to be here? Is it my time to move on?

Should — or can — anyone answer those questions for someone else? I think not. Are we in the disability movement so afraid of death that we will go to such extremes to avoid dealing with it in ourselves?

Doesn't the person who goes public asking to die really need our support and love rather than being told they're "politically incorrect"?

If we're that afraid of the reality of death, then we're no different from the medical and rehab people who're constantly trying to "fix" us. But perhaps our need, as a movement, to convince society that our problems are not all related to "illness" has been so strong that we forget we need not convince ourselves of the same thing.

A person' choice of a time to die is a very personal decision; it is rarely if ever meant to reflect on anyone else.

When my acquaintance with M.S. killed herself I got very angry because I felt her decision as a personal attack against me. Who was she to say that my life was not worth it?

What I didn't understand then was that she wasn't saying anything intentional about my life at all; she was saying only that her time on earth was over; she had gone through her level of pain. If we truly do value people and believe what we say about people having the right to make their own decisions, shouldn't our judgments stop at a person's own decision about how long to live?

A friend with whom I was discussing this recently asked me: if I killed myself, would it be because of the disability, or because of the lack of services I needed? Being the activist I am, and wanting to politicize the issue, I blurted out, "the services!"

Then on another day, a day when I was particularly sick, I thought about it. "No, the problem's the disability itself," I said. "No matter how great the services are, I simply can't live like this forever!"

Then it dawned on me: they're inseparable. While all the access in the world can't stop my fatigue, I would be less fatigued if I could work part-time and collect enough benefits to maintain the lifestyle I want — the lifestyle I have when I work full-time. All the attendant services in the world cannot for me make up for the loss of independence. And knowing how few attendant service options there really are today does little to allay my fear of the future.

What I'm getting at, I guess, is this: Disability as a concept has a side that is very political — and needs voices, votes and action. But it has another side that's very personal. This side needs discussion, support and understanding. And this side is too often met with silence.

The bottom line, for me? Amazingly enough (for me!), I don't have an answer to this one — or even a firm opinion. I've sat on both sides of this fence. I know that I don't like having my quality of life questioned; and was offended when I felt it was being questioned by another's death. But I also know that when my disease progressed to the point where I could no longer deny the time-limits of my own life, I was forced to deal with death. And, this time around, I've been most annoyed that this topic seems such a taboo within the movement.

I also found I was annoyed with myself that I couldn't just have a protest or do civil disobedience to solve my problem. The principles of organizing just don't work here, though: to escalate the action? To where? To make the other side look bad in the press? Well, what other side?

When the issue is one's own death, "organizing" doesn't seem to be what to do. But I so wanted there to be "sides" and for me to be able to "win!"

I've found out that I can't deal with this dying process through planning meetings, press confences, media packets and leafletting. I have to use and discover things that have heretofore been foreign to me: feelings, real relationships with people, letting go. And this stuff is more challenging to me than any bureaucratic policy or any set of stairs. It makes me angrier than any rehab counselor and fills me with more passion than ADAPT. I guess I could say that living while knowing that I may die soon has been the hardest thing that I have ever done.

But the process I've been going through — realizing that I may die from complications of my disability or that I may reach a level of disability that I cannot tolerate — has not made me unable to be an activist. I still fight for access, for transportation and other crip issues. I am still actively involved in my local independent living center.

Making room for people to die in the community is as much a disability issue as demanding that we be allowed to live in the community. Those of us with progressive illnesses need support, regardless of our choices.

We are all oppressed by the physical barriers around us. But we're also oppressed by our own community's silence. To need to deal with the issue of death, and to find others around you unwilling to listen, to find them even leaving the room rather than confront death and dying issues, is also oppressive.

And we do not need to be our own oppressors.

March/April 1991

Silence on the
Psychiatric Holocaust

Steve Mendelsohn

As a Jew and a psychiatric survivor, I am angered by the pronouncements of certain prominent liberal Jews who claim that in National Socialist Germany only Jews and Gypsies were targeted for genocide. Not only are these pronouncements false, but they may also be part of a deliberate conspiracy to conceal the truth.

Last year marked the 25th anniversary of the publication of *A Sign for Cain*, psychiatrist Frederic Wertham's book dealing with human violence. The most significant chapter details the mass extermination of psychiatric inmates by German psychiatrists before Hitler's Final Solution. Wertham estimates the number of people mercilessly killed in what has come to be misleadingly called the "euthanasia action" in Germany and Austria alone at more than 275,000, a figure corroborated by the Czech War Crimes Commisssion.

More recently, Dr. Max Lafont, author of the book, *L'Extermination Douce,* has pointed out that French psychiatrists starved and froze to death an additional 40,000 psychiatric inmates under the Vichy regime. The total number of psychiatric killings will likely never be known.

In order to truly understand the wider holocaust, it is imperative to first understand the psychiatric holocaust. In 1920, psychiatrist Alfred Hoche and attorney Karl Binding coauthored *The Destruction of Life Devoid of Value*, the first book to advocate the systematic extermination of an entire class of people on the grounds of "racial hygiene." Hoche and Binding describe psychiatric inmates as "mentally completely dead" and "absolutely worthless human beings"; they use both racial and economic arguments to justify mass murder.

Hitler's ideas about Jews parallel Hoche's ideas about psychiatric inmates. Psychiatrist Peter Breggin, author of the recent book, *Toxic Psychiatry,* describes Hitler's *Mein Kampf* as indistinguishable from psychiatric propaganda of the time. To quote a representative passage: "Those who are physically and mentally unhealthy and unworthy must not perpetuate their suffering in the bodies of their children."

During the early 1930s, hundreds of thousands of psychiatric inmates and people with disabilities were castrated and sterilized in Germany. German eugenic psychiatrists, led by Ernst Rudin, the person most responsible for Nazi racial hygiene laws, received enthusiastic moral and technical support from colleagues in the English-speaking world. The United States already had a long history of promoting eugenic psychiatry, buttressed by the 1927 Supreme Court ruling in Buck v. Bell (in the famous words of Justice Oliver Wendell Holmes: "Three generations of imbeciles are enough."). Further support for Nazi eugenics came from the Carnegie Foundation and the Rockefeller Foundation. The latter, according to Breggin, gave a huge grant for Rudin's work.

In July 1939, leading German psychiatrists, including Werner Heyde, Max deCrinis, Carl Schneider, Werner Villinger and Paul Nitsche, gathered to discuss the most economical means of killing psychiatric inmates. Three months later, six psychiatric institutions — Sonnestein, Hadamar, Grafeneck, Hartheim, Brandenberg and Bernberg — were turned into killing centers, complete with gas chambers and crematoria. Psychiatrists even devised the technique of extracting gold from teeth of the dead.

German psychiatry's zeal to kill was boundless. When the 10,000th inmate was cremated at Hadamar in 1941, psychiatrists, nurses and attendants celebrated with a beer party.

It is important to remember here that Hitler never ordered the killing of psychiatric inmates. Wertham comments with justifiable outrage: " . . . the psychiatrists did not have to have an order. They acted on their own. They were not carrying out a death sentence pronounced by somebody else. They were the legislators who laid down the rules for deciding who was to die; they were the administrators who worked out the procedures, provided the patients and places, and decided the method of killing; they pronounced a sentence of life or death in every individual case; they were the executioners who carried the sentences out . . . "

In 1941, the psychiatric killing centers were taken over to be used as training grounds for the SS. Soon after, the gas chambers were moved east to the concentration camps. A number of psychiatrists also went to the camps and were the first to select inmates to be killed. Meanwhile, psychiatrists and pediatricians were still murdering people in "hospitals" — only now they were doing it by lethal injection and slow starvation. A large percentage of the victims were children.

American psychiatry lent its support to genocide. The July 1942 issue of *The American Journal of Psychiatry* featured a debate on killing retarded children. Foster Kennedy endorsed killing severely retarded five-year-olds, whom he called "the utterly unfit" and "nature's mistake." Child psychiatrist Leo Kanner opposed "euthanasia"; he supported sterilization instead. In an unsigned commentary, the editors of this official journal of the American Psychiatric Association came out on Kennedy's side for "euthanasia" murders and advocated a psychiatric campaign to alleviate parental guilt. Franz J. Kallman, a leading psychiatrist who had to flee Germany for America because of his part-Jewish ancestry, advocated the forced sterilization of all siblings of people labled "schizophrenic" — a policy far more radical than anything supported by Hitler.

Possibly the most shameful aspect of the psychiatric holocaust is the postwar cover-up. Most of those who committed these crimes against humanity have gone entirely unpunished. A few have even been honored. According to Wertham, one German court exonerated a doctor on the grounds that the victims were merely "burnt-out human husks." Werner Villinger, a leader in the psychiatric killings, was not only honored by the government of West Germany but was invited to and participated in the 1950 White House Conference on Children and Youth.

The reason for the cover-up should be obvious. Wertham cogently asserts that a full accounting of these atrocities would tarnish the reputation of organized psychiatry and possibly pediatrics as well. This is even more true today, with the resurgence of 1930's-style theories concerning the genetic/ biological basis of "mental illness" and brain-damaging and lethal treatments, incuding electroshock and Clozapine. A full accounting would also challenge the ethic that it is preferable to abort a disabled fetus than to allow it to be born. We would be compelled to radically change our dehumanizing policies toward both psychiatric inmates and people with disabilities.

Jewish commentators on the Holocaust, such as Alan Dershowitz in his recent book, *Chutzpah,* should cease their hypocrisy. People who righteously condemn those who deny or de-Judaize the Holocaust must not lend credence to the conspiracy of silence perpetrated by the psychiatric lobby. Psychiatry bears much of the responsibility for the murder of six million Jews. De-psychiatrizing the Holocaust is just as morally pernicious as denying it.

For, as Santayana declared, those who do not remember the past are condemned to repeat it.

January/February 1992

Springtime for Hitler

Kathi Wolfe

April 10, 1993

The flowers are blooming, busloads of tourists are invading Washington and the Holocaust is making a comeback. You can't turn on the radio or watch the tube in this town without getting bombarded with stories on the new United States Holocaust Memorial Museum.

I hear yet another Museum story while I listen to the radio and drink coffee. It's too much to handle when I'm just waking up. I watch "I Love Lucy" for comic relief. It doesn't work. Even Lucy's best sketches can't take away the horror of the Holocaust.

Thank God no one's asked me to write about the Museum. You won't catch me writing about this stuff.

I go with a friend to the grocery. Hydrox cookies are on sale. This cheers me up: surely I won't have to think about the Holocaust while I'm buying bread, Hydrox cookies and milk.

No such luck. My friend glances at the papers in the machines outside the store. *USA Today* has a story on a survey commissioned by the American Jewish Committee. The survey says 22 percent of U.S. adults are "unconvinced that the Holocaust happened." More than one in five Americans, according to the Roper organization survey, are "open to the idea that the Holocaust is a myth."

I remember Holocaust survivors I've met. I think of the

millions of Jews, gays, gypsies and political prisoners the Nazis murdered. I shudder as I recall Hitler's "euthanasia" program. I know that if I'd been a legally blind baby in Nazi Germany, I would have been one of the blinks Hitler killed.

But I can't make myself deal with it today. I go home and boot up my computer, glad for once that an editor needs a story from me by 5 p.m.

April 23

I'm walking out of the Dupont Circle subway stop, on my way to get some flyers on the gay and lesbian rights march that's taking place Sunday on the Mall.

I'm not surprised when I feel someone tap my shoulder. The area's jammed with people buying buttons, selling t-shirts, handing out pamphlets for the march.

I jump, though, when I hear a rough, male voice behind me snarl, "Get out of the way, blind lady! You and these queers belong in concentration camps." He grabs my cane and throws it to the ground.

I stand there stunned for a few seconds. A woman asks if I'm OK; she picks up my cane and hands it to me. A couple of guys go after the thug, but he's long gone. When I stop shaking, I ask, "what did he look like?" Someone tells me "he looked like a skinhead."

To calm down, I go to a cafe. I drink coffee and listen to music. *It was a freak incident*, I tell myself.

April 25

I'm listening to the speakers at the march. A gay man from the South is speaking. He says that while he was walking around D.C. on Friday, a man dressed in a Nazi uniform spat on him and beat him up. His run-in with the neo-Nazi, he says, occurred near the Holocaust Museum.

This is getting frightening. I have visions of Nazis invading the capital. I see them blocking subway exits; taking over "handicapped" parking spaces; spitting on, beating up everyone in sight. When Nazi paratroopers begin storming the White House, I jerk myself out of my reverie. I tell myself to stop being paranoid. I pay attention to the speakers. I enjoy the entertainment. I march along the Mall with hundreds of thousands of gay-rights supporters.

But I can't get the Nazi out of my head. T. S. Eliot said *April is the cruelest month.* This April, with all its Holocaust echoes, is living up to Eliot's dictum.

April 27

The talking alarm clock is saying, "It's 6:40 a. m." The radio is on. And I'm having a bad dream, mixing up Nazis and the television age. It's "Lifestyles of the Neo-Nazis." Nazis are drinking beer on yachts, sunning themselves on the beach, showing off their fancy estates. I want to wake up, so I force myself to listen to the radio. But there's no escape from the Nazis. National Public Radio's *Morning Edition* is running a story on hostilities toward disabled people in Germany. "Fifty years after Germany's gruesome medical experiments and murders, disabled people are feeling a renewed sense of apprehension amid violence by right-wing neo-Nazis," I hear host Bob Edwards say.

Reporter Michael Lawton jolts me awake with his story. I've read something about this recently in *The New York Times* and *The Rag.* But it takes the immediacy of radio for the full horror of this grisly business to sink into my head.

Lawton tells of a couple of skinheads who beat a visually-impaired man to death on his way home from work; of a mentally disabled man tortured for four days; of a man who lost his leg in an accident who kills himself after being repeatedly harassed by neo-Nazis. I start shaking as I remember my encounter with the skinhead. As Lawton tells his story I find myself wondering *What country do I live in? Is this nightmare going to happen here?*

There's no respite. Lawton's report become even more frightening: it's not just the skinheads who are beating up on disabled people in Germany.

Disabled people are being asked to stay out of sight on beaches. And a German judge allowed a couple to get back the money they'd paid on a vacation because disabled people were in the dining room. In his ruling, the judge said, "the unavoidable sight . . . of disabled people . . . reminded the appellants . . . in an unusually intensive way of the possibilities of human suffering. Such experiences are not expected on a typical holiday."

I sit transfixed in horror. The most terrifying thing I learn from the radio is that Germany's new constitution offers disabled people no protection against discrimination.

I get dressed and drink coffee while I try to make something of all that's whirling in my head. I recall the day a few years ago when the owner of a New York City luncheonette tried to throw me out because, as he put it, my "cane would upset the other customers." I'd told him *he'd* be "upset" if I contacted the newspapers or the New York State Human Rights Commission. But what if I were in Germany now? I'd have no legal recourse.

I think of all the crips and blinks I know who can tell a million such stories. *At least in the Americans with Disabilities Act,* I tell myself, *we have some civil rights.* Then I start thinking about all the talk of an ADA backlash and I get really depressed.

I look for more milk, cereal, sugar and hope. Is there anything hopeful in the midst of this horror? Yes. At the end of Lawton's story, he says that, unlike during the Holocaust, disabled people are now fighting back.

May 15

I can't get the Holocaust out of my mind. I'm still having those dreams, the ones with the Nazis. I try to relax by watching old reruns on TV. When I start thinking about Mr. Ed being shot by Nazis I know it's time to turn off the TV.

June 15

I stop running away from the Holocaust and go to the Museum. I've made an appointment with one of the Museum's PR people. If I'm this obsessed with this stuff, I might as well write about it.

It takes three hours to go through the Museum. I know something about the Holocaust already, but am not at all prepared for the horror of seeing the Museum's permanent exhibition. It's more terrifying than I can ever say to stand in that boxcar that took people to the death camps or to look at those thousands of shoes that belonged to people who were murdered.

For the first time in some years of reporting, I am completely overwhelmed. I see, hear and smell the Holocaust. I do something I have never done before on a story: I forget to turn my tape recorder on. So much for accuracy in reporting or grace under pressure.

I learn that the Nazis killed more than 200,000 disabled people. But what makes my hair stand on end is learning that the Nazis developed a system to put disabled people in "euthanasia centers" and gas them in chambers disguised as showers. The technology, the system the Nazis used to kill us served as a model for how to kill millions of Jews and what the Museum PR Person called "victim groups" in the Holocaust.

Gee, I think as I walk to the exhibit on the "euthanasia program," *if I had been in Nazi Germany I would have been part of a model "victim group."*

Then I look at the exhibit on the third floor of the Museum, artifacts from "hospital" rooms from the "euthanasia centers." An archival photo of Hadamar, a castle converted into one of the centers. The PR Person points out the trail of smoke coming from the castle chimney; it's where the Nazis burned the bodies of disabled people after they'd killed them. A blanket and bed from Sachsenberg, a psychiatric hospital in Schwerin converted into a "euthanasia center"; a pair of gloves and wrist and body restraints from the center in Bernberg. A descriptive panel explains the "euthanasia program."

Images of Hitler's "euthanasia program" swim through my imagination. I see Nazis registering disabled children, putting them on buses, taking them to "hospitals" for "special treatment" — and then killing them. Letters from Nazi bureaucrats telling parents of their child's death from "the flu" or "pneumonia" flicker on my mind's computer screen. This comes from listening to the radio.

Talking with Hugh Gallagher, author of *By Trust Betrayed*, made it all real to me in a tangible way, so I can now smell the smoke coming from the crematorium; see the kids not wanting to get on those buses. But coming from the sensual bombardment of the other floors, this small third-floor exhibit doesn't seem very real to me. I feel like I did when I visited Dallas and looked at the "grassy knoll" where Kennedy was shot. It was the TV reports and radio news that brought the assassination home to me; they're what I'll remember. When I looked at that knoll in Dallas, I remember thinking how small it looked.

Yet my reaction is clearly not widespread. The museum staffers I talk with say that the general public is taken aback when they see the exhibit; that most have no idea Hitler set up a system to murder disabled people. The public is very surprised to learn that disabled people were a Holocaust "victim group," staffers tell me.

I go out of the Museum into the sunshine. It feels as though I've gone through a long, deep tunnel. I know for sure now that I'll never be able to absorb the enormity of the Holocaust. But I'm glad to be on the other side of the tunnel.

August 10

I call Hugh Gallagher again. Hugh's been incredibly helpful during this Holocaust odyssey. For something new and different, I ask him more questions about the Nazis, disabled people, the Holocaust and Germany today.

Hugh says Hitler's "euthanasia program" was officially closed down because, as Nazi official Heinrich Himmler said, it was "a secret that was no longer a secret." That certainly has a familiar bureaucratic ring. Apparently parents were getting death notices before their child had died. Or they'd get a death notice for someone else's child by mistake. The official "euthanasia program" was screwed up by bureaucratic glitches.

What about reparations, I ask. Hugh says that no reparations have been paid to the families of the disabled people the Nazis murdered. And neither the German government nor the German medical establishment has ever issued a statement saying that there was anything wrong with the "euthanasia program." A few years ago in a British medical journal, a German doctor called for such a statement; he was subsequently ostracized by the German medical establishment. He now practices in the United States.

I start to ask about something else, but Hugh stops me. "You'll end up writing a dissertation," he says. *You're right, I say, and I really don't want to do that.* I tell him I hope to get a chance to meet him in person some day, then I hang up the phone. It's more than a little weird to make friends with someone because of the Holocaust and neo-Nazis, I think, as I turn off my computer.

August 15

"Aren't you tired of the Holocaust? Don't you want to write about something nice?" my friend asks. *Yes, as soon as this is out of my system!* I'm nearly shouting.

August 23

I've said all I can say about the Holocaust, the disabled and Germany today. For now, anyway. As I look through these notes, I see I've no more answers and little more wisdom than before I started.

Yet I feel more hopeful than I did four months ago. I've learned that you can delve into the most evil realm of human history and stay sane. I've learned that you don't have to be a victim, that you can fight back.

I'm even beginning to look forward to my dreams.

Eugenics and Reproductive Choice

Lisa Blumberg

Sharon, a woman in her early 30s, has had more contact with people with disabilities than many nondisabled persons have. She has been a foster parent to a child with severe cerebral palsy, and her older sister has had multiple sclerosis since age 12. An attorney, Sharon is a partner in a firm that counts people with mental retardation among its clients

When Sharon was pregnant with her third child, her doctor ordered her to have a "new but routine" blood test. She inquired what the test was for, and he told her that it was to help them find out whether the baby was healthy. When she asked him to elaborate, he said it was "to prevent birth defects."

"A vaccine?" Sharon asked.

The doctor said no. The test would indicate whether the baby might have a condition like Down syndrome or spina bifida. If the test was positive, and it was unlikely that it would be, Sharon could then have more conclusive tests and, based on the results, could then make an informed decision in the middle of the second trimester regarding what to do about her pregnancy.

Sharon asked him whether any of the disabilities detected by the test could be treated and ameliorated prenatally. He replied that except in extraordinary cases the only "remedy" was "therapeutic" pregnancy termination.

Sharon, who had discussed prenatal testing and issues

surrounding selective abortion extensively with her husband, said she saw no reason for the test, especially if it might have to be followed by a test like amniocentesis, which would pose some risk to her and the fetus. They wanted another child and, although they hoped their child would not have unusual problems, they were willing to accept a son or daughter with a disability.

The doctor said she should have the test anyway because it would allow her to keep her options open. She declined.

Later, when she was recovering from the uneventful birth of her son, Sharon read her obstetrical records and learned that she had refused the maternal serum alpha-fetoprotein screening test "against medical advice."

Sharon's experience was unusual only in that she was able to successfully insist on exercising what feminist and disability activist Anne Finger calls "the right to choose not to choose."

In 1985, Dr. John Fletcher, assistant for Bioethics at the Clinical Center at the National Institutes of Health, predicted that the screening of every fetus for "birth defects" would soon be routine without saying why it should be routine. Now in the '90s, some form of screening for fetal "defects" is an integral part of the prenatal services most middle and upper middle class women receive. At a time when many low income women do not have access to any health care during pregnancy and may not even be able to obtain the nutrition they need to have a baby of average weight, millions are being spent on genetic tests and sophisticated ultrasound techniques to detect hundreds of conditions ranging from cystic fibrosis to hemophilia to dwarfism to spina bifida to cleft lips to unequal leg lengths.

When amniocentesis began to be used in the early '70s, it was initally seen as an optional test for women who, for their own personal reasons, felt they could not have a child with a disability. Some women had the test, many others did not.

Now, prenatal testing has largely become the decision of the doctor. For example, based on the recommendation of the American Academy of Obstetricians and Gynecologists, amniocentesis is routinely prescribed for pregnant women in their mid-30s or older, and many doctors perform the maternal serum alpha-fetoprotein screening test on all patients who can afford to pay for it.

Doctors now also seem to be less willing to clarify for

parents at the outset that a primary reason for the tests is to permit an abortion should the fetus have a "defect." Similarly, the prospective parents may not be informed that one of the critical limitations of prenatal testing is that, while these tests can place a diagnostic label on a fetus, they can not assess the functional disability that the future individual would have, much less his or her strengths.

A diagnosis of spina bifida, for example, will not indicate whether a child would walk with just some degree of difficulty or use a wheelchair, or whether he would be intellectually gifted, have average intellegence or be slightly retarded. Neither would a finding of cystic fibrosis provide guidance on whether a person's lifespan would be eight years or 58 years or somewhere in between.

Some women do want to make use of the full range of tests, having decided even before conception what they would do if testing yielded an adverse result. Other women are disturbed by the prospect of screening but feel they should not refuse something their doctor recommends. One woman may be concerned that if she is "difficult" now the doctor would not let her make choices during the delivery process. Another may feel that since her doctor is a professional she "should" accept his advice. Yet another who is pregnant for the first time may accept her doctor's view that she "has to have it" because she doesn't have a "track record."

The result of making prenatal tests essentially the prerogative of the obstetrician is that some of the women who have the tests, if left to their own intitiative, would chance having a baby with a disability, or would perceive that they did not have sufficient knowledge to make what Marsha Saxton, who is director of the Project on Women and Disability in Boston and has spina bifida, calls a "rational choice." These women now must risk being in a situation where they will have to deliberately say "yes" or "no" to giiving birth to a child with a disability.

In the relatively rare number of cases where tests do reveal a fetal disability, those prospective parents who are unsure of "what to do" are usually referred to a genetic counselor. Genetic counselors tend to see their role as helping people understand "the risks and consequences" of having a child with a disability.

The advice genetic counselors give, though, may be distorted by the fact that they tend to see disabled persons only in medical settings, where the emphasis is on the person's dysfunction and where the treatment the person is being given may be unpleasant.

Counselors have only minimal awareness that people with disabilities have roles other than as patients, and that there are hundreds of thousands of congenitally disabled people who are attending school, going to work, having relationships, and supporting elderly parents. Some may personally believe that life with a significant disability is not reasonable, and such belief may impact the way they present information to their clients. For example, "A Time to Decide, A Time to Heal," a booklet prepared by a genetic counselor at Michigan State University, advises readers that "one benefit that may be attributed to [pregnancy] interruption is the prevention of the child's mental and physical suffering."

Too often counselors do little more than provide future parents with a dreary laundry list of problems their child could have and express sympathy. Rarely are clients encouraged to discuss disability related concerns with people who are disabled or are parents of disabled children.

Instead, much medical literature seems to assume that the purpose of counseling is to help ambivalent parents to *accept* giving up the fetus just as they earlier accepted testing. Material given out at Yale-New Haven Hospital to couples who have *just* been told their fetus has a disability gives guidance on how to handle the grief that may accompany the termination of a planned pregnancy, thus subtly informing prospective parents that, no matter how much they have wanted a child, they are now on the fast track to abortion. A handbook for genetic counselors put out by the March of Dimes, whose mission is to "fight birth defects," has categorized a decision by parents to carry a fetus with a disability to term as "nonroutine."

Indeed, although abortions due to fetal disability constitute a small fraction of all abortions performed, the overwhelming majority of the fetuses diagnosed as having a "major defect," i.e., a condition that *could* result in a significant disability, are ultimately aborted. For example, when amniocentesis was the only way to detect Down syndrome, about 20% of the fetuses with Down syndrome were aborted. Now that Down syndrome can also be identified by level 2 ultrasound, chorionic villus sampling and blood tests, it is thought that at least 60%

of fetuses with Down Syndrome will be identified. One mother's fear, that her 10-year-old daughter, who is part of the first generation of Americans with Down syndrome to have access to the public schools and to routinely learn to read, will also be part of the last generation of Americans with Down syndrome is not unfounded.

People with disabilities are increasingly aware of and alarmed by the anti-disability bias that underlies much prenatal testing and selective abortion. However, the disability rights movement as a whole has yet to comprehensively address the issue. Part of this is due to the movement's traditional reluctance to deal with medical-related matters, although most of us have been subject to medical oppression. We were late in getting involved in the fight to protect disabled infants from being discriminatorily denied food or treatment in hospitals, and we are less than visible players in the currrent debate over revamping the health care system.

A more significant reason, though, why the movement has not formulated a position on prenatal testing and selective abortion is that the movement for quite legitimate reasons is unwilling to take a stand that could be seen as taking sides in the abortion controversy. The disability rights movement is for the most part a progressive movement and is increasingly cognizant of the need to forge alliances with other progressive movements. People with disabilities, like any other diverse group of people, have varying views on pregnancy termination. However, numerous people with disabilities are pro-choice, and indeed disabled women tend to perceive the same need to have access to abortion as nondisabled women.

Moreover, some of us feel that, if there is any decision where *personal* prejudice can play a role, it is the decision to bear a child. As Adrienne Asch, a sociologist and disability activist, has said: "I consider women who refrain from childbearing . . . [because a fetus may have a disability] to be misguided, possibly depriving themselves of the joys of parenthood by their unthinking acceptance of the values of a society still deeply . . . ambivalent about people with disabilities . . . Yet, I do not support outlawing abortion."

Quite simply put, the movement's dilemma is that abortion is being used to keep people with disabilities from entering the world, and a great number of us want abortion to remain legal.

The solution is for the movement to carefully define the issues that should concern us as disability rights activists. As a movement, we should not take any position on the rights of a fetus verses the rights of a pregnant woman. However, what we can and must do is take a position against any medical, legal or social policy that is based on the attitude that people who have disabilities are categorically inferior to others and therefore would be better off if they did not exist and everyone else would benefit by their absence.

The movement can be abortion neutral and still oppose a geneticist's call for mandatory prenatal testing. Similarly, the movement is not injecting itself into the abortion debate by seeking to prohibit a health maintenance organization from denying coverage for a child because his parents knew beforehand that he might need specific treatment.

Now that we have an administration in Washington that is more receptive to reproductive choice than previous ones, the movement should not hesitate to speak out about eugenics.

We should be able to build consensus around the view expressed by Ruth Hubbard, a retired biology professor at Harvard University, that "a woman must . . . have a right—and more than that, the opportunity—not to terminate . . . [a pregnancy involving a fetus with a disability] in the confidence that society will do what it can to allow her child to live a fulfilling life."

The collective consciousness of the movement was raised to some extent in 1991, when a Los Angeles radio talk show host devoted a program to discussing whether Bree Walker, a prominent anchorwoman, who was nearly 8 months pregnant at the time, should be having the baby. Ms. Walker's reproductive choices were targeted for debate because she has a condition resulting in fused fingers and toes, which has a 50-50 chance of being transmitted to offspring. The incident caused the disabled community to acknowledge and confront the growing social conviction that it is irresponsible to bring children who may have disabilities into the world. Moreover, the incident brought home the fact that, if women are pressured not to have certain types of children, the women who will be subject to most pressure to forgo childbearing will be women with disabilities.

We need to become more aware of how strong eugenics views presently are. According to Elizabeth Kristol, writing last spring in *First Things,* it is the desire of the U.S. Department of

Health and Human Services that screening for "fetal abnormalities" be done on at least 90% of the U.S. population. A society that devalues both women and people with disabilities would not have spent millions of dollars developing and refining prenatal tests just to maximize women's choices and to allow parents to make thoughtful preparations for the coming of a child with a disability.

The social purpose of these tests is to reduce the incidence of live births of people with disabilities. This is recognized, for example, by public health professionals in a report done in connection with a state-wide program in California to offer prenatal screening for spina bifida and other neural tube defects.

The report, which found that more women polled in their study said that they would have an abortion if testing revealed that there was a 100% chance that the fetus had a "defect" than if testing indicated a 95% chance, stated that "if an intended result of prenatal diagnostic technologies is selective abortion of severly affected fetuses, then it appears to be worth the investment to perfect a technology with a detection certainty approaching 100 percent. This is effectively the case today for neural tube defect screening . . ."

The report also found that "significant issues" were raised by the fact that a small number of women said that they would not have an abortion even if the fetus had what the report characterized as "multiple, severe handicaps" such as hemiplegia and incontinence. In particular, the report said that "although there is some evidence that women's attitudes towards abortion shift upon diagnosis of a defective fetus, our results suggest that, at least for certain subgroups of the population, cost benefit and effectiveness analyses of prenatal diagnostic programs should be cautious in making assumptions about high abortion acceptance rates . . ." Nowhere do the writers ask whether preventing the existence of people with spina bifida is an appropriate goal of a program funded by state taxpayers, including taxpayers with spina bifida.

Discriminatory attitudes about people with disabilities are reflected in the willingness of right-to-life groups to propose anti-abortion laws that exempt termination due to "fetal defect," as well as in pro-choice legislation law, which guarantees a woman's general right of abortion until the fetus becomes viable but permits abortion "at any time during the woman's pregnancy if . . . the fetus is affected by a genetic defect or serious deformity or abnormality" (Section 20-209 of the *Maryland Code Annotated*).

It is the courts, though, that have done the most to promote prenatal testing and, by extension, selective abortion by permitting "wrongful birth" and "wrongful life" suits. Such suits, which involve the allegation that a person who is presently alive should not be here, are not allowed in connection with "healthy" children because courts are of the opinion that such suits would damage a child's self esteem and make him an emotional illegitimate. However, judges have decided that it is a different matter when a child is "defective."

The theory behind both wrongful birth and wrongful life cases is that a doctor who "negligently" failed to recommend prenatal tests or to apprise prospective parents that they risked having a "defective" child should be held responsible for the existence of the child and forced to pay damages. However, in wrongful birth cases, it is the parents who are stating that they have been harmed by the child's birth, while in wrongful life cases suit is being brought on "behalf" of the child on the premise that the child himself is harmed by his existence. As a New Jersey court said in the case of *Procanik v. Cillo* 478 A.2d 755 (1984), "the essence of the child's cause of action is that its very life is wrongful." Thus, while wrongful birth suits at least have a certain logic to them, wrongful life suits involve the courts in absurd philosophical speculation and have terrifying implications.

The first state supreme court to espouse the concept of "wrongful life" was the California Supreme Court in the 1982 case of *Turpin v. Sortini* 643 P.2d 954, which involved a little girl who was deaf. The court acknowledged that the question of whether nonexistence was preferable to deafness was a challenging one, but they somehow failed to solicit the views of the only people who are even arguably qualified to answer the question, i.e., people who are deaf. Instead the court, after a lengthy and tortuous analysis, came to the conclusion that if the girl was not alive she would not be deaf, and that therefore she suffers from being in existence. No attention was given by the court to how any child can be expected to cope with either the psychological impact or the social stigma of being judged wrongfully alive.

The fact that it is not the child that the courts are concerned about in wrongful life decisions was revealed a year later by the Washington Supreme Court in the case of *Harbeson v. Parke-Davis* 656 P.2d 483 (1983). This case involved two sisters born a year apart who had "mild to moderate" mental retardation and such physical abnormalities as wide-set eyes, low-set hairlines and small nails and whose mother had not been advised that she risked having "defective" children.

The court dismissed without explanation a concern that prenatal testing and other new reproductive technologies could be "the first steps towards a Fascist-Orwellian societal attitude of genetic purity" and rather decided that these developments "provide benefits to individual families and to *all of society* by avoiding the *vast* emotional and economic costs of *defective children*." (Emphasis mine.) Therefore, the court held that permitting wrongful life suits as well as wrongful birth suits "will promote societal interests in genetic counseling and prenatal testing."

All wrongful life suits to date have been brought against health providers. However, given that the premise of such suits is that nonexistence is preferable to having a disability, there is no reason a court-appointed guardian acting on "behalf" of a child should not be able to bring suit against parents who either turned down a recommendation for prenatal testing or refused to have an abortion when testing identified a fetal defect.

Indeed, Margery Shaw, a lawyer and geneticist and self-styled "fetal rights" advocate, takes the position that "parents should be held accountable to their children if they knowingly and wilfully choose to transmit deleterious genes or if the mother waives her right to an abortion if, after prenatal testing, a fetus is discovered to be seriously deformed or mentally defective." Her reasoning is that "society should decide to wipe out muscular dystrophy, Tay-Sachs disease, cystic fibrosis and sickle cell anemia, just as smallpox, polio and measles have been virtually eradicated." Shaw has been quoted in the *American Bar Association Journal* and published in such publications as *The Journal of Legal Medicine*. Many readers find her views new and thought-provoking.

It is ironic that society is preoccupied with preventing people with disabilities at the same time that it is doing less and less to prevent people from having disabilities. Why is it that we collectively spend so much for ultrasounds when support for nutrition programs for infants and nursing mothers is so lacking? Why is the government embarking on an expensive program to test millions of people for the cystic fibrosis gene when it has not made any similar commitment to make the promising treatments that have just been developed for the symptoms of cystic fibrosis accessible to the limited number of people who have this disease?

Those who want to stamp out diversity among people in the name of fighting physical "defects" don't even know what the real ills of society are.

Some disability rights activists have compared the technology that for the first time in history makes selective abortion possible to atomic power. Yet there has been scant debate on how we should view this new power to predict one tiny aspect of the future, and that which has occurred has been misleadingly focused on whether a woman has an individual right to an abortion. This must change. The real question is whether this technology can be used to impose the view that some groups have regarding what human differences are acceptable or not on all of us. We must not let the eugenicists triumph over disability rights and reproductive choice simply becuse we are squeamish about speaking out.

Proposals for positions to be taken by disability rights groups

There are concrete positions which disability rights groups along with other progressive groups should take to combat eugenics. These positions, which should in no way involve the movement in the debate over whether a woman should have a legal right to abortion, are as follows:

• The decision whether to have prenatal tests must be solely that of the pregnant woman regardless of the woman's age, reproductive history or disability status.

• All expectant couples should be informed as to the purpose of the different available prenatal tests as well as given information on the risks, limitations and expense of the tests, the manner in which these tests will be performed, and when during the gestation period the results will be available. Consent and refusal forms must state that a woman's decision to forgo prenatal tests will not subject either her or her future child to loss of any medical care, insurance, legal benefits or community services that they would otherwise be entitled to. Legislation should be drafted as appropriate.

• The results of all prenatal tests must be strictly confidential and may only be released to a third party with the woman's consent.

• All women regardless of age, reproductive history or disability status must be given the absolute right to continue a pregnancy after prenatal diagnosis. Legislation should be drafted as appropriate.

• Laws regulating abortion should be disability neutral.

• Disability groups should prepare packets of information to be offered to all couples who learn that their fetus has a disabling condition. These packets should contain (1) information that seeks to dispel common misconceptions about disability and to present disability from a disabled person's perspective, (2) information on community-based services for disabled children and their families as well as on financial assistance programs, (3) material on special needs adoption, and (4) a summary of major laws protecting the civil rights of persons with disabilities. People with disabilities and parents of people with disabilities should be available to talk with future parents.

• All medical students should be required to take at least one course in political and social issues of disability and all practicing physicians should be required to take such a course as part of their continuing education requirements. All genetic counselors as part of their specialized training must participate in an activity that will give them contact with disabled persons in nonmedical settings.

• Non-perjorative language must be used when describing persons with disabilities and potential persons with disabilities. The term "defective fetus" should be seen to be in the same category as "kike fetus" and "nigger fetus."

• Wrongful life suits are inherently discriminatory against persons with disabilities and should be prohibited. Wrongful birth suits should only be permitted with disabled children if they are permitted with nondisabled children.

• Family strengthening initiatives such as parental leave, part-time and flextime work, expanded child care alternatives, comprehensive health care programs and programs assisting low income families must be supported. Parenting a disabled child will become a more viable option for more people if society provides more support to parents in general.

January/February 1994

It Can *Happen Here*

John R. Woodward

*A*merican doctors once conducted an experiment that proved you can kill the disabled babies of poor families and get away with it. Their research was funded by the Federal Government. Twenty-four babies with spina bifida lost their lives.

The experiment was declared a success. Yes, it can happen here.

Between 1977 and 1982, four doctors and a social worker at the Children's Hospital of Oklahoma, in Oklahoma City, monitored the births of babies with myelomeningocele (the medical term for spina bifida). Parents who were poor were told that it would not be appropriate to treat their baby and given an extremely pessimistic picture of their child's future life. Parents from better-off families were told more about the treatments for spina bifida and given more optimistic — and more accurate — information about their child's potential..

None of the parents knew they were part of an experiment. Parents who were assigned to the "pessimistic outcome" group chose, by a factor of nearly five to one, not to have their babies treated. The experiment was not conducted to prove that babies with spina bifida will die if they are not treated. Doctors already knew that. The goal of the experiment was to prove that the families would accept a "do-not-treat" recommendation from their doctors.

It was no coincidence that the babies who died were the children of poor parents. To select the families for the "pessimistic outcome group," the doctors conducting the study developed a "formula" which they published as part of their write-up of the experiment in *Pediatrics,* the most famous and influential medical journal devoted to the care of children. This is their "formula": Quality of Life = Natural Endowment multiplied by the contribution of the Home plus the contribution of Society. In a more mathematical style, it reads: $QL = NE * (H + S)$. The doctors measured the "H" — the contribution of the home — primarily in financial terms: family income, family debt, employment and employability of the parents, etc. The parent's "intellectual resources," defined in terms of their educational level, were also included in the calculation of "H," which had the effect of crowding the pessimistic outcome group with parents less likely to challenge the doctors' "facts." Since "Natural Endowment" is multiplied by the other factors, rather than added to them, babies with a greater level of impairment (and hence less "natural endowment") were more likely to be placed in the "pessimistic outcome" group.

The "formula" used non-medical factors to decide which babies ought to receive treatment, which should be a medical decision. The use of a mathematical procedure to create the appearance of an empirical foundation for the decision not to treat is not science. It's "scientism," the dressing up of a moral prejudice in the language and external trappings of science, so as to lend a false credibilty to a value judgment that would otherwise be readily exposed as a mere prejudice. In this case, the doctors arbitrarily assumed that poor families offered a quality of life so much lower than that of middle-class and wealthy families that babies with spina bifida born into them were better off dead.

Frieda Smith, who gave birth to Stonewall Jackson Smith in 1979, remembers being confronted by a doctor just days after a difficult birth, before she had time to come to terms with her baby's birth impairment.

"He [the doctor] told me that I would always have to take care of him, that he would be blind, that he would never know me, that he was more like some kind of an animal than a human being," she says. "He never really sat down with me and explained what the operation would do for Stoney." Ms. Smith was never told that the failure rate for spina bifida treatments is very low, nor did she understand that the operation would reduce the degree of sensory, mobility and intellectual impairment that her son experienced. "He made it sound like Stoney would live longer, but he wouldn't ever get any better."

Ms. Smith signed a consent form agreeing that Stonewall would be fed and given minimal "supportive care," but no antibiotics or surgery. Later, when she had questions about her baby's treatment, the doctor refused to make himself available to answer them. Ms. Smith also says that she did not know that she could have taken her son to another hospital, where he would have been treated at once.

During the five years of the study, 69 babies with spina bifida were born in the Children's Hospital of Oklahoma (now known as the Oklahoma Children's Hospital), a teaching hospital affiliated with the University of Oklahoma. Thirty-three babies were recommended for "supportive care" without treatment; eight of them were eventually treated anyway, either because their parents insisted or because their parents or guardians eventually obtained more accurate information. All of the 24 babies whose parents consented to the "supportive care" regimen died. (A 25th baby in the "supportive care" regimen was moved out of state by his parents and lost to the study. Two of the eight babies that were eventually treated also died, possibly because the treatments came too late.) Most of the babies who were deprived of treatment were born to women in the welfare system, who were paying for their care in the hospital with Medicaid benefits. None of the 36 babies that were given antibiotics and surgery died from the effects of spina bifida. (One died in an accident.)

In addition to being poor, many of the families of the children that were chosen to die were poorly educated. Frieda Smith felt that she was manipulated by a doctor who took advantage of her medical ignorance. Her experiences, and the experiences of other mothers whose babies died, raised serious questions about whether they truly gave "informed consent" when they signed the forms agreeing to the "supportive care" regimen. Indeed, some parents came away from their meeting with the doctor under the false impression that the hospital was not required to treat babies who did not meet the "criteria for treatment" (i.e., the formula).

Ms. Smith and her husband John, who are European-Americans, joined two other parents in a lawsuit against the hospital, the Oklahoma Department of Human Services, administrators in both institutions and the doctors and social workers who conducted the study. Cheparney Camp, a Native American, sued over the death of his daughter Melissa, and Sharon Jackson, who is African-American, sued on behalf of her son Carlton. Carlton, in the words of attorney Jane Brockmann, "beat the odds." He survived for months in a children's shelter, where the nurses and attendants cared for him. Eventually, Ms. Johnson insisted that he be treated. However, the months-long delay caused him to develop more severe impairments than he would have sustained if he had been treated within 48 hours of his birth — which is the standard procedure.

Sadly, the lawsuit was unsuccessful. The National Legal Center for the Medically Dependent and Disabled, in conjunction with Oklahoma attorneys, represented the plaintiffs through nearly 10 years of hearings and appeals, before the Supreme Court decided, last January, not to hear the case. The plaintiffs began in the Federal Courts with an 11-count complaint, charging wrongful deaths, malpractice, violations of fundamental Constitutional rights, a failure to inform the families that their babies were participating in an experiment, discrimination under Section 504 of the Rehabilitation Act and other violations of Federal law. Between 1983 and 1990 the courts threw out all of the counts. When the Supreme Court refused to reinstate the Section 504 complaint in January, they ended the long legal battle.

"What the Supreme Court could have done by recognizing that we had a viable complaint under Section 504 was to send a message to hospitals all across the country, and physicians across the country that you *will* have claims against you if you discriminate against a disabled child in a situation where the treatment is related to that disabling condition," says Jane Brockmann, one of the National Legal Center attorneys who handled the final stages of the case. "We could have scared physicians across the country away from what these physicians did."

Readers of *The Rag* will recall that the European Holocaust of World War II began with the government-ordered murder of persons with physical and mental disabilities, most of whom were killed by their own doctors. This program began two years before World War II and claimed the lives of over 100,000 Germans with disabilities. Ever since the full scope of the Nazi racial crimes was revealed, Americans have insisted to the world and each other that the mass murder of "undesirables" under the authority of State and Science is a crime of which we are not capable.

Indeed, if there is a difference that stands out between the attitudes of the German doctors who murdered their own patients and the "researchers" at the Oklahoma Children's Hospital it is this: the German doctors acted in secret, knowing that their crimes must not be exposed. They hid their killings behind an elaborate arrangement of phony death certificates and other official paperwork. The Oklahoma doctors, on the other hand, proclaimed what they had done openly, in the most prestigious medical journal of their specialty. They understood the attitude of the American public towards persons with disabilities. Evidently, they understood it better than we disability rights activists do today! They know that any furor over their crimes would dissipate without harming their careers, and they knew that in the end their colleagues would admire and emulate them.

"We are beginning to see hospitals going to court, trying to establish 'rights' for themselves," says Ms. Brockman. "Hospitals are seeking the right not to treat some patients." Of course, these patients are persons with disabilities who require expensive, intricate and sometimes long-lasting treatment. In extreme cases, hospitals have sued to have a legally competent parent or spouse removed as the guardian of a person with a disability, so that a new guardian can be appointed to discontinue treatment. Ms. Brockmann sees a trend in the courts: "It seems that when a patient with severe disabilities sues to request that treatment be withheld, the courts are inclined to grant that request; but when someone sues on behalf of such a patient in order to continue treatment, they will have an uphill battle. Treatment should be the default decision in ambiguous cases. The Constitution expressly protects the right to live. As Congress begins to debate the role of rationing in health care reform, the courts will no doubt rule on more "right-not-to-treat" cases.

Today Carlton Johnson, the boy who "beat the odds," is 10. He attends a segregated educational program for children with disabilities, where he is making progress. He does not communicate by speaking, but he is an alert, active and competent child who wheels himself about and plays for hours on an electric organ his family gave him. He recognizes friends and loved ones. He has the capacity for enjoyment and happiness. His life may not be "useful" according to the pseudo-mathematical standards of the doctors who once condemned him to death, but he has one advantage over the men and women who once plotted to deprive him of his life. He will never, ever commit an act of injustice towards another human being as great as the crime they committed against him.

January/February 1994

NOTES ON CONTRIBUTORS

LISA BLUMBERG is an attorney for a major insurance company. She pursues freelance writing on disability and health care issues on the side.

NANCY BIGELOW CLARK is at age 47 still trying to find a place in a world of diminishing space.

JULIE SHAW COLE is an art therapist who has been involved in disability issues since she worked at an independent living center and got into springing people from nursing homes.

TANIS DOE is an alien living in California, recently defected from the land of socialized medicine (Canada) to the home of the brave (no insurance!) to accept a research position at the World Institute on Disability. Her daughter reluctantly came along, hoping not to be discriminated against for being a Jamaican-Canadian instead of an African American.

ANNE FINGER teaches creative writing at Wayne State University in Detroit. Her most recent book is Bone Truth, *a novel (Coffee House Press).*

KENNY FRIES received the Gregory Kolovakos Award for AIDS Writing for his book of poems The Healing Notebooks *(Open Books, 1990).* Anesthesia, *a new book, is forthcoming.*

CAROL J. GILL, Ph.D., is a clinical psychologist specializing in identity, disability and gender issues. She is President of the Chicago Institute of Disability Research and is proudly Disabled.

BILLY GOLFUS is an artiste with beret, disability troublemaker with a bad attitude and rock and roll roué. He doesn't do journalism and he doesn't do windows.

LUCY GWIN is an uppity crip who publishes Mouth *magazine.*

SUSAN HANSELL is currently working on a new play and various poems. She teaches at Brooklyn College.

BRIAN HARTSHORN is disabled, has a part-time job, lives in New York and writes in his spare time. He is currently working on a biographical novel, Hard Gifts.

LAURA HERSHEY is a writer, poet, and agitator native to Denver, CO.

EDWARD L. HOOPER is married to his wife Cindy and has two children, Stacey and Shari. He writes, volunteers, plays quad rugby and is dedicated to disability rights and the disability movement. "As those great ADAPT protesters said, 'I want to go where everyone has gone before.'"

CASS IRVIN is co-founder and past publisher of The Disability Rag. Presently, she is Executive Director of Access to the Arts, Inc., in Louisville, KY.

ARTHUR JACOBS is a graduate of Arizona State University. He has written a collection of short stories and travel stories with Native Americans called Star Walkers.

MARY JOHNSON was co-founder and for 14 years editor of The Disability Rag.

CRIS MATTHEWS is continuing to boldly go where no gimp has gone before.

SUSAN McBRIDE is living with two cats and rheumatoid arthritis in Carmel Valley, CA.

MARY McGINNIS lives in New Mexico where she divides her time between writing and working as a counseling service manager at her local independent living center. She published a chapbook, Private Stories on Demand, in 1988.

STEVE MENDELSOHN is coordinator of Connecticut's Legislative Coalition of Psychiatry and Human Rights. He has twice run for state representative.

MARY JANE OWEN has been involved with the disability rights movement since 1972 when she became active in the Berkeley, CA, CIL. She has worked in the academic, federal, private and religious sectors and is currently director of the National Catholic Office for Persons with Disabilities.

JULIE REISKEN is married to Pamela Carter and, with Pamela, is mother of Tom and Chase Carter. Active with the Colorado Cross Disability Coalition, she earlier organized the Connecticut Coalition for Citizens with Disabilities, founded an ILC and a community center and was partner in a human services consulting firm.

MARGARET ROBISON is a poet and essayist who leads writing workshops for women with disabilities. Her books are The Naked Bear, Here and Red Creek.

S. L. ROSEN is a pseudonym.

MARTA RUSSELL is a freelance writer, producer and photographer living in Los Angeles, CA. She has been disabled since birth.

NANCY SCOTT has been a freelance writer and editor since 1983. She has published articles in the disability press and poetry.

KATHERINE SIMPSON is a writer who lives in California and works for a social service agency.

CHERYL MARIE WADE is the 1994 recipient of a National Endowment for the Arts Solo Theatre Artist Fellowship, a no apologies radical gnarly boned crone and a firm believer in "If you've got it: Flaunt It!"

BARBARA FAYE WAXMAN is an activist and specialist in disabled people's sexual, reproductive and family life rights.

KATHI WOLFE is a freelance writer living in northern Virginia. She learned everything she knows from "crips," Marx Brothers movies and National Public Radio and has told more about herself in The Rag *than anyone should want to know.*

JOHN R. WOODWARD, M.S.W., is a clinical social worker and freelance writer in Tallahassee, FL. He works for Community Dialysis Centers of America, Inc.